Studies in Women and Religion/
Études sur les femmes et la religion : 4

Studies in Women and Religion /
Études sur les femmes et la religion

Studies in Women and Religion is a series designed to serve the needs of established scholars in this new area, whose scholarship may not conform to the parameters of more traditional series with respect to content, perspective and/or methodology. The series will also endeavour to promote scholarship on women and religion by assisting new scholars in developing publishable manuscripts. Studies published in this series will reflect the wide range of disciplines in which the subject of women and religion is currently being studied, as well as the diversity of theoretical and methodological approaches that characterize contemporary women's studies. Books in English are published by Wilfrid Laurier University Press.

Inquiries should be directed to the series coordinator, Pamela Dickey Young, Queen's Theological College, Queen's University, Kingston, ON   K7L 3N6.

COORDINATOR:	*Pamela Dickey Young* Queen's University
COORDINATRICE:	*Monique Dumais* Université du Québec à Rimouski
ADVISORY BOARD / COMITÉ DE DIRECTION:	*Eva Neumaier-Dargyay* University of Alberta
	Monique Dumais Université du Québec à Rimouski
	Pamela J. Milne University of Windsor
	Marie-Andrée Roy Université du Québec à Montréal
	Randi Warne University of Wisconsin Oshkosh
	Pamela Dickey Young Queen's University

STUDIES IN WOMEN AND RELIGION/
ÉTUDES SUR LES FEMMES ET LA RELIGION

Volume 4

"Voices and Echoes"
Canadian Women's Spirituality

Jo-Anne Elder and
Colin O'Connell, Editors

Published for the Canadian Corporation for Studies in
Religion / Corporation Canadienne des Sciences Religieuses
by Wilfrid Laurier University Press

1997

This book has been published with the help of a grant in aid of publication from the Canada Council.

Canadian Cataloguing in Publication Data

Main entry under title:
Voices and echoes : Canadian women's spirituality
(Studies in women and religion ; v. 4)
Includes bibliographical references.
ISBN 0-88920-286-9

1. Women and religion – Literary collections. 2. Women –
Religious life – Literary collections. 3. Canadian
literature (English) – Women authors.* 4. Canadian
literature (English) – 20th century.* I. Elder, Jo-Anne.
II. O'Connell, Colin Brian, 1953- . III. Canadian
Corporation for Studies in Religion. IV. Series: Studies
in women and religion (Waterloo, Ont.) ; v. 4.

PS8235.W7V65 1997   C810.8′0382   C97-931608-1
PR9194.5.W6V65 1997

Cover design by Leslie Macredie

Cover illustration: "Birther" which is panel 6 of the 13-panel *Illuminated Series* by Deborah Fleming. The accompanying text reads as follows: "The ripening cycles continue, migrating through time, connecting the first and the future."

Printed in Canada

Voices and Echoes: Canadian Women's Spirituality has been produced from a manuscript supplied in camera-ready form by the editors.

Order from:
WILFRID LAURIER UNIVERSITY PRESS
Waterloo, Ontario, Canada N2L 3C5

*In loving memory of Edrie Maud (Campbell) Elder, my mother,
who always believed. Spiritual life begins at the breast.*

*For my mother, Helen Jean (Cutbill) O'Connell.
Always there. A person for others.
A beacon in hard times.*

Contents

Contents

Myths

Between Ebony and Ivory

Last Picnic

Second Solitude

Parallel Images

Beginning in Summer

Mother is Sewing

Blood and Chestnuts

Gifts

The Birth Circle

Acknowledgements

Our gratitude to Uta Doerr, for her editorial assistance and her wonderful translation of *Black Moon*. And our thanks to Keith Wilson, Shirley Williams, Susan Parsons, and Joceyline LeGresley at St. Thomas University for their assistance in preparing the manuscript. We also wish to thank Beth Gordon for preparing the camera-ready copy. Sandra Woolfrey and Carroll Klein, at Wilfrid Laurier University Press, were a pleasure to work with. And we admire all the contributors for their faith and patience. Also, thanks go to our families for indulging us. Of course, the usual disclaimer applies.

Jo-Anne Elder
Burlington, Ontario

Colin O'Connell
Ottawa, Ontario

Foreword: Voices

Jo-Anne Elder

What happens when women tell their own stories of spirituality? In attempting to answer this question, to present the ways that women have explored their spirituality, we have entered into a long conversation in which many people participated in different ways. Women who were experienced and published writers and women who had not written before or who had hidden their writing in the bottom drawer or in the backs of their minds have raised their voices. Their words have been reflected upon and reacted to by artists, scholars, and other writers for whom these women's voices resonated in some way in their own thoughts and beliefs. The voices and echoes reflect what Julia Kristeva calls intertextuality.[1] The authors' voices in the first section echo and reverberate from text to text, and on through the whole of the reflections, without being subject to a "master conversation." The participants seem to speak to each other, although, in fact, most have never met. We are reminded of the words of Michael Oakeshott:

> Thoughts of different species take wing round one another, responding to each other's movements and provoking one another to fresh exertions ... There is no symposiarch or arbiter; not even a doorkeeper to examine credentials ... voices which speak in a conversation do not compose a hierarchy ... in it different universes of discourse meet, acknowledge each other and enjoy an oblique relationship which neither requires nor forecasts their being assimilated to one another.[2]

As editors, we saw ourselves as facilitators rather than arbiters. The feminist perspective of this collection highlights the personal, the experiential, and the creative nature of women's writing and, indeed, of feminist scholarship. The ideas of healing, of the journey, of empowerment of the self, and of relations (between characters, between stories, between the self and the other/worldly) are aspects of women's spirituality and experience that traditional scholarship, like traditional religion, has sometimes neglected.

Our functions were to invite and organize the speakers: to send out calls for submissions (sometimes to what I hoped would be "darker corners," sometimes to places where women outside the mainstream might be found, sometimes to writers' groups and journals), to collect them, to sort through them, to select them (the most problematic of tasks, because we didn't want to adhere to overly rigid editorial guidelines), and finally to compile the stories and poems. The division of labour — one of our initial decisions — meant that

I had direct contact with the writers. I thought that this would simply mean that I would write the letters to them and they would reply to my home address to simplify things. I did not expect the phone calls, nor the tenor of the conversations, which I will hold in confidence. I could not have imagined the energy I would feel as some of the women here, and others, joined me one summer in "talking in the round" about women and spirituality. I dream of some day being able to unite all of these creative women, and several of the others whose excellent work we could not include in this volume, in a cosy, if crowded room, and tape the ensuing discussion. But that is another project.

This collection will be read, and is intended to be read, in different ways by different audiences. The collection offers to readers a variety of styles and approaches that has not been heard elsewhere. For some, its originality and usefulness lies in the quality and diversity of the individual stories and poems as personal explorations of meaning and spirituality. The forewords and echoes are intended to be read as the same kind of creative expression (albeit oriented towards reading rather than writing) as the stories. Other readers will be interested in the work of particular writers or in stories that discuss a certain topic, pattern, or perspective. The stories and poems were written by both well-known and lesser-known writers, from several different provinces, with diverse cultural, religious, and social backgrounds; the texts themselves vary greatly in their subject matter and their form. The commentaries, which follow the stories and poems as a group, are responses by readers to the stories, and are simply one reading, not an authoritative reading, of them. They are not meant to pigeonhole the story or to limit its interpretation, and are there to contribute to rather than to silence the conversation. We have tried, however, to make good "matches" between the authors and the commentators, and to respect the wishes of both as far as possible. The readers vary almost as much in their background and perspective as do the writers; some are scholars, working in different fields and different universities; some are artists (a poet, writers of fiction, a photographer); some are women and some are men. Grouped together, some patterns of reading may be detected, just as patterns of writing emerge from the arrangement of the stories. The reflections help the collection to establish some points of contact with a wider readership and with contemporary scholarship, with a view to broadening both the range and scope of the conversation.

This collection has no overriding schema. Women's spirituality cannot be likened to a continuous narrative, a simple structure, or an obvious pattern. If the classical tradition, and modernity, too, are characterized by metanarrativity — a story that is rationally ascertainable, that has a beginning, a middle, and an end — then these stories refuse to be enclosed by tradition. The collection refuses closure.

In the Christian narrative, Christ stands at the centre. Everything else is "before" and "after": after the Fall comes Christ's redemptive birth, followed by Judgement and Consummation. If only as promise, the narrative is nonetheless complete unto itself. As someone once put it, the clock has struck twelve, but the pendulum still swings.

In our postmodern world, however, the clock is faceless. No longer shaped by a Christian metanarrative fused with Greek rationalism, history has become a murky pastiche of constructed stories bearing no witness to a universal history. Truth claims are context-specific, time-bound, and local. Indeed, Christians and Marxists, who both believe in a universal and rational history, have a lot more in common than either group does with this postmodern stress on deconstructing truth claims, especially claims of "objectivity."

Terry Eagleton has written that the Enlightenment's appeal to a universal standard of reason (i.e., objectivity) was rooted in a rejection of the absolutism of the state.[3] A public discourse, so it was thought, could fend off the dictates of the arbitrary ruler. For what could support a universal discourse, if not the belief that reason is universal? Reason itself is capable of penetrating the structure of things as they are. The irony, as Eagleton points out, is that while reason resisted the tyranny of the state, a new tyranny was created by the "implacable model of discourse" instituted by the learned men of the Enlightenment.

"Enlightened" reason, of course, proved to be more exclusive than inclusive. Western white males, for the most part, saw their power consolidated by industrialism and various ruling oligarchies. By defining reality as rational and objective, and defining women as irrational, subjective, and possessing various other faults of human nature that enlightened men thought they had overcome, men could legitimate their hold on power. The enlightened could both appeal to their "higher" natures, their claim on the spiritual realm, and retain greater access to reality as they experienced it themselves. Reason and their claim to power neatly coincided. Patriarchy was as legitimate as the law of gravity.

But if there is no one standard for judging all things, no ultimate authority, as deconstructionists claim, such pretence of reason as universal arbiter must be dropped. Postmodern consciousness must swim instead in the pluralizing waters of radical perspectivism. What once appeared as the law of gravity is now demoted to the status of a perspective: one group's take on *the way it is, and the way it should be.* Honesty requires that metanarrative, ordered and framed through timeless reason, be dropped in favour of the individual voice, anchored in its context, grounded in its status. There are as many points of view as there are voices, as many visions as there are eyes.

In this context, the inner monologue and diary format become genres of choice. For women writers, they are particularly significant because they allow a full and rich representation of perspectives previously suppressed or at least subdued by the *master's voice.* Because validity of voice is no longer based on a fixed set of "objective" facts, especially patriarchal "facts," the insertion of subjectivity into the narrative event is authentic, and even inevitable. That it is Mary, Ashka, or Martha who is telling the story becomes as important as the story itself. This enables the woman writer to regroup her forces, to develop an unalloyed sense of her own voice, to take the first crucial step in remembering her self. As Ellen Messer-Davidow writes, "Feminist epistemology is based on the assumption that we as diverse knowers must insert ourselves and our perspectives into the domain of study and become, self-reflexively, part of the investigation."[4]

But the insertion of subjectivity into the story does not mean that our storytellers' intentions are fully retrievable. If reason has lost its universal status, then timeless truths cannot be found in either the author's intention or the text. Here, Ferdinand de Saussure's writings on the nature of language and Jacques Derrida's attack on the metaphysics of presence have prepared the way for liberating texts from the reification and fixity of meaning.

For Saussure, this has meant liberating language from the theory of correspondence, or the belief that words bear direct reference to what is "out there." Instead, words signify meaning through their relation to other words, and through a complex network of signifiers and concepts in which meaning is produced but also becomes capable of infinite change. Because there is no fixed referent, the play of signifiers is endless, and closure becomes impossible.[5]

Derrida, for his part, attacks what he calls the "metaphysics of presence," or the belief that reality is given directly to the knowing subject. Both Classicists and Modernists hold a common belief that texts totalize complete meanings that can be laid bare by critics and readers, a "definitive interpretation." But where some literary theorists understand meaning as fully present, Derrida finds only dissimulation and dispersal. The protean text escapes our understanding, shifts shape, and cannot be shown to be fully present. Because there are no objective referents, there are no bases at all for metanarrativity. What we are left with are numerous interpretations leaving, at most, intimations and traces. As Derrida puts it, "there is no outside text."[6]

The message here? Reading texts, much like life, cannot be orchestrated. Otherwise one falls back into a metaphysics of presence in which the fixity of meaning, allegedly derived from an objective referent or timeless state of affairs, illegitimately excludes other ways of knowing. The claim of patriarchy is a case in point. So, when women raise their voices to suggest other ways of seeing and being, the consequences to Classicist and Modernist truth claims are almost unspeakable, unimaginable. What happens next? Where do we go from here?

No one knew what tone our conversation would take on as it developed, what topics it would touch upon. If we can find a common definition of spirituality that is woven through these stories, which are so different one from the next, it is the lived experience of religion or belief, and the deeper meaning of everyday experience. The stories are characterized by this simultaneous movement in both directions, from the here and now to the beyond, from the inner world to the everyday, from the real to the imaginary and back again.

When I first sent out calls for submissions I was sincere in my intentions to reach non-professional writers as well as familiar writers, but I was also reasonably confident in what the submissions would look like when they arrived: so confident that I suggested themes in the call and began to plan the book around these subjects. For various reasons, we had to abandon this approach.

The theme that recurred most often, for instance, was one that wasn't even on my list: abuse. *And why wasn't it on my list?* The multiple levels of denial struck me right away. If they hadn't, women I talked to about the project certainly would have reminded me. Explaining that "concerns that are generally labelled therapeutic — recovery from childhood trauma, for example — are a common focus of spiritual feminist thought and ritual action" (p. 66), Cynthia Eller quotes Vicki Noble, author of *Motherpeace*, who concludes that "women are choosing to heal ourselves from the world illness of patriarchy."[7] In other words, the concept of abuse can be expanded to apply more generally to women's position in patriarchy. Rape, spousal abuse, harassment, as well as childhood sexual abuse, are occurrences too common to be marginalized; the fact that they are at the centre of women's spiritual concerns is no accident. The spiritual quest often takes the form of some sort of recovery. In the archetypal heroic quest, the (male) hero is frequently given the role of restoring order to the kingdom or of recovering lost objects. Instead, a heroine's quest might involve restoring harmony to her inner world, of recovering or transforming her self.[8] In this way, recognition of abuse can serve as the starting point of a woman's spiritual journey.

The stories in this collection by Joyce Howe, Melissa Hardy, and Claudia Gahlinger show just how different an all-too-common experience can be. Joyce Howe's childhood voice is so clear, so resonant, that it seems to have been written from inside that other, younger self. How many of us have such demons to confront? Naming the spirits evokes and releases their power, whether in a *catharsis*, as in these stories, or in ceremony in ritual, as practised by Native people who reserve their spiritual names for this use or the matriarchal peoples who protected their Goddess's name.[9]

In Melissa Hardy's case, the demons are definitely Christian ones, and the connection between patriarchal religion and abuse is once again made, as it will be, we are afraid, many more times in our post-Cashel age. A blurring of fantasy, memory, and reality is an apparently common element in the journey from abuse to autonomy. Setting free the voice trapped inside the silent, passive childbody is at once disturbing and empowering. Claudia Gahlinger, like

Hélène Turcotte, uses the power of the goddess as a reference point, a touchstone, as they journey through painful childhood memories towards woman's power, travelling through questions as big as life and death. Interestingly, stories like Joyce Howe's and Claudia Gahlinger's have something in common with Lorraine Coyle's. Distancing one's most inner self from abuse may involve creating another figure or persona to deal with the real world, protecting the psyche from destruction. Psychological case studies recounting the development of multiple personalities are not so different from the kind of out-of-body experience described by Coyle. In these stories, rather than writing from the body, women are writing their way *out of* their physical bodies, which are facing physical or emotional pain, and *into* their inner selves.

It was just as telling to note what subjects did not incite any responses. I came to understand how different women's definitions of spirituality could be, and this served as one of those reminders one's psyche serves up, again and again, until it is properly integrated: women celebrate differences, and women's differences are worthy of celebration. A narrow definition of feminism is certainly inappropriate here, as it is everywhere. Cynthia Eller, in *Living in the Lap of the Goddess*,[10] attempts to define the boundaries of "feminist spirituality," characterizing it as "separatist, in the sense that it is focused on women" and "feminist, broadly defined" because the members of the movement "see themselves as operating out of some sort of feminist consciousness." She also situates it fairly clearly "outside of traditional religions," as "part of an alternative religious milieu." While Christian and Jewish feminists are not excluded from her grouping, "the center is firmly outside, and indeed, sets itself in opposition to traditional religions," often rejecting Jewish and Christian symbols outright (p. 7). It is hard to know whether the women represented here would recognize themselves in these criteria. The texts certainly focus on women, and in many cases, on women *as* women, and many of the stories express elements of a broadly defined feminist consciousness. Many of the writers would define themselves as feminists, although fewer as radical or separatist feminists. However, relations towards both men and traditional religions are more often typified by an attitude of questioning or challenging social roles than by excluding, rejecting, or opposing men and the Church. The exception is stories of abuse that has been perpetrated either by men or the Church (or both). Traditional religions as well as goddess-centred beliefs obviously offer support to women, according to these women's own testimonies. Relatively few of the writer's perspectives were wholeheartedly New Age or Neopagan, although according to Eller the feminist spirituality movement owes a great deal to such sources as the New Age movement, secular feminism, neopaganism or witchcraft, ecology, therapy, Jungianism, Eastern religions, Native American religions, and African religions, as well as Judaism and Christianity. Few of these influences are evident in our selections or other submissions. Lorraine Coyle's out-of-body experience is narrated in a style quite atypical of other astral-travel tales, and from the point of view of an old woman who seems very real and familiar. Susan Kerslake takes a satirical look at some of our New Age, age-old tendencies in her sharp characterization of Tansy, and Sharon Ferguson-Hood's narrator takes an equally curious, fascinated, sometimes sceptical view of Rastafarian beliefs. One interesting feature of these examples is the somewhat ironic (and therefore perhaps typically Canadian) perspective they provide on elements that are taken very seriously by the members of the American feminist spirituality movement described by Eller.

On the other hand, what I would consider a primary source of women's empowerment, mothering, was not so common a subject, or, in such stories as Marguerite Andersen's, its empowerment seems diminished. Louise Holland shares many of my own feelings in her story "The Birth Circle," and the poems "The Weaned Child" and "Mother is Sewing" also evoke the rich warmth of the mother/child bond. The strong, grounded mother figure is rarely foregrounded elsewhere, however, and it is probably because of my preoccupation with mothering that this surprised me. To some degree, Marguerite Andersen's and Louise Holland's stories illustrate a contrast found in other women's texts between somewhat powerless "real" mothers (who may be represented by the heroines' mothers or themselves) and another kind of Mother, empowered or magical. Eller suggests that "having a divine mother is a way of compensating for the frailties of human mothers, giving women a more perfect mother, one who will never separate from them or prove herself inadequate to her daughters' needs" (p. 143). It should be noted, however, that the negative or inadequate mother figure is rarely portrayed in Canadian feminist writing, in which the ideal or powerful Mother is often collapsed into the heroine's self; she is the Mother one is becoming or can potentially become, a symbol of women's strength and empowerment. This tendency, which I have discussed elsewhere, is another reason I found the lack of submissions on the theme of mothering as empowerment somewhat surprising.

Our attempt to present writers of different cultures was only partially successful, in one sense. From a different point of view, however, the idea of boundaries between cultures, defined as nations or dominant religions, is questioned by these women. Just as the women who write about Christianity challenge the stories with which we are so familiar, the notion of a woman "belonging" to a particular culture fails to take into account the fundamentally ambivalent status of women. Moreover, any "multicultural" project also calls into question my own status, not only as a woman, but as a third-generation Canadian white woman (I could add middle class, well-educated, heterosexual, married, anglophone, etc.). Pretending to be neutral and objective would be useless; I do, however, believe myself to be fairly pluralistic, for I am also bilingual (on good days, multilingual), married to an Aboriginal man, and the mother of mixed-raced children; I have been a single mother and "unsalaried" a good deal of my adult life. However, not many of our stories reflected cultural plurality. Maybe I should not be surprised to see that most of our submissions were from Canadian-born white women. After all, Eller points out that the overwhelming majority of members of the feminist spirituality movement are white and middle class. In any case, though, I will not deny the pleasure that Maya Khankhoje's story gave me, from the first time I read it. Whether they come from a Native woman — in both senses of the word — of another country, like Maya, or a Native of our own country, like Beth Brant, who lays claim to the long-forgotten "feminist longhouse tradition" of her Mohawk foremothers, or Anne Ricard Burke, whose story testifies to the often-silenced history of the Métis, such voices have not been heard clearly up until now. I think it is time to listen. The fact that all three writers consciously use Aboriginal myths, though in various degrees of transformation, is interesting.

Another aspect of the anthology worthy of discussion is the inclusion of two stories by francophone writers. We had hoped for more stories in French, German, and Spanish languages we were prepared to translate, and had sent out notices in French as well as English. Originally written in French, Martine Jacquot's and Hélène Turcotte's stories appear here in translation. Jacquot's and Turcotte's story have little in common, but illustrate some tendencies that are stronger in French-Canadian than in English-Canadian writing. Jacquot's story is informed by a different definition of "spirituel" than is commonly understood in English, and is linked with the concept of the imaginary. The relationship described exists both in the protagonist's personal imagination and in the domain of the symbolic, rather than the real. Most of the English-speaking writers in the collection emphasize the links, rather than the gap, between the real and the spiritual, experience and belief, etc. In "Black Moon," which has been beautifully translated by Uta Doerr, there is a more explicit use of myth than is found in many of the other stories; the relationship between the personal and the mythic, the use of symbols and figures invested with meaning in the individual journey, are an important focus. This is also the case in Claudia Gahlinger's story, while Maya Khankhoje uses an existing myth in a more explicit fashion.

Like Jacquot, Janina Hornosty and Liza Potvin work on the level of the imaginary and the surreal rather than the real. Yet the connection with female experience is not lost here; the very human experience of intimate relationships is still the starting point for the flight of the authors' imaginations, which take them into a terrain where dark humour sometimes suppresses rage or resentment.

Where do the stories of women's spirituality come from? Eller discusses some of the needs that the feminist spirituality movement meets, emphasizing the way it validates women's experiences as women and empowers them. Certainly, these stories come both from deep within and from everything around. Writing, whether it is by women who have never written or women who write every day, is an act of affirmation. Whatever she chooses to write about, a woman is, in a very real sense, writing her self. As is any writer. Creativity is living with a higher consciousness, seeing the deeper meaning in acts of everyday life. In art, everything is possible. In this way, through art, women can at once affirm the significance of their daily lives and transcend the limits of reality. Individual stories are woven together into the whole story; the here and now becomes open to myriad possibilities.

The creative expression of spirituality is empowering not only to individual women, to the writers, but also to the readers, and, in a sense, to all women, because they contribute to the bigger picture, to women's "herstory." In this way, creative pieces contribute to knowledge, giving voice to women who, in some cases, have not been heard before. In other cases, the stories and poems have already been published elsewhere, but their voices assume a different timbre and range of meaning when gathered together with other voices.

Some of the stories start out as stories we all know, stories that shape the way we see our own story, our own lives. From the Great Thinkers and those who wrote the Great Books to the old wives and the humble women,[11] biblical tales and Greek and Roman myths echo into everyday wisdom: who could, today, watch a little boy cling to his mother and cower under his father's stern reproach without thinking of Oedipus as mediated by Freud?

Every time we raise our voices, we hear echoes. There are the old tales that resonate through the new tellings, the myths that determine the way we look at what is happening in the here and now. One phrase that is currently popular suggests consensus: *the reality is*. Whose reality? *The world according to whom?* For many of us, the text that still reappears, fragmented and remodelled in our words, is the Bible. Reading the brilliant stories by Ann Copeland, Gloria Sawai, and Donna Caruso, all of which come out of Christian tradition — sticking out like sore thumbs and other wounds as they retell girlhood stories — or poems such as those of Carol Rose that bear witness to a Jewish women's consciousness, makes me wonder how much of the power is in the underlying narrative, the Judeo-Christian mythos that fashions a heritage shared by many Canadian women, and how much in the retelling, the way the story is written anew. In each case, that "way" is very different, thereby challenging the idea of a single path, a "right way"; in every case, however, the "way" is a fundamentally female one, as the writers highlight women's relationship with conventional religion. Ann Copeland's tenderness, Donna Caruso's humour, and Gloria Sawai's more absurdist irreverence contrast sharply with Ingrid MacDonald's re-vision of Christian life.

There are other stories we have forgotten, though perhaps not completely. They have been hidden from us by the powers that be, the Fathers who have built the structures of the world in which we live. The story of the prehistoric peoples who worshipped the Great Goddess was destroyed by idol-smashers and woman-bashers. In the Greek myths that are familiar to most of us, there is a multitude of gods and goddesses conducting their lives in near-human style. Earlier tales, however, focus on an Earth Mother figure. Even sceptical scholars often find this idea of a Mother Creator "well-grounded" in the many senses of that term, although they often consider her demise equally plausible. In Beth Brant's story, the Sky Mother gives birth to the First Woman, a manifestation of the Earth Mother that is consistent with the "feminist longhouse" tradition that Beth claims and re-claims as her own. It is a little more curious that this story seems familiar to some of us who were raised outside these systems. Perhaps it is because such a tradition lies, following Patricia Smart's image of woman in patriarchy,[12] underneath the foundations of many belief systems. What we all know at our deepest level of consciousness, what the various levels of sophistication of our primitive knowledge attempt to cover up in degrees of abstraction and symbolism, is that we are all *of woman born*.[13] Witnessing natural birth, be it human, animal or vegetable, our certainty is whole. It is from the earth, from the physical world, from the body that life and consciousness begins and flows.

This project combined life and art in mysterious ways. Certainly the spirit of the lives of these women comes through in their creations. The process, as well as the product, had a life of its own. Perhaps it is impossible to relate its story and still do justice to the moving and breathing life it took on. The process was interwoven with two central events in my own life: the births of my two sets of twins and the deaths of my parents, which were in turn interwoven with each other and even with the lives of some of the women I made contact with in the course of the project, as well as with my co-editor Colin's life. I have never had a purely academic relation with any subject (I had to throw out a whole chapter on mother figures from my thesis when my first child was born, because I discovered matriarchy physically and emotionally as well as intellectually) and I certainly couldn't with this one, though I admit I tried. (Colin probably tried harder, and succeeded only slightly better, but that's his story.) The time I dedicated to the project taught me a lot about control and flow, as has the time I have spent looking in other places and writing my own stories.

When I first read about the matriarchy, while doing my doctoral research, things suddenly began to make sense: men abused and silenced women because they feared their power. Only women can give life through their bodies, but men can give life through their art. In order to do so, men had to structure social and religious systems differently, and promote their "sterility cult," their fear and hatred towards women and children. Physical life had to be separated from spirituality, and all the ensuing polarities would correspond to the initial gender conflict. Matriarchal and holistic visions of humankind would give way to patriarchal di/visions. For the past decade or so, women writers and scholars have suggested that contemporary society testifies to the demise of goddess-centred beliefs, much in the same way as the arrival of the Europeans destroyed the Mother Earth which Native civilization protected. The assertion of the universality of patriarchy can be well-documented, while the idea that different sorts of cultures (goddess-centred, earth-centred, co-operative, etc.) exist or have existed in the recent past is often vigorously denied. For instance, one anthropologist, questioned more vigorously on his assertion, explained to me that a "culture" was defined by a certain minimum population. In other words, if a linguistic, religious, and cultural system is limited to a very small number of people — a small village, for instance — the members of that community would not have an identifiable culture. Interestingly, the existence of such small villages is quite typical of matriarchal peoples, who needed to keep their numbers down in order to move quickly and easily, who cared painstakingly for the dependent members of their groups, and in whose everyday existence every person played a unique role. Extended breastfeeding resulted in natural child spacing: that is the positive side of population control. Natural conditions were difficult, but the greater threat came from waves of invaders encroaching on the precious land base necessary to survival. *Change the definition, and erase the memory. This does not exist. The reality is ...* Most recently, the anti-politically correct have taken up arms against what seems to be an underground matriarchal consciousness. Wife-beating, spousal rape, incest, and sexual harassment were until recently frequently denied or understated; that the Holocaust, gender harassment, and date rape still are should not surprise me, but I admit that it does. So pagan-bashing will continue: the Wicca M.P. criticized by Christians, the feminists attacked by the men's movement, Native traditionalists still struggling with long-time Christian converts, the goddess-worshippers and others with a spiritual focus who weary liberal thinkers and secular humanists; these are some of the current victims of self-identified left-wing and right-wing thinkers.

Descartes did not invent the mind-body separation. This was accomplished during the transition away from the Great Goddess towards a Father God. For how could she be supplanted unless that fundamental knowledge of our birth was abstracted into symbolism? *We are of woman born, but we must be born again.* Tales of rebirth gradually changed from being attempts to understand life after death — a fairly simple concept, once one realizes that it is the same sun and the same moon that disappear and reappear in the sky — to being doctrines of the proper life. And so, body and soul are split into two worlds, and the physical one becomes less and less important, less valued.

But how can I, as a woman, feel this to be so? Every month, beginning from the sudden end of childhood, blood ebbs and flows. My mother tells me that this is a wonderful thing, that it means I can become a mother. I am not convinced. Like Kathy O'Grady, I am bothered by the fact that it is the opposite of a ritual, a sacrament, although it has all the ingredients for both, being connected with such lofty ideas as the moon, oceans, journeys, eros, and thanatos. But, in my adolescence, blood was an embarrassing stain, an obstacle. Mary was lucky: she did not have to menstruate. Later, it becomes a trial, a recurring tension. Whether I am trying to conceive or not determines my feelings about my body. Like Marguerite Andersen, birth control was a part of my life, a part of the control I needed to have for many years, but the technology was always a symbol of my own ambivalence. I go through long years of living in the world of the mind, regimenting my body with chemicals and long hours of study. I call my activities during the weeks before final exams being in training. Regular meals, long hours of sleep, systematic review. My body exists purely to keep my mind *working*. The real world is a tricky place to live in, as the characters in Martine Jacquot's story seem to find. Love is fantasy, imagination, a story that is never written. Work is real, written down: essays, exams, c.v.'s. Get plenty of rest, my mother says. Think about it as you are going off to sleep. The magic works. The painful wisdom teeth, the bouts of pneumonia, the cramping do not distract me. But when I am ready to *really begin life*, the bleeding brings with it true grieving. There is a happy ending to our story, however. I cannot say the same for the "bigger story." The life-giving memory leaks away, leaving only a stain on patriarchal conscience that can be explained away as a "false memory." For some women, though, there is a feeling that something else is false, is not right, that they do not have the "right fit"[14] into the lives they lead.

Just as the statues were toppled over to make room for the anti-iconic early patriarchs, who seemed bent on destroying both the bodies and the pictures of bodies they found, the familiar stories took on new characters and new endings. Persephone was raped and taken underground, and even her powerful mother could only manage to gain custody for her for half the year. Other tales offer similar explanations for the wrath of winter and the end of the harvest. The goddess took on lovers, and gradually the power shifted to these consorts. Human or divine, the early male figures generally made brief appearances, consistent with their role in conception, but as time went on the consort stayed by the side of *his* goddess: first for a year, until that extra day the solar calendar made possible, then until the curious day of leap year, then finally in a marriage-like union for perpetuity. The story of Athena is another tale, one of the tales of Hellenic middle age. Zeus, certainly, is going through that painful male menopause. Unsatisfied with being Lord of All, he decides he needs a daughter. He is not the first man to be caught in this dilemma, but for him, the new mythical reproductive technologies come to the rescue: *dea ex deum*. His wombless body has nevertheless submitted itself to the magic of pure, parthenogenic thought. Athena, his powerful and full-grown offspring, springs out of his head. Some anthropologists explain that this signified a recognition of paternity, of the role of the father. But surely the power taken on by these fathers was not inevitable: who would expect that monogamy and monotheism would follow so closely behind the arrival of the invaders, often described as the big blond sailors, the Aryan patriarchs? Who would believe that the washing and feeding accomplished as holy acts and everyday blessings by the sacred mothers would be refashioned into holy sacraments performed only by initiated men? Who could guess that women would be told, centuries later, that the era of their pride and power had never existed?

Who? Women.

Women know how their stories are denied. *It is all in your head.* Of course, most knowledge is. The stories of many women, too horrible to consider, have been erased from public and private memory. Whether it is abuse or genius, it will go unrecognized. Patriarchy is a great leveller. Women's lives, marked by tragedy or greatness, fall by its wayside, leaving a single narrative: the hero leaves his mother and father, accomplishes great deeds, and saves the kingdom.

What if the hero is a young woman? What can she save?

Herself.

It is our life's work to write and rewrite the story of who we are: who we have been, who we are becoming, where we are going. Writing, as process and act rather than product, expands the limited territory assigned to women by their conquerors. Rather than saving a kingdom, women writers create new spaces, and many of these new spaces are in herself. By crossing borders, redefining terms, uncovering forgotten knowledge, and providing alternate perceptions, writing by women challenges conventions and conclusions that may have become truisms in patriarchy.

What is the meaning of life? Who are we? Hearing the voices in these stories and poems, we are listening to various ways of asking and answering these perpetual questions. And we are aware that we are not the first ones to wonder about how we got here, and what it is we are here to do. As women, we are painfully conscious that no one can tell us the meaning of our lives, that we can't actually find it in the here and now or even in many of the stories of the world beyond. Rather than learning by rote, we must truly learn it *by heart*. Perhaps it is not *given* to us to know, but we *are* given stories. To give meaning to our lives, we need this ability to imagine and to remember. As Di Brandt tells us, *and already there is no going back.* We have begun the journey. And what we *can* do, what is in our power (read: capacity), is to *give birth* to meaning. And then the ultimate creative act begins: one, new, fresh, innocent, all-knowing meaning-of-life/ life-with-meaning is born. And thereafter, every act is creative, every word pregnant with spirit.

Notes

1. Julia Kristeva, *Polylogue* (Paris: Seuil, 1977).
2. Michael Oakeshott, "The Voice of Poetry in the Conversation of Mankind," in *Rationalism in Politics* (London: Methuen, 1981), pp.198-99.
3. Terry Eagleton, *The Function of Criticism: From the Spectator to Post-Structuralism* (London: Verso, 1989), p. 12.
4. Ellen Messer-Davidow, "The Philosophical Bases of Feminist Literary Criticisms," in *Gender and Theory: Dialogues on Feminist Criticism*, ed. Linda Kaufmann (Oxford: Basil Blackwell, 1989), p. 87.
5. Ferdinand de Saussure, *Course in General Linguistics* (London: P. Owen, 1960).
6. Jacques Derrida, *De la Grammatologie* (Paris: Minuit, 1967), p. 227.
7. Cynthia Eller, *Living in the Lap of the Goddess: The Feminist Spirituality Movement in America* (Boston: Beacon Press, 1993, 1995). Quotation from Vicki Noble, "The Shakti Woman," *Snake Power: A Journal of Contemporary Female Shamanism* (Oakland, CA: Hallowmas, 1989), p. 27.
8. Compare, for instance, Annis Pratt, *Archetypal Patterns in Women's Fiction* (Bloomington: Indiana University Press, 1981), and Carol Pearson and Katherine Pope, *The Female Hero in American and British Literature* (New York: R. R. Bowker, 1981).
9. Robert Graves, *The White Goddess: A Historical Grammar of Poetic Myth* (New York: Creative Age Press, 1948).
10. Cynthia Eller, see note 7 above. Further quotations from Eller's book will be noted in the text.
11. From a song by the female a cappella group *Four the Moment*.
12. Patricia Smart, *Écrire dans la maison du père: l'émergence du féminin dans la tradition littéraire du Québec* (Montréal: Québec/Amérique, 1988; translated as *Writing in the House of the Father*).
13. Adrienne Rich, *Of Woman Born: Motherhood as Experience and Institution* (New York: W.W. Norton, 1976).
14. I am using this term as it used by a group of child psychologists and pediatricians, including Dr. William Sears, in their work on "attachment parenting." The "right fit" is the feeling of well-being an infant has when he is being adequately nurtured and is "securely attached" (according to the

terminology of John Bowlby and Mary Salter Ainsworth) to her/his primary caregiver, generally the mother. See, for instance, Robert Karen, "Becoming Attached," *The Atlantic*, February 1990, pp. 35-70.

Through a Glass Darkly:
Visions and Echoes

Ann Copeland

We were sitting in a busy Connecticut restaurant the evening she sprang the question, with its arcane metaphor, its latent anxiety ...

"Don't tell me, then, that you've slipped out from under Mary's mantle?"

I think of Fran's remark, now, several years later, and again feel its intensity. Immediate context evades me, but the sense of the moment remains.

I should have been able to answer this friend of many years directly. Why didn't I? We sat surrounded by muted voices and laughter, clinking glasses, the thick satisfying smell of Ketchup, onions, and hamburgers, as we savored the taste of our Scotch on the rocks.

But she was serious. That was the problem. I heard her concern.

And dodged.

Took a sip of my drink. Distracted her back to more anecdotes from our shared grammar school days, an exercise that gets me through more than one trip home. Play it again, Fran — the video of our childhood: pigtails, barrettes, spitballs, Peter Pan collars and pastel sweaters, nuns, mortal sin, Spin the Bottle, weekly confession. That was a time of answers, not questions. A time that began in the baptized womb and continued in our parish, a complex of pious neighborhoods, largely Irish, in the better end of town. The town itself — blue collar, immigrant, predominantly Catholic, fed thousands of workers daily to the three large factories at its center. Though we both lived far from the black-belching smokestacks, we heard the three o'clock whistles daily as we lined up to be dismissed in orderly fashion from our square brick parochial school on Willow Street, St. Jerome's.

The parish, fairly evenly divided between richer and poorer, occupied a landscape that emphasized such difference. Up on Snob Hill, as some called it, in a neighborhood of shaded streets, spacious lawns, ample houses and two car garages, my family lived. A zigzag of cement steps, some 200 in all, had been cut into the side of the hill which led down to Willow Street and the rest of St. Jerome's parish. About five blocks down Willow stood our school. Fran lived nearby, in a neighborhood of three family houses with tiny lawns, working mothers, Irish pride, pictures of servicemen on mantels, and hopes for a brighter future. Eternity, just around the corner, promised relief and reward.

Unlike me, Fran never suffered, I think, from grandiose expectations. She often climbed the steps to come home with me after school and she loved what my mother called "nice things": delicate plates displayed in the china closet, silver tea service, needlepoint chairs, miniature demitasse cups with their

1

curved gold legs — all the elements of gracious living for that time — the forties and fifties, and place — New England. We'd barely be in the house and Fran would be at me: "Did your mother do that?" pointing to some needlepoint. Or: "Someday I'm going to have a Duncan Phyfe sofa just like that." Surrounded by things, you don't see them. Fran had an eye for what was there. Her own mother, widowed early, had taken in sewing and raised four daughters, Fran the last.

Blunt and outspoken, she often got in trouble at school. "Bold" the nuns would call her. I was more bookish, earnest to pull A's and please my teachers. Both of us were tomboys, though, both of about equal strength. THE event of our grammar school days was the fifth grade fight.

I turned ten that December day in 1946. It was bitter cold. We were all out at recess in our snowsuits, playing Whip on the steep slope in the girls' playground. We stood at the top of the hill and joined hands. The first girl ran down the hill as fast as she could, pulling us behind her. I was at the end and landed in a pile of snow.

While I was still half-buried, Fran started to sing "Happy Birthday." The ritual spankings began. Fran spanked me hard, until it hurt. She kept it up. To this day I don't know why. Was she jealous? Had I hurt her in some way? Or did she simply, as children can, get carried away? I grew angry, hit her back. What ensued was not a ladylike fight: hair on snowsuits, bloody noses, real pain. Sister Josephine hurried over. "Young ladies!" By then we were going at it hard, both crying. A ring of girls had formed around this diversion usually reserved for the boys' yard. Somehow, we were separated.

Almost immediately the bell rang and we were back in the fifth grade classroom. What a birthday! I really hurt. One eye throbbed, a tooth felt loose, my head stung from pulled hair. The atmosphere in the room was charged. In sailed Sister Marie Louis. I remember her as long fingers and a long thin face. She had extraordinary thumbs, doublejointed. When she was struggling for self-control, she'd bend them way back, each in turn.

"Miss Houlihan," she said, long and thin in the face, "Is today your birthday?"

"Yes, Sister."

"And, Miss O'Connor, do you have anything to say?"

"No, Sister."

We sat a row apart. I was behind Fran, trying to read her shoulders. Were her teeth loose, too? I had socked her once in the face.

"Now, class, you work here at your civics for a few minutes. Page 50. I have something to say to these two outside. I do not expect to hear a sound from you."

She took us outside to the cloakrooms, wire cages where boys and girls hung their segregated coats each morning.

We glared at each other. I didn't want to hate her. Surely she didn't want to hate me. We were friends. This was awful. Her lip was bleeding. A small circle of blood darkened the collar of her white blouse. My throat ached.

"Now, I understand you two have been fighting."

"She ... " I started.

"Nevermind, Miss Houlihan. I don't need to know another thing. What's important is that you two make up."

Make up! How could she force us to make up? Anger had dissolved and left in its place lumps of embarrassment and hurt.

"All right, now, *hug*," said Sister.

We looked at her, at each other. Impossible.

"You heard me," said Sister. She did not say apologize. "You are to hug each other as if you meant it."

I heard the as if.

Fran began to grin sheepishly. I felt plain silly.

"Do I have to push the two of you together?" she asked.

I don't remember who did it first. In the dark cloakroom, surrounded by the heavy smell of wet snowsuits, supervised by long-boned Sister Marie Louis, we hugged and giggled.

Seconds later we returned to the classroom. Eyes watched from behind civics books. We were friends again.

She is the only childhood friend I see on my infrequent trips home. And through her words, her pieties and loyalties, I catch a glimpse of that world ... in which she still lives.

The following year I had my vision.

Sister Imelda, our sixth grade teacher, rightly thought me boycrazy but she didn't realize that I secretly aspired to sanctity. I was up on a number of saints: Teresa, who managed to unite mystical visions and earthly power, thus having it all; Isaac Jogues who lost his fingers; Benedict Joseph Labre who welcomed vermin; Father Damien and his lepers. I'd be no good with lepers and knew I wasn't in a league with Teresa Neumann or Padre Pio. But I longed for a vision.

Sometimes after noon lunch at home, I'd run down the steps and Willow Street to St. Jerome's church and make a visit. It was a temporary church with tan walls, small garish stations of the cross, cracking plaster, dark varnished woodwork, and painted saints with bedroom eyes turned heavenward. Any well-trained Catholic child learned early to look past appearances.

I liked to kneel in the very last pew and fix my eyes on the gold crucifix in the little niche above the tiered white altar.

One noon, as I was kneeling there, I saw behind the crucifix and all around it a kind of golden halo. I shut my eyes, then opened them. Still there. I'd never seen anything like it — a monstrance of light. It must be a vision, I thought, excited and gratified. For years I'd been waiting for this, hardly daring to hope. Voices sometimes accompanied visions. I listened. Nothing. I looked around. Down in front the old lady with bobbed white hair went on rattling her beads against the pew. Over by St. Joseph a man knelt, head bowed. The halo of light remained. No one seemed to notice. I alone had been favored. I backed out of church, eyes on the golden glow lest it evaporate.

For several days I walked around school hugging my secret. I didn't even tell Fran. It was a delicate matter. Unlike Bernadette or the children at Fatima, I hadn't been commissioned to DO anything. I didn't even have the stigmata. How could I prove to anyone the truth of my claim? Better to keep quiet. If God wanted others to know, he'd take care of it. Probably even Sister Imelda didn't have visions. Let her scold me for wearing Tangee Natural and throwing spitballs. She didn't KNOW.

It was wonderfully warm, that feeling of having been singled out by God Himself. I doubt I have ever loved myself so much.

A few days later I made a visit at a different hour. Over near Mary's altar, above the flickering votive candles, a circle of light hovered. The same circle? It didn't move. The crucifix above the main altar was in shadow. The halo seemed to have shifted. On several subsequent visits, depending on time of day and weather, I found that halo in a different spot. I resisted this discovery but there was no denying what I saw. I was forced to an embarrassing conclusion. I had been deluded. It had all been a trick of light. Wishful thinking had produced my vision. I had not been favored. Thank heaven I'd never blabbed, even to my closest friends. Even to Fran.

Who to this day might want to believe mysterious workings behind the arrangement of that light. Nor could I easily explain to her a later moment etched in memory.

Easter Monday, 1966. The basement of a large convent in New York, a room with a cement floor, a furnace at its center, several overflowing trash cans set about. Home from graduate school to celebrate Holy Week and the Easter Vigil with my religious community, I was about to return that day, by bus, to my university.

Aggiornamento was a fashionable word in those days. John the XXIII had called Jews "my brothers" and opened his arms to embrace them. Publicly he'd joked about the Vatican as that "paper bag" he lived in. Nonetheless, for a religious community to entrust a young sister to a secular university was still a calculated risk.

I'd cleaned up my room that Easter Monday morning and carried my trash to the basement. I carried as well an inner burden both heavy and strangely exhilarating. Through the solemnities of that week I'd concealed my secret. At the Easter Vigil I'd stood out in the courtyard beneath the paschal moon watching Father Moriarity cut into the new paschal candle a cross, the year, and alpha and omega. I'd heard his words: "Christ yesterday and today, the Beginning and the End, Alpha and Omega. His are the times and the ages, to Him be glory and dominion through all ages of eternity. Amen." I'd watched him insert grains of incense into the candle to recall the wounds of Christ. Light and shadows played across my sisters' faces as each one lit the flame of her smaller candle from the great darkness-dispelling Easter light. Through it all I'd felt a certainty sharp as pain, heavy as lead: this would be my final stay in that house. In that world.

Now, as I was about to return to graduate school and who knew what else, a bent figure was emptying her basket into the one barrel not stuffed full. Her back was to me. I waited.

She turned, saw me, stopped, leaned against her mop handle.

Mother Justine. Old, crippled with arthritis, nearly blind.

We were friends. The previous summer I'd read to her Bonhoeffer's *Letters from Prison* and a book by Simone Weil. Her habit was going green now and wisps of white hair leaked between her cheek and the starched templets. Her small eyes bulged behind doublethick lenses. Soon she'd be totally blind. Retired, she was waiting to die.

"How are you doing at university, Sister?" she said. "I've been wanting to ask you."

"Fine, Mother." Pointless to tell her I couldn't get through a paper on Milton, that Henry James' rarefied consciousness was doing me in.

"When are you going back?"

"This afternoon. The one o'clock bus."

"Well ... " she narrowed dying eyes, "you know we're very proud of you. The only one of ours away at a secular university. *We're counting on you.*"

I wanted to say, *"Don't."*

Instead, I hugged her. Beneath my grasp, through folds of black, I felt the brittle bones of death.

All the way back up the highway in the stuffy bus that afternoon I stared out through dirt-streaked windows at radiant forsythia and dogwood, haunted by her words. Her wish. I wanted to write to her, warn her. *Don't count. No one can serve as a justification for another's faith.*

It was months before I found those words.

I never saw her again.

Fran can laugh at illusion. She appreciates pain. With rare compassion she succours the sick and the old. Visits my ninety-year-old mother regularly. Takes her to Mass on Sunday. With swift wit she can puncture hypocrisy, mimic pretension. But she has always been thin skinned. Sensitive to slight, she is easily hurt. Perhaps that lies behind the fifth grade birthday explosion. Who knows?

In any case, religious doubt does not seem to be her territory. In a house full of mementos from a pious childhood, she still puts slips of paper under the virgin's statue to hold special intentions — as the nuns in grammar school taught us to do. *Help Mamie Byrne to cope with chemo. Help my niece to find a good job. Bring back Bobbie Kelly to his mother.* I do not object that she includes me and my family there. Who knows what penetrates the veil?

We swap stories when I visit home. Our meetings, in middle age, are largely anecdotal, selective renderings of what's happened since I was last home. We seldom approach the abstract.

Still, I would hesitate to tell her of a later vision of mine, this time set in a small town in southern Idaho. 1979. My first visit to the American west.

The chance to teach there for six weeks had brought me thousands of miles from home, husband, children. I'd never before seen real mountains. Now, having driven through sagebrush desert, seen wild horses running free, admired the Snake River and Lizard Butte, I'd discovered that even Boise, Idaho, has its charm.

I found weekends hardest, when what promised adventure turned suspect and emptiness rebuked fantasy.

I'd learned one way to offset loneliness: take a walk. Let the eye see what it would see.

Sunday morning. I found myself outside a Catholic church. Cars were parked up and down the street. I was in my running suit doing the annual makeover. I was tempted to go in. I hesitated. What discomfort might I be inviting?

On the church steps stood a girl in jeans, battered Nikes, and bright blue windbreaker. Her stringy blonde hair hung almost to her waist. Beside her, a toddler was screaming his head off, his cheeks scarlet and puffy. She tried to pick him up and he kicked.

"Want a child?" she said to me. He kicked her in the stomach.

She looked too young. Sixteen, maybe.

"Thanks, I have two," I smiled. "Has Mass started?" The doors behind her were closed.

"Oh, you can go in," she said. "The crying room is at the back."

Fascinating. A whole room for crying. I'd never been in one. At St. Jerome's we'd been herded to a special children's Mass at nine on Sundays. In the convent we were not distracted by children. I'd always thought crying rooms a Protestant invention.

I went in.

The whole rear of the church had been glassed in. As I entered, I passed two sober-faced men in the last pew busy with papers of some kind. About a dozen people stood on this side of the glass: a few small children, older couples, several denimed adolescents poised for a quick exit.

Through the soundproof glass I saw the snowyhaired celebrant seated behind the altar. The sermon was over. To his right, outside the sanctuary, stood a group of singers and guitar players. Their mouths opened and closed, but the only sound to penetrate the crying room was the godawful voice of the priest setting an example of participation for his flock. The microphone was attached to his chasuble. He looked too earnest to skip a verse.

At the Our Father, people on the other side of the glass stood and joined hands. The friendly West.

The lady next to me, thin and self-contained, eyed me as if trying to decide. I was late, after all, and in a running suit. I reached out my hand and grasped her cool dry fingers.

The child outside on the church steps had begun to scream again.

Time for holy communion. Two men in suits and ties opened the glass doors and nodded toward us. Suddenly I could hear the choir. They were good. People began leaving their pews, lining up in the aisle.

Should I go?

No one in that church knew me. I was merely a visitor stopping by in her jogging outfit. A spectator from Mars. I could sit and watch them approach that table, listen to the singing, think my thoughts. I wanted something more.

What ancient need drew me toward that altar? Childish hopes for visions had long ago given way to the humbler hope of daily bread. I certainly expected neither voices nor comfort, nothing more than the strange dry taste of what the church calls God.

Feeling a bit uncomfortable, I stepped from the pew and passed through the opened glass doors.

I was curious. I knew something special about this church. The nuns who ran the attached school belonged to the order I'd left years before. For the early part of their formation they'd been sent East, to the house where I was trained. I remembered in particular a lanky one from Montana. In those days, Montana seemed exotic. I could imagine Sister Charles riding an Appaloosa bareback around a ranch. Maybe I'd see her here, or someone else I'd once known.

I moved slowly forward in line, scanning heads, faces. How would I recognize nuns? There was one old lady in a white bordered veil. Her head trembled and she wore thick glasses. Before my time.

I approached the altar. The choir was singing a Gelineau psalm. The Magnificat. Seen up close, the priest's face was lined and grainy, his tired eyes bloodshot.

I took the host, sipped from the chalice.

On the way back I spotted another veil in the choir. No one I knew.

I returned to my crying room. The glass doors closed behind me.

I tried to pray for the family back home.

"Go in peace."

The parishioners blessed themselves, moved to escape.

On my way out, one of the solemn men at the back smiled and offered me a pamphlet plus a small red paper flower. For a dollar I could proclaim myself pro-life. Bishop's request.

"No thank you."

When I left the church, screaming baby and young mother were nowhere to be seen.

Our lives abound with echoes.

How to name the moment when a glance, a remark, a passing image, the merest glimpse of a face in a crowd will touch to life the fugue of memory and desire hidden deep in the heart, awakening music lost or long forgotten?

Though her question touched me in an odd way, I couldn't answer Fran directly, level with her. Was this cowardice or wisdom? Or something else I couldn't name? Until that moment, I'd forgotten that way of thinking, of speaking. I'd put away those things of childhood.

Then came her words.

"Don't tell me, then, that you've slipped out from under Mary's mantle."

Scenting danger in something I'd said, she'd responded instinctively.

From our early days we'd been trained to know Mary's place: virgin, mother, not God. You could run to her with silly things, secret guilts, without fear of losing face. What she lacked in augustness she made up for in human understanding, mediating between us children and that inconceivable absolute — God Himself. Her mantle, soft and blue with no rough edges, had room for everyone. Inside it you were safe from cold despair, churning passion, the small ongoing needles of time. It softened life without denying it. Her embrace, gift undeserved, was a place you could count on.

Perhaps Fran longed that I, like her, might feel safe.

She would argue with my formulation: "No, I want you to BE safe."

There was no resolving that distinction over a shared hamburger on a winter night in Connecticut. No way, then and there, to retrace steps leading to the distance she may have sensed between us. How do you recapitulate a life in a word?

Visions dim.

Echoes fade.

In the end, evasion does not satisfy.

The heart would speak the truth ... and be heard.

I might have avoided a direct answer through a familiar dodge: Retreat to Art. Raid poetry to mend life. "The reason can give nothing at all like a response to desire," I might have said — hauling out the ammunition of a privileged education.

It would have availed nothing. Poetry cannot mend life.

Still, evasion does not satisfy. A longtime friend deserves better. Fidelity makes its claim on the soul.

Gestures carry the unspoken.

Perhaps it sufficed that I didn't try to answer.

I nodded to our waitress and ordered another round of Scotch. Then, immersed again in the world of hamburger and onions, clinking glasses and muted conversation, I rejoined Fran — foraging anew in the universe of pigtails and barrettes, saints and earnest piety, lost forever now to all but the play of friends who'd once shared its reliable comfort, the radiant warmth of its fragile shelter.

The reason can give nothing at all like a response to desire.

Angelus,
or
Blessed Are the Uninitiated for They Shall Go Fishing

Donna Caruso

Julia rode sidesaddle on the green crossbar as Anthony peddled through the empty streets. She could hear her own laughter trailing after them like a banner in the soft morning light; could feel Anthony's fresh-washed and smiling face close to hers in the breeze, his breath warm on her cool cheek. Someday Anthony would be a priest and she would be a nun. Julia imagined them riding along on the bike, grown up: he in his cassock, she in her veils, black and billowing like a pirate ship.

Julia had heard Father Bernard speaking quietly to Anthony after mass one Sunday in the sacristy. She had gone in even though girls weren't allowed because she had to go home to pee and Anthony was taking so long. There were no bathrooms in the church because that would be a sin to pee in God's house. She saw Father Bernard was leaning very close to Anthony and saying that if Anthony continued to be a good boy one day he might become one of the black fathers. Father Bernard had asked Anthony if he thought God was calling him to the priesthood. Yes, Anthony had answered so softly, yes he did. Father Bernard said he would pray for Anthony's vocation, and he would have him serve the 5:45 every morning. Getting up that early to serve God would help him, Father had said, help Anthony with his vocation. Anthony had asked Julia to come with him; and so they rode each morning early to the church.

Julia went in with Anthony by the side door. After he had disappeared into the sacristy, Julia proceeded alone up the terrazzo stairwell. At the top of the stairwell, a heavy door separated her from the place where the people sat. She grabbed the door handle, pretending to be Julia the Barbarian, and ripped the door off its hinges as if it were paper, roaring her barbaric yawp into the church's deafening silence. Her eyes, a-fire; her chest, heaving. She would genuflect then beside a pew, cross herself, and sit, a conquering barbarian princess robed in animal skin; and there she would wait for the cup of blood she had heard they served here.

Julia liked to listen to the stillness in the church. It was a thick and billowy stillness that filled the church in its every corner and made every wee little sound boom. Whispers, the softest footsteps, a door opening, all seemed as loud as shouts in the holy silence. Julia's school teacher, Sister Mary of the Immaculate Conception, could make her classroom just as still. Sister Mary used the silence to make it seem like no other sound in the whole world existed except for some kid's poor mumbled excuses, or worse, the kid's pissy, blubbery tears. It was a powerful thing to carry the silence of the church inside you and be able to use it like Sister Mary of the Immaculate Conception did. She could make a kid see the hugeness of a mistake. Julia thought that must be why God put the silence in his church. To show us our noisy sins. Julia knew she needed God to show her how big her sins were because they never seemed very big at all to her. But that was because she was young and didn't know any better. Mama said she would learn. "You'll learn," Mama had said so many times; "One of these days you'll learn." So Julia knew she would. The hard way, because Mama said that, too.

The factory workers came into the booming silence one by one, cheeks flushed from walking. Each laying claim to a pew, they knelt, women mostly, in dull black skirts and sweaters, their swollen feet laced into cracked black shoes, heavy hose hiding their varicose veins. They covered their heads with flowered babushkas and gazed at the Virgin while their thick hands fumbled amongst tissues and pennies for their rosary beads. Banks of beeswax candles alerted heaven to their pleas: pains in need of miraculous cures; children, weak with sickness; the rent money gone for shoes. Then, on the altar, Father Bernard and Anthony appear, their lush white and golden vestments flowing, their hands folded piously in prayer, pointing upwards to God. Julia's eyes look up, seeing only the ceiling deep blue with painted silver stars.

Julia tries to catch Anthony's eye to make him smile; take him out of the ritual, out of the Latin secrets, into her thoughts of sailing the bluest of seas, of riding the fastest of bicycles. Pirates in disguises they were, playing a role till the moment came for throwing off their robes and revealing the truth of their pirate hearts and their private desires. These church women, too, Julia knew, had hearts fit for murder and looting if only given the opportunity. Almighty God would turn his unblinking eye sooner or later; then things could emerge: birds of flaming red and serpents of gold with jewelled eyes. Dancing. Daggers. And flight.

They stood for the gospel. Father Bernard had a strong accent from a country far away and Julia found it hard to understand him. Half the time he turned his voice away from the microphone to the place on the page where he was reading. In and out his words would fade, like voices behind Mama and Papa's bedroom door. When he was finished with the gospel he gave the sermon and they all sat as he spoke; quietly waiting.

Julia appeared to sit still as a stone while Father Bernard spoke, but secretly she would balance carefully on tiptoe on the back part of her pew like the high wire artists at the circus; then she would leap from one pew to the next gathering reds and blues spilled from the stained glass windows by the brightly rising sun. She would make a coloured wreath for her hair. From one pew to the next she would bound, silent as a thief, graceful as a ballerina, scooping colours from the women's shoulders, from the terrazzo floor, from the side of Anthony's smooth beardless face. Father Bernard wouldn't notice, absorbed as he was in his own thoughts about the gospel message. This was Julia's favourite part of the mass, the time for thinking privately, the time for sitting quietly in the fresh coloured sunlight.

She wondered what the women in their plain dark clothes thought as they watched Father Bernard in his gold and white dress. Would they like to tear off a piece of it to wear as a headband or a belt around their waists like the gypsies? Would they like to paint their faces scary with his red and purple wine? One woman, she knew, carried a knife; a shiny long kitchen knife in her boot, and in her purse, a small pistol. At Hallowe'en, no one went to her house for fear of being slit ear to ear like a pig. Julia knew the woman came here to the church to fool God into letting her into Heaven. Julia thought Heaven would be exciting if the mean people were there. Sometimes she was mean herself. It made her feel good, powerful and strong. And if she turned out to be mean when she grew up, she still thought she should get into Heaven just the same as the nice people. God was mean, too; God sent people to Hell forever, forever and ever Amen. That was very mean. They prayed all the time to stop him from doing it to them, to stop him from getting really mad and throwing them into the fire when they died where they'd roast till they dripped, like marshmallows. Rescue us and be gracious to us they all said. Don't burn us on a spit like wieners was what they meant.

Hot, hot, don't touch, Mama said to the baby, Christina.

Hot, hot, don't touch.

Julia realized Mama was telling her about life and death, Heaven and Hell.

Julia wondered how you ever learned everything you had to know to be a grown-up. Mama knew everything. These women in the church probably, too. And Father Bernard knew as well. They could tell things about God, and stories about people who had died long ago, and the whispered stories that were secrets. Julia liked the whispered ones the best because they never seemed to be finished. Although she could hear really well, she pretended not to when Mama told a whisper story because if Mama thought she was listening she would send her away to play. But if Mama thought she was already playing blocks and not paying any attention to her, Julia could hear the whole thing right up to the last part which she never understood because it was so quiet and full of knowing looks. Julia had learned that the grown-ups got into trouble just like the kids. Most of the whisper stories were about that. Grown-ups who ran off or were sent away, grown-ups who were crazy and in love. Lots of the women here in church were in whisper stories because of love and men and running off.

Whisper stories were exciting like Julia's secret hiding places: dark corners, places under beds and forgotten closets. When she and her brothers and sisters played hide and seek, Julia always tried to find the best secret hiding place. She loved it when the others would look for her and look for her. She would pop out when no one was around and they'd never know where she had been hiding unless she told. And she would never tell. Again and again they could try to find her, walk right by her calling her name and never know where she was. She would hold her breath and concentrate on being invisible. Julia loved that. Loved being secret.

Father Bernard was on his feet again, praying. It was the Credo, the "I believe."

"I believe in God, the Father Almighty
Creator of Heaven and Earth ... "

Julia believed in many gods and she didn't believe in any gods. Julia hadn't made up her mind about gods yet and she didn't get how anyone else had. Why weren't the gods and angels coming to her and telling her things, like God telling Moses about the commandments, like God telling Anthony to be a priest. God hadn't told her to be a nun. She just wanted to be a nun because she loved the long dress, the flowing veil; she liked the idea of being a black bride all the time. Even at the grocery store. Even at Eaton's. And never having babies to take care of or live with like she had to at home where there was always some smelly kid around, crying or dirty. She hated that. Couldn't wait to be a nun and live in a clean quiet place where she could hear herself think for a change. A place where maybe at last she could hear God talking to her. Where she could talk to him, and ask about the other gods, if there were any, like a woman god he slept with naked sometimes like Mama and Papa and if there were any god kids and if they were a pain like her baby sisters and brothers.

Anthony was getting the bowl and the towel for Father Bernard now. Father Bernard had to wash up before making the miracle where Jesus came in the host. He couldn't touch Jesus without washing first, it wasn't the holy thing to do. Father was the only one who could touch Jesus at all. Anthony couldn't, even though he was a boy and in the altar boy's dress and up on the altar. He could get close but not touch. Like what Mama says to do when you're visiting somebody and you really like their stuff and you want to pick it up. You can't. Just look. That was the way it was for Anthony on the altar. He could look at Jesus in the host, could look real close, but never touch. Only the priest could do that.

Papa told Anthony not to touch girls either. Julia had heard them talking in the garage. She wasn't supposed to hear but she did. Papa told Anthony stuff about women, about men and women. It made Papa blush and Julia could tell it was secret and really important. He talked about what the men did to the women for babies and how it was for after you were married when you could give babies a house to live in. You can look all you like, Papa had said with a quick laugh, but don't touch; even though girls would make his thing hard, make it ache. Julia heard Papa talk about the changes, and how Anthony would maybe have to touch himself sometimes to let off the pressure. Too much of that, Papa had said, really red and embarrassed, too much was no good for you either. Anthony was real silent and red all through this and when Julia heard Papa ask if there were any questions Anthony wanted to ask, she was so disappointed when Anthony just shook his head no. Julia had lots of questions like what happened to a boy's thing to make it hard? And how did it soften up again once it was hard? And what about the other things the boys had, did they get hard, too? And Mama had had lots of babies; had all this hard stuff been stuck into Mama all those times and hadn't that hurt?

Next, Father Bernard had to mix the water and wine and say some prayers. Then came the time for kneeling and deep solemn silence. Everybody knelt. Julia hated kneeling. She knew this was the holiest time and you had to keep your head down and hit yourself on the chest three times and she didn't mind that, but the kneeling was what she really hated. It made her think of being mean and squishing bugs even though Julia knew that wasn't what she was supposed to be thinking about. Whenever she had complained to Mama about the kneeling at church, Mama had told her to think about God because it was a holy time. To think about Heaven and all the angels and saints. Julia learned about the angels and saints in school because the nuns gave out pictures of them; holy cards they called them, a lot like baseball cards, except prettier. They had the angels and saints, Jesus with a sacred heart you could see; and Mary, Jesus' mother, with a lot of naked angels on a cloud.

None of them were kneeling, Julia had pointed out to Mama once.

Mama told Julia that if she was very good and became a saint, she'd never have to kneel again. Julia thought it was better just to be bad and skip the kneeling altogether. She leaned back on the pew bench. If Mama were here she would yank her upright pronto. But Mama never came to the 5:45.

It was consecration now and Anthony had to kneel on the hard altar steps and be very still. When Father Bernard raised the host and made the miracle happen, Anthony had to ring the bells to let everybody know so they could bow their head and hit their chest. Julia loved this. She watched the women to see where on their chest they hit. Some of them hit right on their left boob and it made Julia wonder if that hurt. She wondered, too, if she'd get big ones or little ones when she was older. The big ones would get in the way, she thought. Small ones wouldn't flop around so much when you ran. But boys liked the big ones better and Julia thought that was important.

Anthony liked the big ones. Julia could tell by how his eyes snuck looks sideways at certain ladies like Mama's friend Muriel. Muriel always went up to Anthony, real close to him, and placed her hand along the side of his face and said something like, "Such a fine one, a fine young man," and Anthony would blush like crazy. You could always see some of Muriel's boobs because her blouses were tight and open in the front and she leaned over a lot. In summer, she wore halter tops and everything was stuck out in front, her shoulders bare. Muriel's boobs were pretty big and Julia saw that Anthony liked them.

Julia wondered if Father Bernard liked big or little boobs. She knew he had a thing because she had asked Mama and Mama had gotten so mad Julia knew the answer must be yes or else Mama would have said of course not like it was a ridiculous thing to think in the first place. Julia knew Father Bernard didn't have a family because priests couldn't because it wasn't a holy thing to do. Julia agreed one hundred percent with that. Having a family was the most unholy thing Julia could think of. But Julia wondered if Father Bernard's thing got hard anyway because of women even if he wasn't going to have kids, or if God made that stop for priests. When Muriel showed off her boobs to Father Bernard did he look sideways like Anthony did? Like Papa?

Soon Julia would be making her first confession and she would have to go into the confessional for a secret talk with Father Bernard. She was supposed to tell him her sins, but she couldn't think of anything she did that was so bad. Maybe she could ask him if it was a sin to wonder about if his thing got hard. Julia knew he would tell her, even though it was kind of personal.

It was communion time and Julia sat in her pew while the others went up to the altar rail. Julia couldn't go because she hadn't made her first communion yet, although she would soon. But today, almost everyone went up but her, her and the ones who had seriously sinned recently and hadn't had a chance to go to confession. That was the catch: once you made your first communion you could have communion free anytime you wanted unless you had done a mortal sin. The kind that condemned you to Hell. Julia wondered what sins the people had done who hadn't gone to communion. In her first holy communion instruction class Julia had asked about the adultery commandment, and Sister Mary of the Immaculate Conception had said, "Adultery is for adults," but she would say no more. Since grown-ups were always telling Julia not to do this or that like steal or lie, Julia thought they must not do those sins themselves; Julia figured they must all do the adultery one, whatever it was. She could ask Mama if she committed adultery sometimes like some of the women in the church at the 5:45. Maybe if she and Mama talked about sins more Julia would understand them better. It seemed to Julia that there sure was a lot to learn about sins.

Father Bernard cleaned up the shining golden chalice and drank a little wine. The church was very quiet, no one even coughed. Julia wondered if they felt better now that God had touched their tongues and was in all the people's bellies. Julia wondered if the quiet came from God being there.

The mass was over and Father Bernard and Anthony left the altar. The women in the pews knelt for one last prayer, heads bowed most deeply. It was as if now they could really talk to God; now that they finally had some privacy. Anthony came back onto the altar in his cassock to snuff out the candles. One by one the flames died, a thin white trail of smoke rising in their place, wafting aimlessly, lost of purpose.

Julia waited outside where cars were beginning to fill the streets. Anthony was taking a long time again but Julia didn't mind so much. She looked into the lighted windows of one of the houses nearby to watch what people were doing. Winter was a better time to spy on the church neighbours; the sun came up later and the lights inside the houses gave the perfect light for watching the father shaving, the family eating breakfast, and the girl upstairs dressing. Now, in summer, there was less to see, but more to hear; there emerged from open windows the voices missing from the winter pictures. Julia would have to put the two together, so that she could understand fully. So much was that way: it came to you in bits and pieces.

Soon Anthony came and Julia hopped onto the crossbar of his bike. Fast or slow he had asked her. Fast, she said, real fast. His strong arms steered them surely, speeding over the flagstone sidewalks and through the familiar streets. She wondered if they could build a raft on the river today, go fishing. Anthony said yes, that would be fun. They would play pirates. Julia leaned back into the curve of Anthony's arms, knowing the game had already begun. Already she could see their billowing sails. Julia wished hard with eyes shut tight and her fingers crossed that she and Anthony could play their game always. Always.

already there is no going back

already there is no going back
the trees curl around your
feet the air is full of messages
you miss the father in your
bones the rain falls warm
on your cheek you stand alone
at the world's edge your soul
is worth diamonds your feet
are heavy with the weight
of it which way you whisper
mother please

Di Brandt

The Day I Sat with Jesus on the Sun Deck and a Wind Came Up and Blew My Kimono Open and He Saw My Breasts

Gloria Sawai

When an extraordinary event takes place in your life, you're apt to remember with unnatural clarity the details surrounding it. You remember shapes and sounds that weren't directly related to the occurrence but hovered there in the periphery of the experience. This can even happen when you read a great book for the first time — one that unsettles you and startles you into thought. You remember where you read it, what room, who was nearby.

I can remember, for instance, where I read *Of Human Bondage*. I was lying on the top bunk in our high school dormitory, wrapped in a blue bedspread. I lived in a dormitory then because of my father. He was a religious man and wanted me to get a spiritual kind of education; to hear the WORD and know the LORD, as he put it. So he sent me to St. John's Lutheran Academy in Regina for two years. He was confident, I guess, that's where I'd hear the WORD. Anyway, I can still hear Mrs. Sverdren, our housemother, knocking on the door at midnight and whispering in her Norwegian accent, "Now, Gloria, it is 12 o'clock. Time to turn off the lights. Right now." Then scuffing down the corridor in her bedroom slippers. What's interesting here is that I don't remember anything about the book itself except that someone in it had a club foot. But it must have moved me deeply when I was sixteen, which is some time ago now.

You can imagine then how distinctly I remember the day Jesus of Nazareth, in person, climbed the hill in our back yard to our house, then up the outside stairs to the sundeck where I was sitting. And how he stayed with me for a while. You can surely understand how clear those details rest in my memory.

The event occurred on Monday morning, 11 September 1972, in Moose Jaw, Saskatchewan. These facts in themselves are more unusual than they may appear to be at first glance. September's my favourite month. Monday my favourite day, morning my favourite time. And although Moose Jaw may not be the most magnificent place in the world, even so, if you happen to be there on a Monday morning in September it has its beauty.

It's not hard to figure out why these are my favourites, by the way. I have five children and a husband. Things get hectic, especially on weekends and holidays. Kids hanging around the house, eating, arguing, asking me every hour what there is to do in Moose Jaw. And television. The programs are always the same; only the names change! Roughriders, Stampeders, Blue Bombers, whatever. So when school starts in September I bask in freedom, especially on Monday. No quarrels. No TV. The morning, crisp and lovely. A new day. A fresh start.

On the morning of 11 September, I got up at 7, the usual time, cooked cream of wheat for the kids, fried a bit of sausage for Fred, waved them all out of the house, drank a second cup of coffee in peace and decided to get at last week's ironing. I wasn't dressed yet but still in the pink kimono I'd bought years ago on my trip to Japan — my one and only overseas trip, a $300 quick tour of Tokyo and other cities. I'd saved for this while working as a library technician in Regina, and I'm glad I did. Since then I've hardly been out of Saskatchewan. Once in a while a trip to Winnipeg, and a few times down to Medicine Lake, Montana, to visit my sister.

I set up the ironing board and hauled out the basket of week-old sprinkled clothes. When I unrolled the first shirt it was completely dry and smelled stale. The second was covered with little grey blots of mould. So was the third. Fred teaches junior-high science here in Moose Jaw. He uses a lot of shirts. I decided I've have to unwrap the whole basketful and air everything out. This I did, spreading the pungent garments about the living room. While they were airing I would go outside and sit on the deck for a while since it was such a clear and sunny day.

If you know Moose Jaw at all, you'll know about the new subdivision at the southeast end called Hillhurst. That's where we live, right on the edge of the city. In fact, our deck looks out on flat land as far as the eye can see, except for the backyard itself, which is a fairly steep hill leading down to a stone quarry. But from the quarry the land straightens out into the Saskatchewan prairie. One clump of poplars stands beyond the quarry to the right, and high weeds have grown up among the rocks. Other than that it's plain — just earth and sky. But when the sun rises new in the morning, weeds and rocks take on an orange and rusty glow that is pleasing. To me at least.

I unplugged the iron and returned to the kitchen. I'd take a cup of coffee out there, or maybe some orange juice. To reach the juice at the back of the fridge my hand passed right next to a bottle of dry red Calona. Now here was a better idea. A little wine on Monday morning, a little relaxation after a rowdy weekend. I held the familiar bottle comfortably in my hand and poured, anticipating a pleasant day.

I slid open the glass door leading to the deck. I pulled an old canvas folding chair into the sun, and sat. Sat and sipped. Beauty and tranquillity floated toward me on Monday morning, 11 September, around 9:40.

First he was a little bump on the far, far-off prairie. Then he was a mole way beyond the quarry. Then a larger animal, a dog perhaps, moving out there through the grass. Nearing the quarry, he became a person. No doubt about that. A woman perhaps, still in her bathrobe. But edging out from the rocks, through the weeds, toward the hill, he was clear to me. I knew then who he was. I knew it just as I knew the sun was shining.

The reason I knew is that he looked exactly the way I'd seen him 5000 times in pictures, in books and Sunday School pamphlets. If there was ever a person I'd seen and heard about, over and over, this was the one. Even in grade school those terrible questions. Do you love the Lord? Are you saved by grace alone through faith? Are you awaiting eagerly the glorious day of his Second Coming? And will you be ready on that Great Day? I'd sometimes hidden under the bed when I was a child, wondering if I really had been saved by grace alone, or, without realizing it, I'd been trying some other method, like the Catholics, who were saved by their good works and would land in hell. Except for a few who knew in their hearts it was really grace, but they didn't want to leave the church because of their relatives. And was this it? Would the trumpet sound tonight and the sky split in two? Would the great Lord and King, Alpha and Omega, holding aloft the seven candlesticks, accompanied by a heavenly host that no man could number, descend from heaven with a mighty shout? And was I ready? Rev. Hanson in his high pulpit in Swift Current, Saskatchewan, roared in my ears and clashed against my eardrums.

And there he was. Coming. Climbing the hill in our backyard, his body bent against the climb, his robes ruffling in the wind. He was coming. And I was not ready. All those mouldy clothes scattered about the living room, and me in this faded old thing, made in Japan, and drinking — in the middle of the morning.

He had reached the steps now. His hand touched the railing. His right hand was on my railing. Jesus' fingers were curled around my railing. He was coming up. He was ascending. He was coming up to me here on the sundeck.

He stood on the top step and looked at me. I looked at him. He looked exactly right, exactly the same as all the pictures; white robe, purple stole, bronze hair, creamy skin. How had all those queer artists, illustrators of Sunday School papers, how had they gotten him exactly right like that?

He stood at the top of the stairs. I sat there holding my glass. What do you say to Jesus when he comes? How do you address him? Do you call him *Jesus*? I supposed that was his first name. Or *Christ*? I remembered the woman at the well, the one living in adultery who'd called him Sir. Perhaps I could try that. Or maybe I should pretend not to recognize him. Then he spoke.

"Good morning," he said. "My name is Jesus."

"How do you do," I said. "*My name is Gloria Johnson.*"

My name is Gloria Johnson. That's what I said, all right. As if he didn't know.

He smiled, standing there at the top of the stairs. I thought of what I should do next. Then I got up and unfolded another canvas chair.

"You have a nice view here," he said, leaning back against the canvas and pressing his sandaled feet against the iron bars of the railing.

"Thank you," I said. "We like it."

Nice view. Those were his very words. Everyone who comes to our house and stands on the deck says that. Everyone.

"I wasn't expecting company today." I straightened the folds of my pink kimono and tightened the cloth more securely over my knees. I picked up the glass from the floor where I'd laid it.

"I was passing through on my way to Winnipeg. I thought I'd drop by."

"I've heard a lot about you," I said. "You look quite a bit like your pictures." I raised the glass to my mouth and saw that his hands were empty. I should offer him something to drink. Tea? Milk? How should I ask him what he'd like to drink? What words should I use?

"It gets pretty dusty out there," I finally said. "Would you care for something to drink?" He looked at the glass in my hand. "I could make you some tea," I added.

"Thanks," he said. "What are you drinking?"

"Well, on Mondays I like to relax a bit after the busy weekend with the family all home. I have five children you know. So sometimes after breakfast I have a little wine."

"That would be fine," he said.

By luck I found a clean tumbler in the cupboard. I stood by the sink, pouring the wine. And then, like a bolt of lightning, I realized my situation. Oh, Johann Sebastian Bach. Glory. Honour. Wisdom. Power. George Frideric Handel. King of Kings and Lord of Lords. He's on my sundeck. Today he's sitting on my sundeck. I can ask him any question under the sun, anything at all, he'll know the answer. Hallelujah. Hallelujah. Well now, wasn't this something for a Monday morning in Moose Jaw.

I opened the fridge door to replace the bottle. And I saw my father. It was New Year's morning. My father was sitting at the kitchen table. Mother sat across from him. She'd covered the oatmeal pot to let it simmer on the stove. I could hear the lid bumping against the rim, quietly. Sigrid and Freda sat on one side of the table, Raymond and I on the other. We were holding hymn books, little black books turned to page one. It was dark outside. On New Year's morning we got up before sunrise. Daddy was looking at us with his chin pointed out. It meant be still and sit straight. Raymond sat as straight and stiff as a soldier, waiting for Daddy to notice how nice and stiff he sat. We began singing. Page one. Hymn for the New Year. Philipp Nicolai. 1599. We didn't really need the books. We'd sung the same song every New Year's since the time of our conception. Daddy always sang the loudest.

The Morning Star upon us gleams; How full of grace and truth His beams.
How passing fair His splendour. Good Shepherd, David's proper heir,
My King in heav'n Thou dost me bear Upon Thy bosom tender.
Near — est, Dear — est, High — est, Bright — est, Thou delight — est.

Still to love me, Thou so high enthroned a — bove me.

I didn't mind, actually, singing hymns on New Year's, as long as I was sure no one else would find out. I'd have been rather embarrassed if any of my friends ever found out how we spent New Year's. It's easy at a certain age to be embarrassed about your family. I remember Alice Olson, how embarrassed she was about her father, Elmer Olson. He was an alcoholic and couldn't control his urine. Her mother always had to clean up after him. Even so, the house smelled. I suppose she couldn't get it all. Anyway, I know Alice was embarrassed when we saw Elmer all tousled and sick-looking, with urine stains on his trousers. Actually, I don't know what would be harder on a kid — having a father who's a drunk, or one who's sober on New Year's and sings "The Morning Star."

I walked across the deck and handed Jesus the wine. I sat down, resting my glass on the flap of my kimono. Jesus was looking out over the prairie. He seemed to be noticing everything out there. He was obviously in no hurry to leave, but he didn't have much to say. I thought of what to say next.

"I suppose you're more used to the sea than to the prairie."

"Yes," he answered. "I've lived most of my life near water. But I like the prairie too. There's something nice about the prairie." He turned his face to the wind, stronger now, coming toward us from the east.

Nice again. If I'd ever used that word to describe the prairie, in an English theme at St. John's, for example, it would have had three red circles around it. At least three, I raised my glass to the wind. Good old St. John's. Good old Pastor Solberg, standing in front of the wooden altar, holding the gospel aloft in his hand.

In the beginning wass the Word,
And the Word wass with God,
And the Word wass God.

All things were made by him;
And without him wass not anything made
That wass made.

I was sitting on a bench by Paul Thorson. We were sharing a hymnal. Our thumbs touched at the centre of the book. It was winter. The chapel was cold — an army barracks left over from World War II. We wore parkas and sat close together. Paul fooled around with his thumb, pushing my thumb to my own side of the book, then pulling it back to his side. The wind howled outside. We watched our breath as we sang the hymn.

In thine arms I rest me, Foes who would molest me
Cannot reach me here; Tho' the earth be shak — ing,

Ev — ry heart be quak — ing, Jesus calms my fear;
Fire may flash and thunder crash,
Yea, and sin and hell as — sail me,
Jesus will not fai — l me ....

And here he was. Alpha and Omega. The Word. Sitting on my canvas chair, telling me the prairie's nice. What could I say to that?

"I like it too," I said.

Jesus was watching a magpie circling above the poplars just beyond the quarry. He seemed very nice actually. But he wasn't like my father. My father was perfect, mind you, but you know about perfect people — busy, busy. He wasn't as busy as Elsie though. Elsie was the busy one. You could never visit there without her having to do something else at the same time. Wash the leaves of her plants with milk or fold socks in the basement while you sat on a bench by the washing machine. I wouldn't mind sitting on a bench in the basement if that was all she had, but her living room was full of big soft chairs that no one ever sat in. Now Christ here didn't seem to have any work to do at all.

The wind had risen now. His robes puffed about his legs. His hair swirled around his face. I set my glass down and held my kimono together at my knees. The wind was coming stronger now out of the east. My kimono flapped about my ankles. I bent down to secure the bottom, pressing the moving cloth close against my legs. A Saskatchewan wind comes up in a hurry, let me tell you. Then it happened. A gust of wind hit me straight on, seeping into the folds of my kimono, reaching down into the bodice, billowing the cloth out, until above the sash, the robe was fully open. I knew without looking. The wind was suddenly blowing on my breasts. I felt it cool on both my breasts. Then as quickly as it came, it left, and we sat in the small breeze of before.

I looked at Jesus. He was looking at me. And at my breasts. Looking right at them. Jesus was sitting there on the sundeck, looking at my breasts.

What should I do? Say excuse me and push them back into the kimono? Make a little joke of it? Look what the wind blew in, or something? Or should I say nothing? Just tuck them in as inconspicuously as possible? What do you say when a wind comes up and blows your kimono open and he sees your breasts?

Now. There are ways and there are ways of exposing your breasts. I know a few things. I read books. And I've learned a lot from my cousin Millie. Millie's the rebel in the family. She left the Academy without graduating to become an artist's model in Winnipeg. A dancer too. Anyway, Millie's told me a few things about body exposure. She says, for instance, that when an artist wants to draw his model he has her either completely nude and stretching and bending in various positions so he can sketch her from different angles. Or he drapes her with cloth, satin usually. He covers one section of the body with the material and leaves the rest exposed. But he does so in a graceful manner, draping the cloth over her stomach or ankle. Never over the breasts. So I realized that my appearance right then wasn't actually pleasing, either aesthetically or erotically — from Millie's point of view. My breasts were just sticking out from the top of my old kimono. And for some reason that I certainly can't explain, even to this day, I did nothing about it. I just sat there.

Jesus must have recognized my confusion, because right then he said, quite sincerely I thought, "You have nice breasts."

"Thanks," I said. I didn't know what else to say, so I asked him if he'd like more wine.

"Yes, I would," he said, and I left to refill the glass. When I returned he was watching the magpie swishing about in the tall weeds of the quarry. I sat down and watched with him.

Then I got a very, very peculiar sensation. I know it was just an illusion, but it was so strong it scared me. It's hard to explain because nothing like it had ever happened to me before. The magpie began to float toward Jesus. I saw it fluttering toward him in the air as if some vacuum were sucking it in. When it reached him, it flapped about on his chest, which was bare now because the top of his robe had slipped down. It nibbled at his little brown nipples and squawked and disappeared. For all the world, it seemed to disappear right into his pores. Then the same thing happened with a rock. A rock floating up from the quarry and landing on the breast of Jesus, melting into his skin. It was very strange, let me tell you, Jesus and I sitting there together with that happening. It made me dizzy, so I closed my eyes.

I saw the women in a public bath in Tokyo. Black-haired women and children. Some were squatting by faucets that lined a wall. They were running hot water into their basins, washing themselves with white cloths, rubbing each other's backs with the soapy washcloths, then emptying their basins and filling them again, pouring clean water over their bodies for the rinse. Water and suds swirled about on the tiled floor. Others were sitting in the hot pool on the far side, soaking themselves in the steamy water as they jabbered away to one another. Then I saw her. The woman without the breasts. She was squatting by a faucet near the door. The oldest woman I've ever seen. The thinnest woman I've ever witnessed. Skin and bones. Literally. Just skin and bones. She bowed and smiled at everyone who entered. She had three teeth. When she hunched over her basin, I saw the little creases of skin where her breasts had been. When she stood up the wrinkles disappeared. In their place were two shallow caves. Even the nipples seemed to have disappeared into the small brown caves of her breasts. I opened my eyes and looked at Jesus. Fortunately, everything had stopped floating.

"Have you ever been to Japan?" I asked.

"Yes," he said, "a few times."

I paid no attention to his answer but went on telling him about Japan as if he'd never been there. I couldn't seem to stop talking about that old woman and her breasts.

"You should have seen her," I said. "She wasn't flat-chested like some women even here in Moose Jaw. It wasn't like that at all. Her breasts weren't just flat. They were caved in, as if the flesh had sunk right there. Have you ever seen breasts like that before?"

Jesus' eyes were getting darker. He seemed to have sunk farther down into his chair.

"Japanese women have smaller breasts to begin with, usually," he said. But he'd misunderstood me. It wasn't just her breasts that held me. It was her jaws, teeth, neck, ankles, heels. Not just her breasts. I said nothing for a while, Jesus, too, was not talking.

Finally I asked, "Well, what do you think of breasts like that?"

I knew immediately that I'd asked the wrong question. If you want personal and specific answers, you ask personal and specific questions. It's as simple as that. I should have asked him, for instance, what he thought of them from a sexual point of view. If he were a lover, let's say, would he like to hold such breasts in his hand and play on them with his teeth and fingers? Would he now? The woman, brown and shiny, was bending over her basin. Tiny bubbles of soap drifted from the creases of her chest down to her navel. Hold them. Ha.

Or I could have asked for some kind of aesthetic opinion. If he were an artist, a sculptor, let's say, would he travel to Italy and spend weeks excavating the best marble from the hills near Florence, and then would he stay up night and day in his studio, without eating or bathing, and with matted hair and glazed eyes, chisel out those little creases from his great stone slab?

Or if he were a curator in a large museum in Paris, would he place these wrinkles on a silver pedestal in the centre of the foyer?

Or if he were a patron of the arts, would he attend the opening of this grand exhibition and stand in front of these white caves in his purple turtleneck, sipping champagne and nibbling on the little cracker with the shrimp in the middle, and would he turn to the one beside him, the one in the sleek black pants, and would he say to her, "Look, darling. Did you see this marvellous piece? Do you see how the artist has captured the very essence of the female form?"

These are some of the things I could have said if I'd had my wits about me. But my wits certainly left me that day. All I did say, and I didn't mean to — it just came out — was, "It's not nice and I don't like it."

I lifted my face, threw my head back, and let the wind blow on my neck and breasts. It was blowing harder again. I felt small grains of sand scrape against my skin.

Jesus lover of my soul, let me to thy bosom fly.
While the nearer waters roll, while the tempest still is nigh ....

When I looked at him again, his eyes were blacker still and his body had shrunk considerably. He looked almost like Jimmy that time in Prince Albert. Jimmy's an old neighbour from Regina. On his twenty-seventh birthday he joined a motorcycle gang, The Grim Reapers to be exact, and got into a lot of trouble. He ended up in maximum security in PA. One summer on a camping trip up north we stopped to see him — Fred and the kids and I. It wasn't a good visit, by the way. If you're going to visit inmates you should do it regularly. I realize this now. Anyway, that's when his eyes looked black like that. But maybe he'd been smoking. It's probably not the same thing. Jimmy Lebrun. He never did think it was funny when I'd call him a Midnight Raider instead of a Grim Reaper. People are sensitive about their names.

Then Jesus finally answered. Everything seemed to take him a long time, even answering simple questions.

But I'm not sure what he said because something so strange happened that whatever he did say was swept away. Right then the wind blew against my face, pulling my hair back. My kimono swirled about every which way, and I was swinging my arms in the air, like swimming. And there right below my eyes was the roof of our house. I was looking down on the top of the roof. I saw the row of shingles ripped loose from the August hailstorm. And I remember thinking — Fred hasn't fixed those shingles yet. I'll have to remind him when he gets home from work. If it rains again the back bedroom will get soaked. Before I knew it I was circling over the sundeck, looking down on the top of Jesus' head. Only I wasn't. I was sitting in the canvas chair watching myself hover over his shoulders. Only it wasn't me hovering. It was the old woman in Tokyo. I saw her grey hair twisting in the wind and her shiny little bum raised in the air, like a baby's. Water was dripping from her chin and toes. And soap bubbles trailed from her elbows like tinsel. She was floating down toward his chest. Only it wasn't her. It was me. I could taste bits of suds sticking to the corners of my mouth and feel the wind on my wet back and in the hollow caves of my breasts. I was smiling and bowing, and the wind was blowing in narrow wisps against my toothless gums. Then quickly, so quickly, like a flock of winter sparrows diving through snow into the branches of the poplar, I was splitting up into millions and millions of pieces and sinking into the tiny, tiny, holes in his chest. It was like the magpie and the rock, like I had come apart into atoms or molecules, or whatever it is we really are.

After that I was dizzy. I began to feel nauseated. Jesus looked sick too. Sad and sick and lonesome. Oh, Christ, I thought, why are we sitting here on such a fine day pouring out sorrows into each other?

I had to get up and walk around. I'd go into the kitchen and make some tea.

I put the kettle on to boil. What on earth had gotten into me? Why had I spent this perfectly good morning talking about breasts? My one chance in a lifetime and I'd let it go. Why didn't I have better control? Why was I always letting things get out of hand? Breasts. And why was my name Gloria? Such a pious name for one who can't think of anything else to talk about but breasts. Why wasn't it Lucille? Or Millie? You could talk about breasts all day if your name was Millie. But Gloria. Gloria. Glo-o-o-o-o-o-oria. I knew then why so many Glorias hang around bars, talking too loud, laughing shrilly at stupid jokes, making sure everyone hears them laugh at dirty jokes. They're just trying to live down their name, that's all. I brought out the cups and poured the tea.

Everything was back to normal when I returned except that Jesus still looked desolate sitting in the canvas chair. I handed him the tea and sat down beside him.

Oh, Daddy. And Philipp Nicolai. Oh, Bernard of Clairvaux. Oh, Sacred Head Now Wounded. Go away for a little while and let us sit together quietly, here in this small space under the sun.

I sipped the tea and watched his face. He looked so sorrowful I reached out and put my hand on his wrist. I sat there a long while, rubbing the little hairs on his wrist with my fingers. I couldn't help it. After that he put his arm on my shoulder and his hand on the back of my neck, stroking the muscles there. It felt good. Whenever anything exciting or unusual happens to me my neck is the first to feel it. It gets stiff and knotted up. Then I usually get a headache, and frequently I become nauseous. So it felt very good having my neck rubbed.

I've never been able to handle sensation very well. I remember when I was in grade three and my folks took us to the Saskatoon Exhibition. We went to see the grandstand show — the battle of Wolfe and Montcalm on the Plains of Abraham. The stage was filled with Indians and pioneers and ladies in red, white and blue dresses, singing "In Days of Yore from Britain's Shore." It was very spectacular but too much for me. My stomach was upset and my neck ached. I had to keep my head on my mother's lap the whole time, just opening my eyes once in a while so I wouldn't miss everything.

So it felt really good having my neck stroked like that. I could almost feel the knots untying and my body becoming warmer and more restful. Jesus too seemed to be feeling better. His body was back to normal. His eyes looked natural again.

Then, all of a sudden, he started to laugh. He held his hand on my neck and laughed out loud. I don't know to this day what he was laughing about. There was nothing funny there at all. But hearing him made me laugh too. I couldn't stop. He was laughing so hard he spilled the tea over his purple stole. When I saw that I laughed even harder. I'd never thought of Jesus spilling his tea before. And when Jesus saw me laugh so hard and when he looked at my breasts shaking, he laughed harder still, till he wiped tears from his eyes.

After that we just sat there. I don't know how long. I know we watched the magpie carve black waves in the air above the rocks. And the rocks stiff and lovely among the swaying weeds. We watched the poplars twist and bend and rise again beyond the quarry. And then he had to leave.

"Goodbye, Gloria Johnson," he said rising from his chair. "Thanks for the hospitality."

He leaned over and kissed me on my mouth. Then he flicked my nipple with his finger. And off he went. Down the hill. Through the quarry, and into the prairie. I stood on the sundeck and watched. I watched until I could see him no longer. Until he was only some dim and ancient star on the far horizon.

I went inside the house. Well, now, wasn't that a nice visit. Wasn't that something. I examined the clothes, dry and sour in the living room. I'd have to put them back in the wash, that's all. I couldn't stand the smell. I tucked my breasts back into my kimono and lugged the basket downstairs.

That's what happened to me in Moose Jaw in 1972. It was the main thing that happened to me that year.

Discriminatio Spirituum

Melissa Hardy

Isabel Smythe, a pupil at the school, and Sister Blandina, her teacher, lay on their stomachs on the stone floor of the small Romanesque chapel, their arms extended to either side of them in imitation of the Holy Cross. They were adoring the Sacred Heart — that was the mandate of the Little Sisters, after all; the Perpetual Adoration of the Sacred Heart. They accomplished this in shifts. As for the object of all this Perpetual Adoration, it sat high on the high altar like a egg in an egg cup — a Fabergé egg in a rococo cup. Some deep, inward part of it turned now blue, now green, now purple — the Sacred Heart operated on principles similar to those governing lava lamps.

Sister Blandina always chose this, the graveyard shift, for the Adoration because it presented her with an opportunity to mortify what flesh still remained to her after years of conscientious fasting. In addition, she was an insomniac and had been since childhood when she used to lie awake at night waiting for her several brothers to steal into her room under cover of dark and molest her. *(Pad, pad, pad. Feet down the hall. A board which creaked. The doorknob turning.)* Because of her brothers, Sister Blandina did not much like men.

As for Isabel, she was supposed to be asleep in her cubicle at such an hour, but, truth was, she had a thing for Sister Blandina. This was not surprising as Sister Blandina was unspeakably lovely. She owed her unsettling beauty not so much to individual features — the long, straight nose, the crumpled mouth, the round and softly dented chin, and eyes the color of a dense fog — as to the absolute serenity of her expression. Her face closely resembled a saint's death mask.

The devotion of the Perpetual Adoration was supposed to be performed in silence, and for some time Isabel and Blandina kept this rule, lying side by side in the aisle that ran before the altar, their bodies separated by the length of their two arms, their fingertips nearly touching. Sniffing covertly, they sampled one another's perfume. Isabel, being a young lady of Family, wore "Miss Dior;" Blandina affected a more painful fragrance — the odor of sanctity, Isabel supposed. A more practised nose might have detected "Taboo."

It was Blandina who at length broke the silence. "I'm sure," she said, "that you will get it." (Her voice was somewhat muffled; she was, after all, lying on her face. *If you don't look, it's not happening. "Go away! No, stop it!"*)

"What?" asked Isabel.

"Discriminatio spirituum," Blandina pronounced softly. "The ability to see demons," she explained.

33

"Pardon?" asked Isabel, a bit startled.

"The ability to see demons," Blandina repeated. "I've been seeing them for years. Shall I tell you about the first time I saw them?"

"I'd rather you didn't," said Isabel, who was easily spooked.

But Blandina seemed not to notice. "I remember it quite clearly," began the nun. "As if it were ... not yesterday, but a dream I have dreamt ... always. Even when it happened, it had that quality of a dream — the clarity, the intensity of some vision invested with a larger proportion than usual of reality, less diluted than is ... quotidian experience."

Isabel had observed that Blandina did not speak as people usually do.

"I had not been well," the nun continued. "A fog of long duration had settled on me. I heard voices as if they were fog horns — at a distance, but sometimes one would float quite nearby, and I would be startled, for I hadn't known anyone was there.

"And I had headaches — big, booming headaches. Boom! Boom! I was in the Motherhouse then, in Belgium. 'It's just her sinuses,' they said. But do you know what *sinus* means in Latin? A bay, a lap, a cavity. It was not my sinuses but my cavities, my empty spaces.

"So they sent me here; they sent me there, to this convent and that, hoping that the fog would lift, that I would leave it behind me in some strange port, or succumb, if succumb I must, at some great distance ... Thus it was that at last I came to Venice.

"And there it was worse. Far worse. 'Keep me afloat,' I cried, but they ... they strapped me down and said, 'Take this, Little Dove. Swallow that.' That's what they called me, The Dove, and they put me in the dovecote."

Her voice was low, sweet, a terrible cooing.

Isabel rolled up onto one side and looked at Blandina. Her feet were cold, her nipples squashed out of shape, bent to one side.

Blandina too rolled to her side. "It was wintertime," she said. "The evening of Epiphany. God Made Manifest. The Little Sisters took me to San Marco, airing me, I suppose, but doing it at night so that no one would see a novice of their order beneath such a load of ... I don't know ... madness? Perhaps they meant to cure me. There are relics in San Marco's; thumbs and skulls and such.

"It was sleeting. We carried big black umbrellas which glistened like domes of mica beneath the street lamps. The drowned piazza steamed cold, and water washed the wrinkled stones of the narthex. It was as though Venice were a ship which had sprung a leak and was slowly sinking, waves riding the desk that was the piazza. The ship tossed. I felt quite unsteady on my pins. We entered the basilica. What with the roll and swell, I had to seize hold of objects as I made my way down the aisle ... to keep upright. Sometimes they proved to be the arms of people — soft, spongy and then hard bone. I had no way of telling — what with the pain, the fog — what lived and what didn't. And suddenly I saw them."

"Who?" asked Isabel.

"The demons," replied Blandina. "They emerged from the fog. Wafted into slow focus. They blew towards me like the diaspora of a dandelion clock, and the next thing I knew, they had attached themselves to me, as if with suckers. They hung from my arms; they clambered over me like monkeys, licking me with tongues ... tongues not like tongues but ... you know what I mean ... like the ... the private parts of men (have you ever seen these things? Oh they are *disgusting*)." Blandina's elegant nose wrinkled finely at the bridge.

"Is that a fact?" Isabel asked, swallowing hard.

"Oh, yes," said Blandina.

"What do demons look like?" Isabel asked in a hoarse whisper.

"Like men," Blandina whispered back. She shuddered. "Like awful boys. But their skin is metallic, their features more finely chiselled than those of men, and their eyes are so disconcerting. Demons' eyes have no pupils. Did you know that? All eyeball and silver, almost shiny. They catch the lights. I've often wondered if they are really mirrors and not eyes at all. Mirrors reflecting some great, some hideous light."

(The light from the hall in a column on the floor. The door cuts it in two, closing. Now it is dark, and there are hands, pulling at her.)

"Now, however," said Blandina, and at this she shifted, sighed, glanced around her, squinted. "I can't see them too clearly. They look like long streaks of grey, trembling, insubstantial matter, rather like darkish fluid barely gelled."

"Demons? Here?" cried Isabel softly. Terrified, she surveyed the tiny chapel: the Sacred Heart glittering darkly in the guttering candlelight; behind it, a twelve-foot mosaic Virgin, looming, veil whipped back to reveal marcelled hair. The Mother of God's eyes glowed red with rage as she ground the triangular head of a serpent against the jagged rock. And to one side of the altar, the eastern, votive wall ... It was so thickly hung with gilt hearts holding here a snapshot, there a lock of hair, that it seemed to palpitate. *Remember me*, the silent cry went up from the little hearts. *Remember Gino! Remember little Mary Ann who died just three days before her first communion! Oh, great Mother of Mercy. She was a good enough girl!*

"But we are surrounded by demons," Blandina assured Isabel, as if that were no cause for alarm. "There's no place they prefer to a chapel. It's an interesting thing, you know," she said in a somewhat more conversational vein, "but I find I see them more or less clearly depending on the state of my soul. When my heart is pure, I see them quite clearly, as clearly as I see you. At other times I can barely make them out ... But don't worry," she assured the girl. "Demons can't hurt you unless you mistake their voice for that of your soul. Of course, that's a mistake people often make. As for me, I never have that problem because I can see them. At the very least I can see their lips move. So you see, I'll protect you."

Blandina looked long at Isabel then. Some emotion, well-mastered but too strong for the nun to suppress entirely, wavered across her face. It altered her expression as subtly as a change of light might have introduced new concavities, places to catch and hold shadow. For a moment the only sounds to be heard in the chapel were those of wax dripping on the floor of the dais, the chapel settling in a series of crotchety, old squeaks, and below the stone slabs of the floor against which their ears were pressed, something scraping against stone with metal. Then Blandina lifted her hand and, laying it on Isabel's wrist, encircled it with her long icy fingers, running her thumb up and down a stretch of blue vein on the underside of the girl's forearm for a moment before taking hold of the pink satin ribbon that held her peignoir together at the throat. She wrapped it around her finger, let it unroll and fall free.

"Such pretty hair," she murmured. She touched Isabel's blond hair. "I had long hair. Once. Not so pretty. Straight and brown. But long. It came to past my waist. They cut it off." Blandina's soft, crumpled lips bumped along Isabel's forehead, leaving in their wake a trail of heat.

(Hands that sought her in the dark, separating her from the bedclothes; she lies, knees to chest, like a baby in the womb, like a body in a burial jar.)

"We must not let men touch us," Blandina told her, "for they are impure." Her hand, dry and fever hot, stroking Isabel's nipple into shape.

("Come on, 'Dina, now! Open up!" Hot hissing in her ear; the voice of snakes. And when she didn't ...)

"Don't you see?" the nun implored her, pulling Isabel close, holding her to her, scanning demonic lips over the girl's shoulder to discern the purport of their muttered discourse, vaporous mouthings that look like the shimmers of heat off a sidewalk. "I must protect you from men!" she told her. "Seal you so they will not defile you. Your body is a temple, Isabel. And these ... " Her hand on Isabel's white thigh.

(Her brothers pry her knees open. One of them holds them down.)

"Corinthian columns," the nun whispered. She parted Isabel's thighs with her hand, touched her where it's sweet. "Let me seal you with this sharp ecstasy that is ours to give," she urged her.

("You will like this," her brothers tell her. "Be quiet, 'Dina!")

"But you mustn't scream," insisted Blandina, her hand pressed tight on Isabel's mouth.

* * *

After Isabel left the chapel, after it was over, in the huge emptiness that is the night, Blandina gave in to those pesky demons. She had kept them at bay for so long. It was impossible to hold out longer. Useless. And so they grew their familiar circle tighter; knelt; pulled her lovingly to them; rolled her in the loose transparency of their arms. They would not stop laughing. This had always been the case, and Blandina had never been able to convince them to stop.

("It's not funny, what you're doing!"
"C'mon, 'Dina. You like it! Don't lie to us!"
"Someone will hear!")

But, though she protested, she made no move to push away the liquid fingers which tested her as if she were some ripe fruit, which reached for her throat, her hands, her bosom, with fingers that melted at her touch like snow. They kissed her cheeks, her eyes, her lips with their lips like stinging nettle. *"Dina! 'Dina!"* they crooned in strange, tuneless voices, as they straddled her with wet, warm legs that grew around her like vines and held her tight.

the challenge

women have always been home
to our children   our men
finding themselves the centre
of our own wisdom
is a challenge
one that begins with the Mothersource
buried in years of fear
about the Goddess
waiting to unearth
Her power

when we accept the challenge
She unsheathes Herself
belches from the earth
deception & fear
fall from our skirts
ochre & moist

old myths heal us
thorns from the witch's tree
crown our heads
adorn us in wisdom

carol rose

the wall

In Jerusalem
I always come
Face to face
With my longing

It never fails
The hunger   desire
The frantic search
For doorways

I seek Your heart
Find only cracks
Stuffed with prayers

I become a prayer
Folded   tattered
Small enough
To fit Your wounds

I shape myself
In secret hollows
Cling mosslike
To Your ancient contours

Body on body
We lovers loosen
Rocks that separate us

In the morning
Only doves and beggars
Come to witness
Your return to stone

carol rose

scenting You

i carry Your scent in a crystal jar
jasmine blossoms sand & sage

i open the lid   especially
in winter   sniff the air

i discover Your smell
in tall prairie grass

catch a hint of Your musk
on the flesh of new wheat

even corn reminds me
i inhale Your perfume in its hair

                    carol rose

hallel*
(dedicated to the Women of the Wall)

the taste
of your
tear soaked
stones stays
on my tongue
not tied
to palate
my right hand
not withered
holds fast
& remembers
Jerusalem
where men
preen their
prayershawls
like peacocks
as women wail
in labour
birthing
songs
of hope
under a new
moon

carol rose

*traditional song of praise

breaking the rules

when

    they soar

lore

    of light

instead of

    and full

law

    moist

guides

    wings

life

    butterfly

there's a

    grow

gentle

    themselves

breaking

    rules test

(on the inside)

carol rose

Margaret's Dreams

Susan Kerslake

Tansy (her new name) had been there for only two days and already Margaret couldn't stand her. "My husband's dear sister who's been away around the world finding herself, 'communing,' 'being,' 'into' the exotic and esoteric, who should have something interesting to say to those of us poor slobs who have stayed put, some wisdom, reassurance that our role is important, if for nothing else than to subsidize!" But Tansy was busy with her early morning order of tai chi, a cleanse of yoga, perhaps a pre-jog, then breakfast and a meditation on the night behind and the day ahead. The bathroom was strewn with little bars of soap, each for a different part of her body, handmade, balms, ointments, unguents, brews, tinctures. Some smelled good enough to eat, others seemed to have seeds about to sprout. Tansy wore only cotton and her clothes must be washed in environmentally safe soap. Had they sprayed anything on their lawn that would prevent her sunbathing? Margaret only wished.

They'd given her the guest room. Margaret had taken pride in it actually, nice touches of silk flowers, a colourful Morris Louis poster, even a note pad in the shape of a musical note. When she peeked in, the room was a shambles.

Tansy wore only yellow, a colour that hardly suited anyone. This was her sun period, sort of like the Chinese associations of animals with years, she explained. The lunar phase would be next when she would dress all in silvers, then would come Mars. "Her Martian stage," Margaret said to Alan who had longer hours away from home than she did and found it all amusing. "She's just flinging her wild oats," he said, which confirmed her belief in that family's lack of knowledge of quotable quotes.

Was she always like this? Margaret thought this would be a gentle question with room for explanations and then some small attempt at understanding on her part. Alan said, "Selfish? Yes." That's why I married him, she thought.

Just before she left for work in the morning, Margaret dropped hints about things that could be done, that needed to be done around the house, thirsty plants, dusting, errands that were within striking distance, her own brother's favourite corduroy jacket at the cleaners.

When she got home, fevered and fed up, not only had nothing been done, not even the breakfast dishes, but Tansy said, "Finally you're back. Can I borrow the car?"

Margaret didn't know why she couldn't, though she wondered in a stage aside why the automobile was exempt as a bad machine. Airplanes and home electricity seemed to be O.K. too.

"Fresh, fresh," Tansy was saying. She'd checked the fridge and there was practically nothing she could eat.

Tansy could always bring up a fresh, fresh flash of sunny smile. She was happy — remember, the quest was a joyful one; that morose stuff was behind everyone now. There were ups and downs as discovery of the self would dictate, but basically ... and she felt so good. Her body was so fresh.

The third morning Margaret was in the kitchen at the same moment. "I dreamed about you last night."

Tansy seemed to shudder and turned attentively. "What do you mean?"

"I had a dream about you."

"On purpose?"

"I had a dream and you were in it." Margaret was busy and didn't see the acute angle Tansy was making with her body.

"So?"

Margaret raised the glass of orange juice to her lips and got a fixed look of recall on her face. "It was night. There was a huge field of mown grass ringed with people. Torches blazed. Spotlights were aimed on a white square that seemed to be made of canvas in the centre of the field. Nothing was happening but everyone was concentrating on the white square. We needed to get across the field and couldn't go around, it was too dark to see what was there, trees or cliffs. You were going first. No one in the crowd knew we wanted to get by; it was something we had to do ourselves. But we knew it would be disturbing to them, that they wouldn't like it. They might get very angry and we were afraid in that way we are of an unknown but perceived danger. The tarp square was so white, just like it was waiting for a sacrifice; it was so obviously a target ... " She sipped her juice, the astringent wrinkle of her lips may have been due to that. "The people were so far back in the darkness, but the looks on their faces — "

"And then?"

"That's all, then I woke up."

Tansy made a funny sound in her throat. "That dream makes me really uncomfortable."

"Why?"

"I wonder if I'm going to have a trial of some sort?"

"I thought that's what all this was about?"

"Well it is, but it's more of a quest. It doesn't have to be trial."

A trail instead of a trial, Margaret mumbled to herself.

"What was that?"

"Nothing."

"Was that something more from the dream?"

"No no."

The kitchen stirred with a yellow light reflected from Tansy's clothes. She moved in little circles, picking out nuts and seeds and grains from plastic bags. There was butter and honey. Water boiled on the stove. She poured it over a spoonful of blunt cut leaves.

Margaret squeezed her glass onto the counter. As she left with her briefcase, Tansy flashed her a stunning smile of white teeth and bestowed, in earthly breath, a syllable that sounded like "jai."

"I'm not looking forward to coming home anymore." She should have been shouting, but she had to whisper and put her hand on the face of Alan's magazine forcing it down into his lap. "Can't you come home any earlier?"

He gave his steady tolerant you-know-better-than-that look. "Think of it as practice."

"Practice for what?"

"Our children."

Margaret had forgotten to make juice. How nice it would have been, she thought, if ... but Tansy was seated quietly at the table in an island of paper. Beautiful quality stuff, some of it handmade, muted colours, ragged edges. Expensive. "Letters?" she asked.

"No. This is for my journal. It's a new form. I learned about it at the workshop. Instead of chronologically, you write on single sheets and keep them in a box. That way you can shuffle them around, rearrange them. It's totally changed my perspective on my life. That's what they said would happen. Suddenly time isn't as important, well it is, but I can look at each entry as a fluid event in my life. Its emotional content is more important. And you can colour-coordinate the entries — "

"The workshop people papermakers?"

"Their friends are — "

"Gave you starter kits?"

"And we could buy boxes too."

"What a nice idea."

"If you study colour you find out it's quite spiritual too."

Margaret hardly recognized the inside of her own fridge — whole plants lounged in plastic bags, dirt on their roots, cold sluggish bugs surprised. Her system cried for citrus. There, a puckered nectarine.

"Oh well, I guess I can get another one this morning," said Tansy.

"I guess so," Margaret bit it. The she remembered, "I had another dream about you."

"Really?" An uneasy stillness.

Margaret chewed the fruit, soothing the receptors on her tongue. "Ummm," an ambiguous sound, nodding her head.

"What was it?"

"I'm just trying to remember."

Tansy watched her mouth.

"You had a tracheotomy. You were in a tunnel in a hospital and at the end of the tunnel an anaesthetist was trying to put a wick of cotton in the hole to put you to sleep, but when he did that, your tongue flattened back in your throat like a stopper. He didn't see that happening. You couldn't breathe. I grabbed you up, you were sort of child size then, and ran after the doctors to show them what had happened."

"Your throat looked like vocal cords, those ridges of pink flesh and your tongue was flipped back, all those blue veins — but the doctor said it was perfectly alright like that."

"But what happened to me?"

"I don't know—nothing—that's all I dreamed." She threw the stone in the garbage. There was barely room for it. She shook the bag, tied it up and took it out to the can. If that new bag is full when I get back, she thought; who is her maid usually? Or is she one of those people who can live in a sty? I can't believe mother Muriel brought her up this way, I know she didn't; she's always offering to help if there's something that needs to be done, she can't sit still for a minute.

"Just how long does she plan on staying?" Margaret asked Alan. It had been a week. She had not expected — "I dread coming home — "

"Dread?"

"When I came home today, I couldn't get in. My own house. She had bolted the doors because she wanted to take a bath and was afraid someone might come in while she was communing in herbs — "

"How did you get in?"

"It's not funny. I yelled and pounded. When she appeared, she said, 'Oh hi!' OH HI!" Margaret couldn't think of the words to describe the beatific smile that coalesced through the vaporous golden steam that floated from Tansy's body. "Come."

The bathroom looked like "before."

"What is this?" she traced her finger through an oily film that coated the tub.

"Cleanser should fix that."

It was rainy and cool the next morning. Tansy was upside down in the living room. Incense reeked from three wands and from the stereo, gongs meditated on two or three notes. As Margaret watched, a finger of ash dropped to the carpet and collapsed. Yellow clashed in her muted colour scheme. Tansy must have dyed everything at once in the most garish Rit offered. She had talked about the reputation of yellow, maligned as the colour of madness; it was equally important to creative people or those on the verge, reborn people; a slight reticence to include herself until Margaret said, "like you." "Why yes!" grateful, surprise, surprise. Could she really be that ... innocent?

Alan had suggested leaving a note with things that could be done. She put it down on the stereo.

"Oh, had another dream about you. It's weird isn't it? Almost every night now I dream about you. You'll have to start a box of other people's dreams about you. Maybe all kinds of people are dreaming about you each night, but they don't recognize you, they don't know what your name is — that stranger in my dream they'd say ... maybe they write down their dreams too and there are diaries all over the world with you in them."

Tansy was still upside down, her body rigid, her eyes thrown open.

"It was dark. You were wandering around. Everywhere you went the light bulbs burnt out. You'd turn on a lamp, it would flicker and go out. It was a large house or hotel, a rambling building anyway, with lots of rooms. It seemed that if you wanted to you could wander all night, perhaps endlessly, trying to find the lamp that wouldn't go out when you touched it."

The rain had freshened things; a pleasant odour and coolness rose from the wet sidewalk. Margaret had had a good day. She looked forward to telling Alan this and that. Their house looked pretty in this light, the little tree was making seeds this year for the first time; the annuals had bushed out and blossomed. This was their starter home. They hadn't planned on staying here this long, but it'd grown on them and the neighbourhood had proved terrific. Almost as good as an old fifties sitcom. They deserved it though. Damn it anyway; they worked hard and obliged the ethic.

The note was still on the stereo.

"This was for you," Margaret said steadily.

"Yes, I saw it." Tansy smiled. Her hands remained folded in her lap.

"So what did you do?" Margaret was smiling too; she could feel the idiot grin grease her face.

"Oh, I didn't have time. Everything has become relative you know, to me. Time has lost its old archaic tyranny over me. I can control it by ignoring it," she said brightly.

Alan and Margaret ate out. He took her to the Vegetarian pizza place; deep-dish spinach, her favourite, a pitcher of pop, and kept saying, "She wasn't this bad before; she's gotten worse." The baseball game on T.V. he'd wanted to see had already started.

"Every pore is explored, each memory provoked, each thought analyzed — "

"Anal-ized."

"Alan!"

"Childlike."

"Childish. Children don't examine their thoughts, they just have them."

"You have to love her."

"I have to what?"

"Not you. If you do then you can stand it, I mean."

"You've got to do something."

"But what?"

On Tansy's closed door there was a sign "Do not disturb." Margaret rolled her eyes and grabbed her fist back with her other hand; I'll not disturb you, she thought.

It was Saturday. When Margaret returned from shopping, Tansy was out in the yard. "Sleeping in, were you?" Her body buttered in a yellow bikini.

"I just didn't want to hear another, yet another damn dream that you'd had about me."

"Funny you should mention that, I — "

"I don't think I want to hear."

Margaret felt herself give a little wiggle like a worm on a hook in the vicinity of an uncertainty. After just long enough, she said, "Well, let me know."

The screen door creaked when Tansy came in and lodged her hip against the kitchen counter.

"Yes?"

"Did you have one again last night?"

"Sure did."

"Doesn't it strike you as odd; that you would dream about me every night, night after night?"

"And these are the ones I remember? Imagine all the ones — well we had that conversation before."

"Are you worried about me or something?"

"Ohhh ... I don't know?" She reined back wondering what would be next.

"I mean in the dreams, I'm always having trouble."

"Yes, it seems that way."

"Dreams are about how things are — or could be. I had a friend who foretold things in her dreams."

"Really."

"None of the things you've dreamed about me have come true."

"Dreams are supposed to be symbolic aren't they?"

Tansy swooned into a thoughtful trance, a dalliance. "Dreams can be lots of things."

"Well, in one I had last night you were keeping a book like your diaries, except it was paintings — "

"I have a friend who does that, a sketchbook — "

"These were finished paintings, details, the whole page filled with colour, shadows — "

"Shadows?"

"More like a fog, but it was night. You'd painted the front of a building the way a child does, no top or sides, and it was full of little square windows. In each window there was a face. There were people with babies milling all around the outside of the building. At first I was trying to see their faces but it was too dark; yellow light shone out from behind the people in the windows. Then I noticed you in the lower right hand corner crawling towards me, one hand reaching out, imploring — "

"Imploring — "

"You were hollering something, I couldn't tell what you were saying, your mouth was open crying or pleading," Margaret curled her lip as if she couldn't describe it any further. "You were hurt somehow, I couldn't tell. Page after page of paintings like that, crowded, busy, but damp with a kind of sadness. You were in each one, but always separate, bigger than the rest of the people who seemed the right size to fit. It was odd, at first I couldn't find you in them, but then I realized you had to be there, it was like one of those 'hidden in this picture is — ' usually something in great contrast to the rest, a lamb or a beast — "

"Beast." Tansy spit on the word. "There are beasts in my life."

Margaret put her head down in her hands on the counter.

"Are you feeling alright?" Tansy was concerned, she was worried. Sick people were interesting, but they became unavailable.

Margaret waved one hand in the air, a gesture of reassurance.

"Did you used to dream about me?" Tansy touched things on the counter, lightly, straightening them, lining them up.

"Before you came?"

"Yea."

Margaret considered. Out of the corner of her eye she could see the beast in innocent's clothing; the menagerie: cow's eyes, coltish limbs, golden mane. She saw the sharp beak, the quick pink tongue, the stretched membranes in the throat right down into the maw of hunger, a moist and shiny, blossoming, amorphous, rapacious hunger. She heard her peeping: whole health, sublime states, acupressural alterations, restorative regressions, lyrical love, miracles. A creature whom, it was true, she didn't love.

"I want to understand," said Tansy.

"I don't understand it myself," Margaret stood up straight, "what can be happening, what does this mean? Is it a reflection of my psyche or yours? What if I did have powers to direct people's lives? So far the dreams have been passive, a sort of past-tense quality, but what if I started dreaming of you doing things that could happen. I don't understand; this has never happened to me before; it's scary really. I don't have any control, as you can see. Night after night. Before I go to sleep I think, is it going to happen again, will it be like the last one? I've tried to remember things that might have happened in the day, that might've influenced the dream. I don't know what to do. You ask if I used to dream about you; I've never had this kind of experience before. It's frightening."

Tansy blinked. "You have no control." She didn't, couldn't believe it. Margaret was supposed to. Her life was so ordered, appeared so perfectly if stupidly shaped, yet here she was in the grip. This might be interesting, it had potential, but she couldn't chance it at the moment, not while she had so much work to do on her own life. Ill-timed, inconsiderate, but there was that woman she'd met at that workshop ... Alan would give her bus money, or maybe even drive her, just a weekend trip; mostly he'd been home during her meditation time; he would want to know what she was doing. It had turned out that she didn't care that much for Margaret who seemed stressed and hardened, even sort of dangerous. She went to get something.

"I think you should think about this," she said to Margaret, handing her a brochure.

The Death of a Husband

Liza Potvin

LISTEN. I might as well tell you from the start: I no longer believe in Romance. It's a plot designed to keep us chained to the same lifelong partners, to grease the wheels of capitalism, to keep us buying, buying, buying. And I know that you don't really buy any of those feeble plots that limp miserably across your television screen, the kind that send you dashing to the refrigerator during commercials in search of more genuine sustenance and comfort. Even there you are confronted by heart-shaped boxes of stale chocolate and overripe camembert that call for someone else's fingers and a bottle of heavy Bordeaux. I mean, really, life is nauseating enough without seeking out some ersatz hero who breathes heavily on the late night show and glares suggestively at his female sidekick.

Admit it: what really turns you on these days is death. You've plotted your husband's at least a hundred times. Not the actual details. You're not into murder, of course, unless it's a good murder mystery, and then it always has to be someone else's. No, it's his absence that you find titillating, and the funeral itself. And all that money from the insurance company. I dare you to deny this: you even know exactly what you'll wear at his funeral. You've pictured yourself in black, looking forlorn but mysterious, sexy even, standing by the side of his grave, over and over. The setting is vaguely misty, just enough to give it that soft-blur focus. You will be the perfect spectacle of the bereaved, in your long flowing black cape and the stunning black fedora that covers just half of your face.

You picked out the underwear some time ago, your best black lace high-cut French panties, the ones he gave you for your birthday several years ago, the ones that wait at the back of your drawer between sachet bags of lavender. The kind that you perpetually hope will give you that seamless, sleek look: no hooks, no snags, no catches, nothing to interrupt the smooth gaze of the eye, as promised. Some haunting feeling prevents you from selecting them on a regular basis, as if you were saving them for a special occasion. Like the seduction scene you replay in your imagination every time you envision yourself wearing them. In this scene, you have on your best black stockings too, or maybe your white ones, the kind that are so sheer and so expensive that they would run all over the place the moment you put them on in real life.

This fantasy is the reversal of the night when you met him, the night when you lay in your tepid bath water, debating whether or not you should even go to the party. How bloated you felt, how tired, too lazy even to shave your legs (I'll be wearing trousers anyway," you thought). "I'll just stay for one glass of wine, then come right home and get a good night's sleep," you said, as you reached for your oversized white cotton briefs. You know the ones I mean: the underwear your mother ordered from the Eaton's catalogue for you when you were in grade ten, with the elastic all stretched out, but they never seem to wear out, and they're so damned comfortable that you cannot bring yourself to throw them out. On that night, despite your mortification, he never seemed to notice what you were wearing, but from that moment forward, you vowed to choose black over white, the future over the past, the unknown over the known.

You see what I mean. About the romance and consumerism crap. And this craze for striking parallels, as if our whole lives were bound up in finding perfect symmetry. Next you'll be wanting a happy ending to this story. Give me a break! Anyway, this is a story about death.

Back to the funeral: there you are, standing there so wearily, holding back your tears, looking so lovely and vulnerable, while all your friends gather about you with an endless litany about love, death, life and other profundities. The usual sort of banal soliloquies that people utter to satisfy themselves when they are hungry to speak. But there is one tall, rather attractive man in the crowd, a former cohort of your husband's, who approaches you and says absolutely nothing, merely clasps your hand tightly, looks you in the eye searchingly for what seems an eternity, and then ...

Honestly, you're so prurient and predictable, waiting there. Drooling for the details of someone else's sordid fantasy. You're either all a bunch of hopeless romantics (I noticed how your hearts were thumping away back there, as if mere words could restore the lustre to your pathetic love lives), or you're silly degenerates who have not yet caught on to the fact that romance and the author are dead, that in this age of Velcro, zippers no longer get inconveniently stuck, and closure has become a moot point.

The point here is that you do want him gone from your life, and dead seems the only way to do it. For the entire following day, you are lost in the details of your new life. You envision long, drawn-out afternoons over cups of aromatic, freshly roasted coffee, where your time is completely your own. No interruptions. True Independence. Glorious Self-Sufficiency. All that space to yourself, the luxury of solitude. You have long ago separated the possessions you value from his, determined what you could get for his Harley, sold off all his toys for imaginary sums, given away what you consider his junk to the Salvation Army. The living room expands in your head, the bedroom already seems tidier without any of his clutter. You have remodelled the kitchen in a new colour scheme, dispensed with those hideous shelves he built for you "as a temporary measure only," indulged yourself in multitudinous and varied extravagant sensations. You picture yourself taking strolls through your favourite district, stopping at cafés whenever the whim should sweep you away. No mandatory meals. No regular sleep patterns. In fact, no clocks. And if you should choose, the occasional lover between your sheets, who will always leave early and never complicate your life with his insistencies, his demands to know how things between the two of you will end up. For it is a fact that many in that crowd will consider you a heroine, admire your stoic patience. How beautifully you hold up under such duress! What a tragedy! Such a young widow, with four children to raise all on her own! ...

But wait a minute! Is that his car you hear coming up the driveway? His key in the lock? In a panic, you scramble around the kitchen, adjust the silverware, place the wine on the table, set the garnish delicately on the salad dish, slip the plates into the oven to warm. Such reveries have made you famished, inordinately greedy, anxious to please. The candles are lit, and the flame mocks the surrounding darkness. Like magic, his face appears before yours as you encounter one another like intimate strangers, in that warm, familiar way ...

Enough drivel. After all, we know how long your private dinner will last before the procession of kids comes barging in. We also know who it is who will be stuck in the kitchen, scraping that candle wax off the linen, washing those dishes, digesting that hoard of complaints about brown-bag equality ("Well, if he gets peanut butter cookies, how come I only get a banana? It's not fair!"). And your beloved skilfully avoids confrontation through his long-standing technique of sprawling out on the chesterfield and turning up the volume on the hockey game, the organ chords chanting their tireless refrain beneath the commentator's agitated but controlled analysis. Even hours later, the kids all miraculously asleep, their whining rhythms curiously echoed in the jarring stillness, there is a longing that you cannot quite put your finger on. Even as you tug him toward you, ignoring his protests that the Leafs are actually ahead, that you may be witnessing history in the making, you recognize that something rare is transforming your spirit. A crisis of faith. And look at the bewilderment in his eyes when you lead him to the bedroom, where you have lit dozens of tiny candles in random patterns on the bureau, the nightstand, even the floor. Is it guilt that arouses your ardour now? You stroke that pale brow, that warm flesh, and chastize yourself inwardly for having imagined this body cold and six feet under. And who can blame you if you believe you hear the orisons of the cherubim and the seraphim when you cry out, Oh God?

Yes, something unearthly has possessed you. You cannot fall asleep after, in spite of the reassuring rhythm of his snoring. You pace back and forth in the kitchen, staring mournfully out the window at the waning moon. Then you retreat beneath the covers, where you find him once more and shape his astonished sleeping form to your pleasure. His breathing nearly regular until his lashes flutter and he stammers, "My God, you are going to kill me!" You are almost reduced to a fit of passionate weeping.

Finally, somewhere in the nascent hours of the morning, as the light outside begins to overtake the darkness at a compelling speed, your memory sifts mental photographs, takes stock of cherished experiences, replays in slow motion, and then in inexplicably hastened flashes, those moments you have hoarded like shiny pennies. Slows to a halt at one. When was it? Fourteen years ago? Can't be. Yes. All of you were there: the picnic basket of sandwiches from the deli, the buttery cheese, the silky chartreuse grass, the smell of such indefinably sharp, pulsing colours, too strong to be real, almost hearing the sizzle of the sun on the back of your neck, how pungent and rusty the moist black earth smelled as you sat with him, leaning against a tree whose bark was born of a texture neither of you could accurately describe, though it teased the tips of your tongues. The photograph fading to black and white now, its stark colours absorbed into the salt-and-pepper of the t.v. screen's effervescence, as you slide heavily and pleasantly into that tingling state that precedes sleep. Only the afterglow of the picture remains, as when you turn off the tube abruptly and a white ghost lunges off the screen at you, its distorted shape behind the lids of your eyes, but you can distinguish quite clearly the outlines of two figures: you and your beloved, strolling hand in hand through that first day of spring, and onward into eternity.

Disturbing the Peace

Janina Hornosty

The man in his underwear and T-shirt and the woman in her nightdress took the stand. The judge asked them a question and the man answered it. The woman's intense glance ran the short circuit from her husband to the judge, and back, over and over again. This circuit would have included the defense lawyer, but there was no defense lawyer, just the row of men dressed in shiny black leather, inevitable as crows.

"It was about three-thirty in the morning. That's when he woke up. I looked out the window and there they were, revving up their engines, calling out to each other, making one hell of a racket. And decent people trying to sleep."

There was a pause in the proceedings while the judge shuffled some papers and glanced around the room, pausing in various corners to think, or muse, or something akin to these things.

"*Are* you decent?"

At this the man turned crimson and involuntarily shuffled his heavy slippers on the hard marble floor of the witness stand. He couldn't speak. Suddenly, he had become immensely ashamed of his slippers. They had seemed so much part of him, he hadn't thought about them, and now he couldn't remember when he had been without them. He panicked. He was twenty-eight.

His wife, startled by her husband's failure to reply, tried to think of something to say. When she said it, it wasn't quite what she thought it would be:

"They came with their egos a-hulking
They came with their discontent skulking
With a hoot and a holler
With erect expertise
They came at the heart of our uneasy peace."

The judge was quiet again, pausing to consider, or reflect, or something like that.

"Yes, there is some truth in what you say. But why didn't you, you and your husband that is, just turn to each other, put your arms, silken with sleep, around one another, and make love, each lulling the other into a warm wet dream? Why didn't you do that? Why didn't you do that thing?"

Now the woman couldn't speak. Her heart smote her, and she turned her face away. The judge watched her, and the soft footlight of the witness stand touching her lovely cheekbone, inviting it to play. It was too sad to play, just then, of course.

The man and the woman were dismissed. As they descended the stairs from the witness stand and made their way to their seats, the man was very careful to pick his feet up with each step so that no one would look at his slippers, attracted by the flopping sound. Some people did look anyway. Not everyone, not no one. Some, as is natural.

The row of dark shiny defendants was next asked to come to the stand. There were six of them and only three chairs, so three of them had to sit on the floor. It was alright though; they were still visible to everyone in the room, a motley collection of black angles. One of them, one that didn't get a seat, had his hands grasped around what appeared to be a steering wheel. It soon became evident that this was a permanent fixture; somehow the wheel had adhered to him, passive to the embrace of his hands. The judge asked about this:

"What do you love?" the judge asked, addressing the man with the wheel.

"Speed," the man answered, without hesitation or expression.

The judge then turned to another one of the men.

"Do you have any poems?" the judge asked, a little wearily.

The second man answered almost as quickly as the first had, and with nearly as little inflection:

"Yep — one poem:
Black as night
Fuck and fight
I'm a knife
Jump on life
Or it'll jump you first, oh ya."

The judge didn't feel the need to ask any more questions. The whole case was becoming tediously clear. The men were dismissed from the witness stand. As they clumped to their seats, the judge thought, mused, and considered, and at last threw the thing out to the room at large.

"Does anyone have anything he or she wishes to add?"

Nobody stirred for a moment or two. Or it seemed this way until people realized that a very, very old woman from the back of the courtroom was slowly making her way to the witness stand causing barely a ripple as she hobbled along in her beautifully cut suit of dark green velvet. Its lines were exquisite, showing off the woman's tiny form to best advantage. And she had on the loveliest, most peculiar shoes imaginable. They squeezed the heart with their graceful and daring curves of green satin, and rows of tidy aggressive points, like amethyst teeth. Truly winning.

"I would like to talk about my grandmother."

There was a subdued but general stir in the courtroom. Alright, yes, she *was* very elegant, this very old lady, but did she have to *push* things by recalling, summoning into the room, someone even more ancient than herself? People twisted a touch nervously in their seats. Only the judge looked entirely comfortable, even hopeful. All, however, were polite and came to attention with the merest tap of the judge's gavel.

"When I was about eleven or twelve," the tiny grand woman began, "I was taken by my parents to the house of my grandmother and left there for a few months while my parents tried to decide whether or not they still loved one another." The voice of the woman was as frail and shaky as the stereotypical voices of old people in T.V. sitcoms, but there was a powerful undertone, arresting as goose flight.

"I must say I was a little afraid of her at first. She was very tall, and strong and beautiful, like a hawk. She was, I soon discovered, exquisitely gentle — with a hawk's gentleness. I had been used to the hen-gentleness of my other grandmother.

"For the first few days and nights, my visit was delightful, but fairly ordinary. We went for long walks in my grandmother's extraordinary garden and then brought home herbs and flowers from it to make teas. My grandmother made a special tea for me, to help make me well again, she said. When I said I hadn't known I was sick, she chuckled at me wonderfully. I had never fancied being laughed at, but I didn't ever mind *her* laughing at me. And the tea *was* rather marvelous. I always felt queer but happy after sipping it, as if ... as if the garden, and my grandmother with her big, steady gold eyes, and the animals she kept, with their black-rimmed, knowing eyes, as if *these* were real and the other, the polite Sunday dinner other: the crystal dishes filled with stubby limp lumps of father's stewed, hapless genitals, the high white hysteria we had for music, and my mother whizzing around the ceiling fan in a flatulent race from her dangerous, thwarted ambition, as if all that, that hell-in-a-handbasket, were merely a nasty dream."

The courtroom was very quiet now, allowing the strange voice its way.

"One evening, a cool October evening it was, my grandmother told me that we were to attend a very special religious service, and that she would dress me properly for it. Having been raised an Anglican, I was most surprised when she brought out a loose-ish black silk shift (that rustled against my skin) and put it on me, wrapping what seemed like hundreds of bright scarves of every colour and description around my waist and arms and head. I remember looking in the mirror, lifting my arms this way and that, turning my head, both afraid and delighted by what I saw. My grandmother dressed herself similarly and we went outside into the garden. The moon was high and full; it startled me with its insistent silver gleaming.

"'Chagall! Chagall!' my grandmother called to her favourite cat, and soon he trotted up to us. A graceful yet substantial tabby, Chagall was wonderfully made. His short thick fur glistened, and from between his boldly striped haunches, bunched and powerful as he sat looking up at us with luminous green moons, projected a marvelous black tail. It was utterly erect and yet capable of the most subtle expression.

"Kneeling toward a bush that grew near, my grandmother picked some reddish-brown berries and then knelt to the cat, opening her hand. The cat ate them up with relish and soon after, to my amazement, he began to expand, filling up space with his catness, until he was almost the size of a small pony. His tidy haunches had become powerful flanks; his delicate feet now left tiger tracks in the wet grass. In one leap my grandmother was astride the animal's sinewy back and before I understood what was happening, she had pulled me up in front of her, wrapping her arms around me."

The old woman shifted slightly in her chair, put her head on one side and smiled slowly, as if her mind were now nibbling towards the most hidden, succulent, treacherous part of her memory. Momentarily, she looked up and continued. The quiet in the room had deepened.

"We all but flew, bounding off into the darkness. I knew it was cold, but I felt no discomfort, wrapped in the warm arms of my grandmother, nestled against her full proud breasts scented with some wonderful stuff — it was so unlike the flaccid pillowy embrace of my other grandmother, with its sweetly nauseating powdery asphyxiation.

"We were entering deep woods and travelling, I soon discerned, towards some kind of firelight. I don't know how long we travelled or what we took; for me the journey was a timeless whirl of darkness, musk, moonlight and furry speed. But then we were there. In the place.

"I still don't know what it all meant, or how it meant. There were many others — men, women, children, animals — in a loose kind of circle around a blazing fire, and they were all like my grandmother, all magic. I don't know, or can't say, what exactly they were doing or how exactly they looked when they were doing it, what their expressions were in the moonlight, how their cheekbones looked. I can't say. It isn't possible for me to say. There was a shimmering and a movement, and a wonderful violence of colour and sound and feeling. This keen healthy violence, untainted by despair, or the familiar resounding thump of limitation — smack into the walls of ourselves, our ignorant wills — this wonderful violence was, I knew, what my mother in her hopeless hysterical whizzing had really wanted. I began to cry.

"My grandmother put her arms around me and soothed me, and I was still. Then she took me to one of the men in the circle, tall and grand as she, and introduced me to him as her mate.

"He graciously shook my hand, and then kissed my grandmother. When he kissed her, he put his hand on her breast, absorbedly. She kissed him back, absorbedly. I felt strange; my body glowed.

"Finally, when she stopped kissing her mate, my grandmother took me into the middle of the circle and told me to sit down in the wet grass. I supposed that many creatures were watching, in their way, but I didn't mind. This place seemed very far from the place where I had minded.

"But then a great hush descended over the circle, and I felt their watching grow keen. Something was beginning. I began to feel afraid.

"My grandmother began a slow circular dance around me. With mysterious motions of her hands she made symbols in the air. Her fingers were like fire, weaving a tapestry of curves and points around me, strange signifiers that hung in the air like bright smoke. Her dance became frenzied as she wove tighter and tighter circles around me. The people and animals in the circle were singing; the strange thrilling noise grew louder and louder, sharp with pumpkins and crucifixes. I sat in my bright, living cage of symbols, my body aching with desire and fear. When her voice finally came, it was ferociously gentle: 'Do you want to be born? Do you want to be born?'

"That is what she asked, and I must make an answer. Which, at length, I did."

Silence. There was no more. The little woman nodded politely at the judge to indicate that she was done. She adjusted her collar and smoothed a wrinkle in the skirt of her dress, and then went on sitting.

That was her contribution to the proceedings.

The way it ends is, everybody is utterly still. The spectators, the judge, the men in black, the man in his floppy slippers, his wife, and the tidy old woman on the witness stand, who has not yet been asked to step down. The courtroom is thickening in its stillness, like a womb where something is deciding whether to be.

The Stations of the Cross

Ingrid MacDonald

I.

December 25. 1991. It is late in the night and we are in bed. Talking for hours. Visionary one: you say our deaths will be gifts, one to the other, whoever goes first. I try to accept your idea, death as a gift, but it is hard to reconcile with my idea, death as a loss. There are so few women who love the way we do, who we can compare our lives to, and how could I imagine the world without you? Alice B. Toklas had to live as a widow without her Gertrude Stein for twenty years after Gertrude Stein gave her the gift of her death. Alice's autobiography, which Gertrude Stein had elected to write, was left unfinished. I suppose it's enough of a book on the shelf at our public library without the last decades. During those years Alice walked their big white poodle, its nails clacking on the cobblestone, and she wrote a cookbook of European delicacies, often calling for the yolks of eight eggs. Later she converted to Catholicism in the hope of finding Gertrude Stein in the afterlife.

Mountain: In the Home Country, Grossmutti pulls two pair socks onto strong legs. Red kerchief over strictly combed hair. Butterbread in pocket. Stick peeled smooth by bone handled knife. Grossmutti, butterbreaded, red kerchiefed, taps the path up the mountain every day with her dog and a small herd of brown and white cows. Work becomes the life of any woman and Carrier of Stick Walker Up Mountain keeps twelve cows each named after the apostles with a Matthias, of course, instead of Judas. In summer the Alm is higher up, in fall, not so far. Twelve cows beget milk, which begets buttermilk and chocolate. In the woods, bells on their leather collars clang the sound of cuckoos. Tomorrow, wearing her second best dress, a smock with buttons that dot her girth like flies on a bedsheet, she'll enter the hospital. The white part of her eyes is milky yellow, a few long hairs grow from her drooping goitre chin. She is sixty-seven years old and this is her first time in surgery.

II.

December 26. 1991. For the past month I have carried a box of kleenex wherever I go. Not much is happening, but there's so much to cry about. I cry at the dentist, on the subway, in the grocery store. Like stones found at the bottom of a lake, I excavate years of pain and put words or tears to them. One after another these memories come, flying out of the pocket of my childhood, tied together like a magician's handkerchief. After making love, I cry in your arms for half an hour. I did this last night, I am doing it tonight and will likely do it again tomorrow. Encompassed by this feeling, this being fully loved, I cry for the years and years of feeling no love at all. I smell your warm skin dampened by my tears. I say I can't imagine being with anyone after you. You say, there is no such thing, 'after you.'

Hospital: Grossmutti has been admitted, her flowerprint dress exchanged for a hospital gown. In the hallway a very old man in a wheelchair, straight backed, tongue lolling, says *Schlagen mich nicht*, over and over, his eyes fixed elsewhere. He begs someone not to hit him. Grossmutti folds her stockings carefully and then the nurse gives her an enema, which inflates her belly until her bowel exhales, gushing tepid water and shredded shit into the latrine. A sedative is brought in a paper cup. The curtain is drawn around the bed, but it is soft and pale, like wind. Sound seeps underneath it. The very old man weeping. Soft shoes on green linoleum. A tree outside. The sound from childhood of her own mother coughing in a kitchen where she sits and sews.

III.

December 27. 1991. At breakfast I resume the discussion. Coffee, soft boiled eggs, cornbread toast, and the problem of death. I relate the story of Rosa de Bonheur, from an obscure reference in an art history textbook, the French painter who refused to dress like a woman. The Empress Josephine heard of Rosa's reputation and asked her to court, but the grandeur of the occasion unnerved Rosa. She changed out of her trousers and tie, and wearing a dress, disappointed Josephine. Rosa had a true love, a woman who died. Their love endured but they were separated by two worlds: this world where Rosa wandered room to room with dry paint brushes, and the next. Into this great hole in Rosa's life came Anna Klumpke. A devoted younger woman with a clubfoot and considerable artistic merit. Anna went on a trip to the New World, taking the train to the west, hanging off the back of it, grabbing what she could to bring back home. See? Unfolding a shirt full of wheat grass and brown-eyed susans in front of Rosa. This is the New World. I went there and came back. Rosa instructed the masons to carve their initials above the doorway of their painting studio: RdB, AK, intertwined. In Anna's portrait of Rosa, Rosa is smiling and vibrant.

Death: Grossmutti can't remember where she left her walking stick. This is what bothers her as she is wheeled into the operating room. The mask of anaesthetic covers her nose, turns her face to warm stone, and blots to silence the knives and needles on the other side of the cloth screen. The room is lit only in the middle, and there is an intimacy to it, as if a glow comes from Grossmutti's opened abdomen and there is gold in there shining. A nurse checks the monitors, We're starting to lose her, she says, her voice plain but alarmed. Grossmutti's body is there, warm and sleeping like the barn in winter with its doors opened, but her vital signs grow faint on the screens.

IV.

December 28. 1991. If you were to die, where would you go? Would I still be able to feel you near me? When P. died, I denied it. He was an artist. He couldn't have died, he wasn't finished his career yet. But a deeper part of me knew he was dead even before anyone phoned to say so. I was in front of the mirror putting on a pair of earrings, and my whole body succumbed to a sadness. P. is dying, I said, steadying myself on the dressing table, my hands on the polished wood. I quickly put the feeling away, guilty I wasn't helping him live longer, sending positive visualizations: P.'s gaining weight, P.'s white blood cells multiplying, P.'s blood thick and warm. Since his death I've wanted to give him something: a coat, a butterbread, some mittens. I imagine it is cold there, where death is, a house made of ice and Lapps living nearby. But death is even farther than the Lapps. Traditionally, when a Lapp died, a reindeer was killed on the grave, so the soul would have an animal to take them across the snow.

Moon: The surgeon calls for intervention. His voice barks in the quiet room, the sound of a dog in an empty street. But Grossmutti is not coming back to her body. A moon come unstuck from its orbit, she whirls away into space, away from the planet of her body. Another doctor, drying his hands with a white towel, hurries into the room. Pumps urge a rhythm and then the intermittent beeping of the monitor changes to a single sustained note. The second doctor is still drying his hands on the towel.

V.

December 29. 1991. I have made a plan: What I Will Do If You Die First. I will stay with your body, watching the animating force of you slip away. I will cry. Then, when you are so far away that you are small enough to be breathed in the air with the dust, I will make my way, still crying, to a barber and have all my hair shaved off. My hair is nearly down to my waist and I cannot tell you how much better I feel since I've made this decision, to cut it all off. Like a nun who renounces the world when she takes her final vow, in great dignity, I'll give you my hair. I see you in your coffin, my beloved, with my hair crossed over your heart. In the Haida tradition, the women cut their hair when they mourn their dead. They take a stone for a pillow and blacken their tear-stained faces with pitch. They give gifts to the dead soul who travels to a new world to marry a new husband or a new wife. I can't imagine that, that you would go to another world and take another lover. I see you waiting for me, carrying my hair towards me, which I take from you and wear like a life.

Earth: Grossmutti is grandmother to a girl named Olive who lives far from the Home Country in the New World. They have never met. When news comes, of Grossmutti dying like that, going into the anaesthetic and never waking up, her son, who is Olive's father, is glad she didn't feel pain. This is important to him, that she didn't suffer. Knowing that God would welcome her into His Kingdom, is also important to him, even though he himself does not believe. He has no use for religion and gives his cows secular names: Girt, Hilde, Brownie, Fritz. But he looks at Olive, she is seven. What will become of her without any God? He has the problem of death too. Where will he go when he dies? Into the ground? Just into the earth like a beast? He looks at the ground outside the window. It looks hard and cold.

VI.

December 30. 1991. We want to have enough time to properly die, and I suppose when I say that, I mean enough time to properly live. Some nights I feel sadness just letting you go, as we fall to sleep, drifting off after our bedtime prayer: *We give thanks for this day, for all its sorrow and its joy. We ask the great spirit within to surround us with sleep, bring peace to our bodies and bless the sacredness of our bed. We call our dreams into our hearts that we may live them in our lives. May the love that is between us touch others in the world.* A life seems like so much and so little at the same time. Once, when I was thinking of the rest of our lives in terms of years it seemed like so little. So I calculated it in days, hoping it would feel like more, but I was still disappointed. Here, you said, give me the calculator. 50 times 365 equals. Only 18,250? Is that all? you said. See why I'm sad?

Fountain: Sunday afternoon the father and mother take Olive into town, to a modern church built in grey stone in the shape of a triangle. Olive in saddle shoes stands on tiptoe over a deep stone fountain. Water and oil is poured onto her forehead by a priest. She can only see the black wool of her father's suit and the white frill of a baby's gown, who is also here to be baptized. Olive feels her life sundered as the priest wipes his hands on a cloth held by an altar boy. He speaks quietly, his hands passing over her, but Olive knows the operation didn't work. The priest was supposed to take away her sins, but as Olive raises her head from the deep stone bowl she can tell something has gone wrong. For the first time in her life she has the urge to steal something or break a window.

VII.

December 31. 1991. That other side of life, which we get to by dying, has its place in our love but I'm not sure how. Is it part of what makes our love so tender? St. Teresa of Avila loved God so intensely that she floated off the ground. The Convent Superior gave instruction to the younger nuns, to watch Teresa and grab her by the skirt, should she start to go. Morning bells chiming, church doors opening, Sister Superior did not want the local women with their hardworked eyes and blacklace collars seeing a nun that way. Teresa didn't like floating either, it drew too much attention to herself. Though she was his servant, she asked God to make it stop. Though she was wretched, she courted him like a beloved and filled her wretchedness with his light. She saw him standing before her, a figure in a darkened room. When I'm away from you I try to imagine your face, your features. Though I have looked into your face for hours, for weeks, for years, it is remarkably difficult to imagine you precisely or in all your parts. I retain this: the sound of your voice, a gesture, the feel of your cheek against mine, the warmth of you in bed beside me, and the image of you walking towards me, with light of the sun behind you, drawing you in outline. It is a kind of wretchedness, when I compare these to the real you.

Grave: Olive, now called Mary because Olive is not a Christian name, finds a dead bird in the yard. A speckled hedge bird, her brown body soft and limp, like a loose bean bag. Olive carried the bird carefully about the yard, then gouges out its eyes and buries it, so she may return to the Great Mother of All Birds. When her mother comes out, Olive shows her the birdgrave and tells her about the Great Mother Bird who is represented by a stone on the tiny mound. Never to say such nonsense again, her mother says, leading Olive into the house for a vigorous handwash. When Olive goes to bed, her mother brings her a picture of a man with bleeding hands and big soft cow eyes. From now on, there is no Great Mother of All Birds, there is only Jesus. In the morning Olive is spanked, because she gouged the picture, poking Jesus' eyes out with a pencil.

VIII.

January 1. 1992. In the forest, a hunt is underway. I can hear the hooves and the barking of dogs. I am walking with you, my lover, when we meet an old woman. I wish we could leave the forest without her, this woman in coarse brown woolens, but once we've made eye contact, it is inevitable. She should be with us. We take her to our house and I make a bed for her, as I would for a cat, putting pillows and blankets in the corner on the floor. She sleeps there and surprises me at first by bathing everyday. I ask if she would like me to help her with the cows, but she points out the window and says no, you should plant seeds instead. You need more flowers. By the end of the week she prefers to sleep with us in our bed. We lie, the three of us in a row, the old woman of the forest in her woolens, lightly resting one of her hands on my belly.

Fatherland: The kitchen radio plays the Sunday sermon of a local preacher. Olive's father argues back at the radio, kicks it, turns it off in disgust. Such socialist mishmash. Olive's father takes it upon himself to educate her. Her job is to hold the bible open so her father can use his hands while he preaches. He really doesn't know much about the bible but he is determined, since Grossmutti died, to instill Olive with values. His real passion is for the Fatherland, and so he preaches of God as if God were the Fatherland and their family were the obedient subjects of God's country. A Christian girl does what she is told. The bible grows heavier by the hour. A Christian girl obeys her Mother and Father. Sometimes her father leans his elbows there, on the bible, as if she were a lectern. In moments of oratorical passion he grips the edges of her with his big thumbs.

IX.

January 2. 1992. At night a burnt-sugar smell wakes me. Have we left a pot on the stove? Drowsy, I make my way downstairs. From the kitchen I hear the sound of water being poured into a hot dry pot. A brilliant light comes from the kitchen, and I'm astonished to see the kitchen is filled with people, men and women in their best dark clothes, drinking strong coffee from cups and saucers. They've gone to my funeral and this is my wake. I'm terrified because I've entered another existence. They turn and look at me, as if they've been waiting, but I am terrified. What if I can't return to you, my lover? When Buddhist Master Takkan was dying, his disciples asked that he write a death poem. He refused. They insisted. He wrote the character *Yume*, which means *Dream*, and died.

Stones: How much damage can a thumb do? A sensitive teacher notices something strange when Olive, who she has to remind herself to call Mary now, volunteers to stay after school and clean the blackboards. She cleans the boards and then stays in her seat for a long time, looking out the window. Actually the teacher noticed something strange outside earlier, when she saw Olive by herself, deliberately throwing stones at a pigeon. She mentions it discreetly to another sensitive teacher, not the business about the pigeon, but that the girl is not herself. The librarian Miss Fitzgerald is engaged to be married soon. Well keep an eye out, she says from behind recipe cards organized in the dewey decimal system. If it gets worse, something might have to be done. What are you seeing anyways? Hard to say. Looks like. Thumbmarks.

X.

January 3. 1992. At a museum with A. who is seven years old. Passing a statue of Buddha, she says, Is that the God you guys are always talking about? Well, he's one of them. Buddhists see death as a culmination. In "Practical Instructions for Dying," the dying person is advised not to take treatments which numb pain at the expense of consciousness. I think love should matter as much as consciousness, as in the psalms, where it says, what you love, you bring forward, if you did not love something, you would not bring it forth. But so much courage is needed to love consciously. Buddhist Master Fugai asked one of the monks to dig a deep pit. Fugai, who felt death coming towards him on its wheel, climbed into the pit. Lovingly, he instructed the monk to cover him with earth.

Pool: Their friends, the Muhldorfs, own a motel in town, and it has a pool. In summer, Olive and her parents drive in for a swim and social. They have two kids, the Muhldorfs, and the father comes from the Fatherland as well, but Olive thinks all fathers come from there, and mothers, in a much less talked about way, from a Motherland. Her parents drink drinks in pink and green swirled see-through plastic tumblers with ice that clatters down when the glass is emptied. A woman staying at the motel sits by the edge of the pool, sunning herself and reading. Olive and the Muhldorf boys have races, which Olive wins. The woman gathers her towel and sun oils, and puts on a short terry-cloth robe, readying herself before going back to her room. She says hello and what's your name? Olive, says Olive. You swim so well Olive, the woman says. She crouches by the edge of the pool with her towel over her arm. Olive touches the ledge, her body in water. The woman touches one of Olive's fingers, sweetly, she says, look you're wrinkled like a prune.

XI.

January 4. 1992. All things have the ability to be sacred if we choose sacredness for them, and give them a place to be. In the morning, you light a candle on the altar and we sit on the floor for a few moments. Our altar is a simple table in front of the window with our sacred things on it: candles; stones and shells; a large shell filled with dry green lentils for burning incense; sweetgrass; a Tibetan prayer wheel; three feathers, of a magpie, a bluejay and an eagle; a piece of purple silk; a hand painted glass bottle from India; cards we have given each other; an Amish inspired 'plain and simple' journal which we keep together, each writing in it when we have something to say; and a few crystals. I blow out the candle and we begin our day's work. A letter comes from our friend Jill. She's Jewish, but is staying at a Christian monastery in Saskatchewan where she's writing a play. After some days she approaches one of the ancient monks. To us she writes: So I said, Brother Gregory, what's it all about? And he said, just love yourself. God is Love.

Reflection: Olive's father says, Mary, come here right away. Olive presents herself, dripping. What did the woman say to you? Nothing. Her father's chest hairs show through the opened Hawaiian style shirt he wears. He shakes his head. I don't want you talking to her, do you hear me? Olive pats the sand between cracks with her big toe. She was just being nice. Her father snorts, That's just a put on. She's trying to get information out of you by being nice. Olive folds her arms. We didn't talk about anything. He looks at her through his mirrored aviator glasses and very carefully says, there is a certain kind of people in the world who don't like us, and she's one of them. But why, Dad? Because I'm telling you. Olive looks at the woman who is unlatching the gate to leave. The woman has dark hair, brown eyes, and fair skin. Everything about her looks pleasant and ordinary. She doesn't look like a particular kind of person at all. Olive puts her fists into a tight ball. She hits her father's arm and says, I hate you Daddy.

XII.

January 5. 1992. A. suggests we go to Sunday service at the gay community church. I'm not sure I want to go. I'm sceptical of what organized religion can do for me, as we arrive and take the last few seats available. The church is packed, more men than women, and precious winter light streams through yellow windows. A. has been here before with her mother. A. likes church. She writes a story in her notebook during the readings and sermons, drawing a picture of our rented summer cottage. At communion I walk uncertainly to the front. I watch the man in front of me, the minister gives him the host and then whispers in his ear, her head bowed. I imagine she must know him, the way he smiles, the way she talks to him. But when I get there she puts the host in my mouth and then her arms on my shoulders. My arms are raised up to her. My sister, she says, remember your gifts, fill yourself with blessings here and take them with you, into the world. When I get back to the pew, A. wants to know what the woman said to make me cry.

Key: What did you say? Her father goes from a drowsy recline to his full six feet in less than a second. There is a little shed off the pool, decorated in faux cabana motifs, filled with pool hardware, hoses, pumps, lost and found bathing suits, Mr. Muhldorf's chlorine tester kit and his bottle of schnapps. Olive's father grabs her arm and pushes her into the dark cabin, into its hot musty chlorine smell, and closes the door behind them. He isn't a violent man, so he doesn't have anything in mind when he pushes her in the hut but the objects all around him inspire him. He picks up a plastic diving flipper that is on a shelf near his hand and hits her across the face with the back of it. A Christian girl never speaks back to her father. Then he turns to leave her in the shed, thinking she can cool down in there, when he sees the key hanging on a hook. You'll stay in here young lady until you can prove you're willing to listen to your father. He locks the door. The brightness of the day hurts his eyes. When he hears the ruckus that Olive makes in the shed, throwing cans and hoses onto the floor, he takes the key and throws it into the pool.

XIII.

January 6. 1992. Epiphany, a day for gifts. The day the Magi arrived at the stable and saw a king glowing inside the body of a wee little baby. That kind of glow makes you tremble. I'm trembling a bit right now in the face of your great gift to me. Relaxing in your arms, looking in your face, I see the beautiful face of a loving mother, there inside your normal face. It glows and then diminishes like a star at dawn. Then you get up normal as anything, and prepare toast and eggs for the morning. I'm humming a Christmas song as the coffeemaker burbles. *Do you see what I see? A star. A star. Way up in the sky with a voice as big as us all.* I've come to a place inside myself where it's enough to live only to dream. Where to dream is to live. Before now I had thought of dreaming as a gate with only one side, a gate which I passed through, alone, for reasons of self-enhancement. Last night I found an opening on the other side, and a great big wind whooshing. Doors banged on their hinges and the curtains were sucked against the windows. That's when I saw God. She had big hair and huge breasts swaddled in a loud outfit. She's a good shopper, God is, and she wore a nice, if bright green, set of clothes. She wasn't very happy with the size of the gate. She had to jam

her shopping bag in front of her, and really push to squeeze her big and
glorious hips through that narrow, difficult space.

Tomb: At this point, the experience of the compassionate spectator is all that
is left of this story. The child Olive is not here. Do what you must now, go
back to your work, or hurry home to your dinners. It's no longer early and
the cold comes on suddenly, often bringing snow. Button up well, don't get
caught in the cold. The child is no longer here. Go home now. Later we will
learn that her spirit lives, that a life miraculously survives inside her body.
The women who come to do the washing see it early that Sunday morning.
They find the stone has been moved away from the tomb. They run to you,
leaving their things on the ground, shouting to you, they've seen her again
and alive.

This Is History
for
Donna Goodleaf

Beth Brant

Long before there was an earth and long before there were people called human, there was a Sky World.

On Sky World there were Sky People who were like us and not like us. And of the Sky People there was Sky Woman. Sky Woman had a peculiar trait: she had curiosity. She bothered the others with her questions, with wanting to know what lay beneath the clouds that supported her world. Sometimes she pushed the clouds aside and looked down through her world to the large expanse of blue that shimmered below. The others were tired of her peculiar trait and called her an aberration, a queer woman who asked questions, a woman who wasn't satisfied with what she had.

Sky Woman spent much of her time dreaming — dreaming about the blue expanse underneath the clouds, dreaming about floating through the clouds, dreaming about the blue color and how it would feel to her touch. One day she pushed the clouds away from her and leaned out of the opening. She fell. The others tried to catch her hands and pull her back, but she struggled free and began to float downward. The Sky People watched her descent and agreed that they were glad to see her go. She was a nuisance with her questions, an aberration, a queer woman who was not like them — content to walk the clouds undisturbed.

Sky Woman floated. The currents of wind played through her hair. She put out her arms and felt the sensations of air between her fingers. She kicked her legs, did somersaults, and was curious about the free, delightful feelings of flying. Faster, faster, she floated toward the blue shimmer that beckoned her.

She heard a noise and turned to see a beautiful creature with black wings and a white head flying close to her. The creature spoke. "I am Eagle. I have been sent to carry you to your new home." Sky Woman laughed and held out her hands for Eagle to brush his wings against. He swooped under her, and she settled on his back. They flew. They circled, they glided, they flew, Sky Woman clutching the feathers of the great creature.

Sky Woman looked down at the blue color. Rising from the expanse was a turtle. Turtle looked up at the flying pair and nodded her head. She dove into the waters and came up again with a muskrat clinging to her back. In Muskrat's paw was a clump of dark brown dirt scooped from the bottom of the sea. She laid it on Turtle's back and jumped back into the water. Sky

77

Woman watched the creature swim away, her long tail skimming the top of the waves, her whiskers shining. Sky Woman watched as the dark brown dirt began to spread. All across Turtle's back the dirt was spreading, spreading, and in this dirt green things were growing. Small green things, tall green things, and in the middle of Turtle's back, the tallest thing grew. It grew branches and needles, more and more branches, until it reached where Eagle and Sky Woman were hovering.

Turtle raised her head and beckoned to the pair. Eagle flew down to Turtle's back and gently lay Sky Woman on the soft dirt. Then he flew to the very top of the White Pine tree and said, "I will be here, watching over everything that is to be. You will look to me as the harbinger of what is to happen. You will be kind to me and my people. In return, I will keep this place safe." Eagle folded his wings and looked away.

Sky Woman felt the soft dirt with her fingers. She brought the dirt to her mouth and tasted the color of it. She looked around at the green things. Some were flowering with fantastic shapes. She stood on her feet and felt the solid back of Turtle beneath her. She marveled at this wonderful place and wondered what she would do here.

Turtle swiveled her head and looked at Sky Woman with ancient eyes. "You will live here and make this a new place. You will be kind, and you will call me Mother. I will make all manner of creatures and growing things to guide you on this new place. You will watch them carefully, and from them you will learn how to live. You will take care to be respectful and honorable to me. I am your Mother." Sky Woman touched Turtle's back and promised to honor and respect her. She lay down on Turtle's back and fell asleep.

As she slept, Turtle grew. Her back became wider and longer. She slapped her tail and cracks appeared in her back. From these cracks came mountains, canyons were formed, rivers and lakes were made from the spit of Turtle's mouth. She shook her body and prairies sprang up, deserts settled, marshes and wetlands pushed their way through the cracks of Turtle's shell. Turtle opened her mouth and called. Creatures came crawling out of her back. Some had wings, some had four legs, six legs, or eight. Some had no legs but slithered on the ground, some had no legs and swam with fins. These creatures crawled out of Turtle's back and some were covered with fur, some with feathers, some with scales, some with skins of beautiful colors. Turtle called again, and the creatures found their voice. Some sang, some barked, some growled and roared, some had no voice but a hiss, some had no voice and rubbed their legs together to speak. Turtle called again. The creatures began to make homes. Some gathered twigs and leaves, others spun webs, some found caves, others dug holes in the ground. Some made the waters their home, and some of these came up for air to breathe. Turtle shuddered, and the new place was made a continent, a world.

Turtle gave a last look to the sleeping Sky Woman. "Inside you is growing a being who is like you and not like you. This being will be your companion. Together you will give names to the creatures and growing things. You will be kind to these things. This companion growing inside you will be called First Woman, for she will be the first of these beings on this earth. Together you will respect me and call me Mother. Listen to the voices of the creatures and communicate with them. This will be called prayer, for prayer is the language of all my creations. Remember me." Turtle rested from her long labor.

Sky Woman woke and touched herself. Inside her body she felt the stirrings of another. She stood on her feet and walked the earth. She climbed mountains, she walked in the desert, she slept in trees, she listened to the voices of the creatures and living things, she swam in the waters, she smelled the growing things that came from the earth. As she wandered and discovered, her body grew from the being inside her. She ate leaves and picked fruit. An animal showed her how to bring fire, then threw himself in the flames that she might eat of him. She prayed her thanks, remembering Turtle's words. Sky Woman watched the creatures, learning how they lived in community with each other, learning how they hunted, how they stored food, how they prayed. Her body grew larger, and she felt her companion move inside her, waiting to be born. She watched the living things, seeing how they fed their young, how they taught their young, how they protected their young. She watched and learned and saw how things should be. She waited for the day when First Woman would come and together they would be companions, lovers of the earth, namers of all things, planters and harvesters, creators.

On a day when Sky Woman was listening to the animals, she felt a sharp pain inside of her. First Woman wanted to be born. Sky Woman walked the earth, looking for soft things to lay her companion on when she was born. She gathered all day, finding feathers of the winged-creatures, skins of the fur-bearers. She gathered these things and made a deep nest. She gathered other special things for medicine and magic. She ate leaves from a plant that eased her pain. She clutched her magic things in her hands to give her help. She prayed to the creatures to strengthen her. She squatted over the deep nest and began to push. She pushed and held tight to the magic medicine. She pushed, and First Woman slipped out of her and onto the soft nest. First Woman gave a cry. Sky Woman touched her companion, then gave another great push as her placenta fell from her. She cut the long cord with her teeth as she had learned from the animals. She ate the placenta as she had learned from the animals. She brought First Woman to her breast as she had learned, and First Woman began to suckle, drawing nourishment and medicine from Sky Woman.

Sky Woman prayed, thanking the creatures for teaching her how to give birth. She touched the earth, thanking Mother for giving her this gift of a companion. Turtle shuddered, acknowledging the prayer. That day, Sky

Woman began a new thing. She opened her mouth and sounds came forth. Sounds of song. She sang and began a new thing — singing prayers. She fashioned a thing out animal skin and wood. She touched the thing and it resonated. She touched it again and called it a drum. She sang with the rhythm of her touching. First Woman suckled as her companion sang the prayers.

First Woman began to grow. In the beginning she lay in her nest dreaming, then crying out as she wanted to suckle. Then she opened her eyes and saw her companion and smiled. Then she sat up and made sounds. Then she crawled and was curious about everything. She wanted to touch and feel and taste all that was around her. Sky Woman carried her on her back when she walked the earth, listening to the living things and talking with them. First Woman saw all the things that Sky Woman pointed out to her. She listened to Sky Woman touch the drum and make singing prayers. First Woman stood on her feet and felt the solid shell of Turtle against her feet. The two companions began walking together. First Woman made a drum for herself, and together the companions made magic by touching their drums and singing their prayers. First Woman grew, and as she grew Sky Woman showed her the green things, the animal things, the living things, and told her they needed to name them. Together they began the naming. Heron, bear, snake, dolphin, spider, maple, oak, thistle, cricket, wolf, hawk, trout, goldenrod, firefly. They named together and in naming, the women became closer and truer companions. The living things that now had names moved closer to the women and taught them how to dance. Together, they all danced as the women touched their drums and made their singing prayers. Together they danced. Together. All together.

In time the women observed the changes that took place around them. They observed that sometimes the trees would shed their leaves and at other times would grow new ones. They observed that some creatures buried themselves in caves and burrows and slept for long times, reappearing when the trees began their new birth. They observed that some creatures flew away for long times, reappearing when the animals crawled from their caves and dens. Together, the companions decided they would sing special songs and different prayers when the earth was changing and the creatures were changing. They named these times seasons and made different drums, sewn with feathers and stones. The companions wore stones around their necks, feathers in their hair, and shells on their feet, and when they danced, the music was new and extraordinary. They prepared feasts at this time, asking the animals to accept their death. Some walked into their arrows, some ran away. The animals that gave their lives were thanked and their bones were buried in Turtle's back to feed her — the Mother of all things.

The women fashioned combs from animal teeth and claws. They spent long times combing and caressing each other's hair. They crushed berries and flowers and painted signs on their bodies to honor Mother and the living things who lived with them. They painted on rocks and stones to honor the creatures who taught them. They fixed food together, feeding each other herbs and roots and plants. They lit fires together and cooked the foods that gave them strength and medicine. They laughed together and made language between them. They touched each other and in the touching made a new word: love. They touched each other and made a language of touching: passion. They made medicine together. They made magic together.

And on a day when First Woman woke from her sleep, she bled from her body. Sky Woman marveled at this thing her companion could do because she was born on Turtle's back. Sky Woman built a special place for her companion to retreat at this time, for it was wondrous what her body could do. First Woman went to her bleeding place and dreamed about her body and the magic it made. And at the end of this time, she emerged laughing and holding out her arms to Sky Woman.

Time went by, long times went by. Sky Woman felt her body changing. Her skin was wrinkling, her hands were not as strong. She could not hunt as she used to. Her eyes were becoming dim, her sight unclear. She walked the earth in this changed body and took longer to climb mountains and swim in the waters. She still enjoyed the touch of First Woman, the laughter and language they shared between them, the dancing, the singing prayers. But her body was changed. Sky Woman whispered to Mother, asking her what these changes meant. Mother whispered back that Sky Woman was aged and soon her body would stop living. Before this event happened, Sky Woman must give her companion instruction. Mother and Sky Woman whispered together as First Woman slept. They whispered together the long night through.

When First Woman woke from her sleep, Sky Woman told her of the event that was to happen. "You must cut the heart from this body and bury it in the field by your bleeding place. Then you must cut this body in small pieces and fling them into the sky. You will do this for me."

And the day came that Sky Woman's body stopped living. First Woman touched her companion's face and promised to carry out her request. She carved the heart from Sky Woman's body and buried it in the open field near her bleeding-place. She put the ear to the ground and heard Sky Woman's voice, "From this place will grow three plants. As long as they grow, you will never want for food or magic. Name these plants corn, beans, and squash. Call them the Three Sisters, for like us, they will never grow apart."

First Woman watched as the green plant burst from the ground, growing stalks that bore ears of beautifully colored kernels. From beneath the corn rose another plant with small leaves, and it twined around the stalks carrying pods of green. Inside each pod were small white beans. From under the beans came a sprawling vine with large leaves that tumbled and grew and shaded the bean's delicate roots. On this vine were large, green squash that grew and turned orange and yellow. Three Sisters, First Woman named them.

First Woman cut her companion's body in small pieces and flung them at the sky. The sky turned dark, and there, glittering and shining, were bright-colored stars and a round moon. The moon spoke. "I will come to you every day when the sun is sleeping. You will make songs and prayers for me. Inside you are growing two beings. They are not like us. They are called Twin Sons. One of these is good and will honor us and our Mother. One of these is not good and will bring things that we have no names for. Teach these beings what we have learned together. Teach them that if the sons do not honor the women who made them, that will be the end of this earth. Keep well, my beloved First Woman. Eagle is watching out for you. Honor the living things. Be kind to them. Be strong, I am always with you. Remember our Mother. Be kind to her."

First Woman touched her body, feeling the movements inside. She touched the back of Mother and waited for the beings who would change her world.

Journey into the Vortex

Maya Khankhoje

They had told her she would come out on the third day. That is what the mediators of the Lord of Xibalba had led her to believe. At least, that is what they themselves wanted to believe. The hunger of their hollow power could only be assuaged with their own lies and delusions. It is true that the war of the heavens is the opposition between night and day. It is also true that the stars have to be conquered and sacrificed, so that the sun can drink their blood and the day begin all over again. In order to keep the universe in movement, people have to spill their blood so that it does not perish. But she knew them to be wrong when they said she would be out in three days. She had grasped this truth as firmly as she had grasped and held on to her mother's breast soon after she was born.

Her birth had been auspicious. She had exited the real world of the void to start her journey through the world of illusion on 12 baktun, 16 Katun, 8 Tun, 7 Uinal and 5 Kin, under the round and radiant face of Ix Chel, the moon goddess who wanders endlessly through the dark night so that the sun, her consort, does not burn her into oblivion.

It is to Ix Chel's care that her own mother entrusted her, shortly before she was sucked back into the vortex of creation. Her poor mother, who had to pay for the honour of birthing her with a torrent of sacrificial blood that drained her body as her hungry child drained her breast dry for the first ... and the last time. At least her mother had been transformed into a lovely butterfly which is the reward bestowed on a brave who dies in battle or a woman who exchanges her own life for that of her newborn child.

This is one of many truths that she understood but failed to accept: that men are rewarded for destroying life and women for creating it. But that seems to be in the nature of all dualities, for how can we see the radiance of goodness when there is no shadow of evil to set it off?

Birthing her had indeed been an honour. It was written that this female child born under the sign of Ozomatli, the monkey who invented fire, was to be a great medicine woman. So the midwife swaddled the baby carefully in her mother's blanket, hurriedly buried the cord that tied her to her unborn twin in the very centre of the house, and stole into the night, with a little bundle in tow. Under the complicitous gaze of Ix Chel.

The midwife had acted out of kindness, for she knew that power is a good and strong thing, but not before its time and not in the wrong place. Before its time, power can turn upon itself, which in this case would hurt this lovely child who would now be hers. And when power is used in the wrong place it can be misused by the enemy. For the midwife knew that she alone could pass on to this child the knowledge that she had acquired from the Final Mother, without any interference from the child's father and his high-born clan.

So she was named Sac Nicte and was brought up in the neighbouring temple city of Tulum, where the breeze blows cool air from a turquoise sea and children grow big and strong. Sac Nicte grew to be as pretty as her namesake flower and as strong as its fragrance although her secret name was to remain hers alone. It is in her secret name that she nursed her power while it grew and took shape, whereas her public name only held her outward appearance, which, by the way, enchanted many men and made the maidens envious.

But Sac Nicte paid scant attention to her body or her face. At least, not in the way it was expected of her. She had been nursed by a kinswoman of the midwife until she was about three, when she playfully started biting the very breasts that had made her teeth so strong. Her nurse, who had many children of her own, was glad to wean this strange child and send her to her Tata, the midwife. Under her Tata's loving hand, she grew up to be wilful and sure of herself.

It is thanks to her Tata that no pebbles were strung from her soft baby head to a midpoint between her eyes, to make them crossed. Crossed eyes might be beautiful, but she needed to see straight for the arduous tasks that awaited her. Her teeth were also spared being polished with stone and water to make them sharp like the teeth of a baby shark. It was also her Tata who refused to encase her forehead between two planks of wood, to give her the gallant elongated look of the temple friezes. For that she was very grateful. In any case, she did not intend to carry heavy baskets slung from her forehead over her back. She did not know why, but she sensed that the source of her strength and her understanding lay somewhere behind her forehead, in a point between her eyes. After all, she had observed that people fall into a deep dreamless sleep when they are hit hard on the head. And babies whose heads get stuck in their mothers at birth often grow up to be dull.

Sac Nicte was not vain but she was sensuous. She liked to sit at her Tata's doorstep and allow the old woman to oil her hair and braid it into two long braids that fell all the way below her waist. And after bathing in the sea, she would rinse herself in sweet water and anoint her body with pungent red resin which would start a fire in her loins if she happened to be thinking of him.

His name was Can Ek and he was a son of one of the Lords of Xibalba. Can Ek was as tall as she was full and his skin had the burnished look of a dying sun. His mother had burnt the roots of the scanty hairs on his face before he reached his manhood and now his face was as smooth and soft as hers. His lips were round and red and his eyes were as black and as sharp as an obsidian knife. So was his rod.

He had come from far away to visit his kinsfolk and to plunge into the jade sea and he had plunged into her soft flesh instead and tasted the salt on her lips. The first time she had felt him inside, she had cried out in pain and the blood between her legs was not blood that was preordained by the rhythm of the moon. After that, she had marvelled at how he could be hard and soft at the same time, a lesson she, as a medicine woman, still had to learn. At times she imagined that what she held in her hand was a plantain that was not yet ripe; at others, she accused him of being like a slippery eel not wanting to be caught.

But his very beauty was her undoing. They said that he had an evil streak. How could it be that she, a medicine woman, had not detected it? They said that when he turned seven, he killed a butterfly, who could have been her own mother! And at fourteen he had killed a deer, merely to possess the gland which holds the secret of all life. But as a grown man he had met Sac Nicte and his eyes filled with tears. A man who could be thus moved was a man to cherish.

He was her undoing not because he had shown the cruelty that was often mistaken for courage and expected of men, nor because their limbs had entwined around each other like the roots of the mangrove tree, but because he was her kin. At least, that is what everybody thought, except for herself and her Tata, who knew that it was not so. It was carved on stone for eternity to see that no man and no woman was to come together with a member of the same clan.

"You must be good at making corn bread," he had said, as he stared at her while she bathed in the river. "Those breasts ripe for children are only given to those who grind corn every morning of their womanly lives."

Sac Nicte had smiled and stared back at him, not making any attempt at covering her private parts.

"I do not make bread at all," she had replied earnestly. "I am a medicine woman. I can help women in childbirth, remove warts and help people polish their shields against their enemies. I can also call on Ashana to keep the evil spirits at bay. I am good at helping people find their secret twins to translate their dreams and visions. I can also weave as fine a cloth as the gossamer web of a spider and fashion quetzal feathers into adornments fit for a queen. I can even count in twenties and predict the movement of the heavenly bodies. I can do that and a lot more, but I cannot make bread. That is not my calling."

Can Ek had remained silent. Knowledge is recognition and Can Ek had recognized her and this is why tears had streamed down his face like the first rains of summer. The Lord of Dualities had decreed it so. A man and a woman must join each other just like the water of the earth ultimately meets the water of the heavens in the distant horizon. This was the woman who was his true opposite and the twin of his soul.

Sac Nicte recognized him too. She had seen him many times even without the help of sacred mushrooms or generous portions of the brew prepared by the goddess Mayahuel. She had seen him and she had imagined the feel of his smooth skin but was not prepared for the richness of his voice or the headiness of his scent.

It was then and there that they had touched for the first of many times, before he even knew her name, before she had pulled him by the hand and taken him home to her Tata.

"I want the priest to tie our tlimantli and if he will not do so, I will do it myself," she had announced in a defiant tone.

"Have you gone out of your mind!" her Tata had scolded. "He cannot marry into our clan because he is a kinsman of my brother."

Sac Nicte smiled and leaning over towards her Tata, grabbed the old woman's feet and squeezed them gently. "Didn't you tell me that when my mother died you took me away from my father's clan because their rank would not have allowed a child of theirs to have become a medicine woman? Didn't you once swear to me that even though there was nothing more in common between us than the bonds of love and wisdom you were willing to spill your blood to spare mine? I'm not asking you to spill your blood for me. I am merely asking you to help me meet my destiny with Can Ek."

The old woman nodded. "If I reveal your origins, the priest might be willing to bless your union, but your father will claim you first. And then I will lose you and you might lose your man. You must go away, my child."

Sac Nicte held the old woman in a tight embrace. "You cannot lose me ever, Tata. You were the one who taught me that essential life and love can never leave you, because you are that."

Three nights after that conversation, Sac Nicte and her lover left Tulum and made their long journey to Chichen Itza, under the cover of a dormant Ix Chel. In Chichen Itza they hoped to blend in with the crowds that had thronged the sacred city to celebrate that moment when the day and the night are of the same duration, before winter arrives. It is known that on that day, as the sun moves over the horizon, the shadow of the great plumed serpent Kukulkan, Father of all of the Maya people, makes his ascent in seven laborious segments up the steps of the main pyramid. When he reaches the top, on the 365th step which marks the completion of a solar year, a new cycle begins.

So Sac Nicte had arrived in Chichen Itza, with her man and their meagre rations of dry bread and peppers and ground chocolate and some honey and a gourd which they filled with the sap of the maguey cactus to quench their thirst along the way. And they stood there in front of the pyramid, marvelling at the sight of Kukulkan and dreaming of a new life for themselves.

But love had made Sac Nicte drop her guard. It is there that the mediators of the Lords of Xibalba had grabbed her and dragged her across the main square and taken her through the paved road that leads to the sacred cenote of Chichen Itza. She did not need to be a seer to know what awaited her. Nor did she wonder about Can Ek's fate.

Can Ek had tried to stop the men from leading her away, but others had materialized from nowhere and dragged him away too. Except that they had taken him up the pyramid, where Lord Kukulkan had snaked his way up in an eerie play of light and shadows, and gouged his heart out in a deft cut with an obsidian knife, as dark and sharp as his lovely eyes.

Sac Nicte stood before the cenote while the priests droned their worthless drivel. She knew why they had chosen them to propitiate the gods. They were recognized for their uniqueness in spite of their anonymity. She understood that to be different means to share the fate of kings, who are destined to taste the bitter drink of sorrow. So Sac Nicte and Can Ek were called to return to the whirlpool whence the powers of the universe have evolved.

She understood the hidden designs of nature and the eternal fires within all things. She also knew that the priests were wrong. They had told her that she would return within three days but it was not true. Nobody ever returned from this cenote, which was a well so deep and green and airless that even the fish could not live within.

But Sac Nicte also knew how to count time and read the stars. She understood the circular nature of time. Time was really like a spiral, like a whirlpool, that sucked you in and down until you resurfaced again, but in another form. When you measured time by the moon, you could count your holy days and when you measured it by the sun, you could calculate the seasons of the harvest. But everything started all over again every fifty-two years. More than the sum of her age and that of Can Ek's but less than her Tata's.

Just as childhood and youth are the promise of form and old age the ruin of physical form, death is the fall into formlessness. Life begins with surprise and ends with questioning. Would Can Ek's heart live on in an eagle or a jaguar? Would her formlessness take on another form, and if so, when?

All these thought forms disintegrated at the very moment in which she was thrown into the green pool. Before she went back to the liquid womb of the Great Mother. Before she left the dry world of illusion to return to the liquid depths of the primal source.

The water felt warm and soothing against her limbs. It seems that she swam and swam forever in a wonderful underground grotto which was mottled with light from holes that looked up to an azure sky. The sea bed was carpeted with undulating coral which swayed gently as fish passed by. The colours were pink and yellow and blue and green, comparable only to those you get under an electron microscope. The vaulted ceiling of that grotto was dripping with stalactites that looked like the strings of sugar candy in her Mexican childhood.

She was glad that she had conquered her irrational fear of water and learned how to scuba dive. A holiday in Cancun without this vista of marine life was unthinkable, honeymoon or not. They had finally made it, her Kanuk and herself. They had met in a sociology congress in Mexico City and it was love at first sight.

Marriage had really been quite beside the point. But the Mexican government did not issue work permits to foreigners unless they were married to Mexicans and her Kanuk often spoke longingly about his home in Oka and his job in Ottawa with the Council of Native Peoples. They decided to commute back and forth, like migratory birds, until the children arrived.

So they had married to please their respective tribes and meet official requirements. This is why they were in Cancun, in a pyramid-shaped hotel where the food was good and the crowds abominable.

Their one concession to their sanity was staying as close as possible to the sea and visiting the Mayan ruins.

So this is how Maya came to be swimming in a lovely grotto which formed part of a network that turns into subterranean rivers and feeds the cenotes.

She got out of the water, dried herself and applied Coppertone to her body before lying next to Kanuk. It never failed. The slippery oil on her skin and the sun beating on her pubis always seemed to arouse her. She turned to one side and started tracing the moon-shaped scar that Kanuk had under his left nipple with her index finger. She then pinched his nipple gently, noticing that it had already hardened.

Kanuk stopped pretending that he was asleep. He kissed her hungrily and seeing that there were not many people around, he eased his shorts to one side and penetrated her right there near the ruins in Tulum. They then fell asleep in each others arms, like the tangled roots of a mangrove tree.

When Maya woke up, she started tickling Kanuk's face with a flower that was lying next to them.

"Stop it," he said, "or you will get me started all over again!"

"Thanks for the lovely flower," she whispered. "I didn't notice when you got up to get it."

"I didn't. Someone else must have given it to you."

"You mean when we were making love? Or asleep? Look around you, the beach is almost deserted."

"It is a strange flower. I've never seen anything like it. What's it called?"

"It is called Sac Nicte," replied Maya. "They say there was once a Mayan princess by that name who ran away with her lover to the forest of Peten, fleeing her father's wrath. When she died, this flower sprouted all over Chichen Itza, commemorating their love."

"Why do you suddenly look so sad, Maya?"

"I just had a strange and haunting dream in which I recognized myself a long time ago. Tell me, Kanuk, you have never explained how you got that scar under your left breast."

"Oh, that, it's nothing really. When I was a kid in the reserve, my friends were always taunting me to prove my courage by pushing me to go deer hunting with them. I just couldn't bring myself to killing anything, so one day just to show them I wasn't a coward I took a jagged can top and cut myself hoping to gouge my heart out. Fortunately, I botched it up and the ambulance had to take me to a hospital in Ste-Anne-de-Bellevue to get it stitched. Now that I've told you my secret tell me yours: who gave you that flower? Was it the guy who was ogling your breasts this morning?"

Maya kissed him gently on his round red lips and shrugged her shoulders.

"It was Sac Nicte herself," she finally said.

"Who?"

"Sac Nicte, my secret twin."

Myths

There is a story of a swan.
See the birthmark on the back of my neck
under my hair. That is where the great bird
pinched me in her beak, snatching me from the sea
and carrying my wet, salty body to the shore.
This is a story I could believe.
Sometimes the wings of a bird beat against
my skull. Feathers fill my mouth and eyes
with a whiteness like winter.

Or I was carried on a dolphin's back.
She pushed me to shore with her soft nose
then turned and disappeared under the waves,
the notes of her song hovering above the water.
In the blue light of evening, alone in the house,
I float through rooms, my sides sleek and slippery.

I was not made from a thin, dry rib
white and bare as if chewed and sucked
by a small dog. These breasts did not come
from a man's side, this round belly, this
hollow at the centre. We dreamed each other
at the same time and we dreamed a garden.
When we awoke there was wind in the leaves
above us apples glowing like red moons
as we turned to one another in the sweet green air.

Lorna Crozier

Between Ebony and Ivory

Martine Jacquot

Everything began at dawn on the 27th. Everything always began, in a way, at dawn on a 27th. No matter which one. That morning, however, the uncertain moment before the break of dawn was to hold special meaning for each of them.

The couple in the story barely knew each other, but they already sensed that neither time nor distance could break what flowed between them like liquid in communicating vessels.

The path in the middle of the public gardens crunched under their step. The sky was fading behind the arches of roses, the stardust sky hanging above the night. The air was still and the couple no longer noticed the tourists dwindling in the distance after the night show, as the chandeliers dimmed slowly behind them one by one. They tried to conceal their uneasiness at the magic of this encounter. To avoid the silence, they broke into a crystal-clear laughter under the still, star-studded sky already turning pale. Making sure they would not arrive at the hotel too fast, sauntering under the green foliage as long as possible. Avoiding those bright neon lights from the heart of the city. Like lovers at a railway station, they sensed the clear-cut break was yet to come, a throbbing pain that would draw that fine border between ebony and ivory when morning light shines on a night like no other. Without it being said and still without knowing, the couple had decided that fiction would become real. Later the rage would follow, and later still the awareness that they'd never retrieve this moment, lost forever. Desperate, not knowing what they might do or say that could change it. Sooner or later, one way or another, comes a rupture.

The rhythm of the footsteps on the gravel path was irregular. Wavering. Vague, uncertain pauses of doubt. The man and the woman were unaware of the changes taking place, when passion is still resisted. When for every word a strange echo rings in the innermost self. Ordinary words, usually meaningless, but suddenly so laden with meaning they're almost unbearable. Veiled words, yet sounding more true than the usual "I love you."

Harboring no logic, the story unfolds, giving more depth and meaning to a new day on the verge of dawn. Beyond all reason and promises already made and almost forgotten. She will follow him anywhere, she would follow him anywhere if he only asked. But he dares not, not yet, maybe never. Yet during this time she will go crazy, crazy for him.

There were steps on the gravel everywhere that night. Happy groups of people passed them by. Night celebrations had drawn to a close, yet revellers wanted to carry on, along every path in the gardens, on every street, all over the city. For the man and the woman, it was only the beginning of a story, although they hadn't quite realized it yet. Deep down, what the truth might hold frightened them. To them, they had already experienced everything. From the shadows of the trees to the silver light of the moon and to the shade. Alternating between the crucial point of the day, between ebony and ivory.

Amongst these people they felt like newcomers. They had never met before, yet they shared common memories: unfulfilled dreams somewhere on the blurred horizon of uncertainty.

Yet the azure of this serene statement; the peacefulness of a childhood storybook; the innocence that follows the moment of awakening; the soft brushing of shoulders, the fragrance of roses, the shivering in the cool early morning hours. Not having a past or a future, a culture or a name; just long enough to cross the gardens until silence spreads over the path behind them.

The benches were wrapped in shade. Only the Milky-Way-like path remained in the middle of the gardens; the rustling of the footsteps on the gravel path, the flowing of a long skirt, the dance of shade and light through an arbor. Yet there was also the bewilderment of love springing up in the midst of people indifferent to one another, those who have the unhappy privilege of living out their indifference together. The feeling of a newborn passion that struggles to survive. The silence that follows. The loneliness that accompanies nightfall. The desire to understand, to recreate the impossible in order to better understand.

Write the story of this couple, doomed to understand how passionate their love was only after they part. Write their story which never was, since they grasped their love for one another only too late, once they have separated perhaps forever, and there is nothing left but the hope that at least the memories will last forever. Write the story that they will try to recreate in their minds and in their dreams, in their numerous letters in which they will look for each other, in which they will try to understand and to love each other.

Recreate the time when they were still unaware, when they were afraid of knowing. Because of the others, because of the unknown of the new day dawning.

Write this story so that we may believe it really took place. So that these lovers who never made love together and probably never will, will have something on which they can build their own love story. So that they won't be forgotten. Transforming what could have been into what is, since what has been written is the only proof that they ever met. Replacing what time will erase. Only the written words will bear witness to what they were afraid of exploring.

Write what they hadn't realized yet and what they were afraid of knowing. For it was still too early, yet already too late.

But one thought, one instant, the hint of a thought would have been sufficient reason for this story to have been written. It would speak for all the impossible loves that have existed if only in a passing glance, because of the others, of a world that is too large, of the dizziness of having constantly to start all over again. As if it were forbidden. As if those love stories could live only in despair and loneliness and in the memories of what did not happen. Nothing happened, yet everything was real.

The sound of their footsteps in the night. They were not saying anything. They were not even looking at each other, but they could feel the other looking into their innermost self. They had travelled so far that they did not know whether they had arrived or if their encounter was just another port of call. Yet they felt the innocence of falling in love for the first time, always the first time. Not to destroy that innocence, even by the passing of time.

It was better to say nothing than to pretend they never noticed or felt anything. The desire to know, to understand, as well as the fear of it.

Write this story because it had become so important that no other could compare, not even in one's imagination.

On the gravel pathway in the middle of the gardens, the couple in the story hesitated between the laughter of finally having met and the tears of knowing of their impending separation. Imminent and inescapable.

Write their story as an excuse for a love which does not have any right to live, but never wants to die.

The happiness of meeting each other. The despair of loving each other in silence. Not to dare because of uncertainty and fear.

Ignore that the present is as important as the passage of time. Write how impossible it is to explain anything when the characters themselves do not understand.

Write their unintelligible, incoherent story, to mask the incomprehensible, uncontrollable truth. Lose oneself in writing as one takes an airplane for an unknown destination, with a one-way ticket. Love without ever turning back.

Make this love come alive in a story, being untruthful to everyday life, colouring the washed-out faces of faded, paltry relationships legitimized by society. Find in a pair of eyes the same fragile beauty as in a rose just before the storm tears it to shreds. Frightening happiness, this encounter, for nothing will ever be the same.

Make this dawn into an encounter unlike any other, a possible adventure different from so many others. Write it to make it immortal, to turn it into a true story.

Hang on to this silent love, to the untold words, write it instead of crying as if life had been lost.

Write as one sleeps. To avoid everyday life emptiness. A kind of escape. An inner sunshine.

They were unaware that they had saved a secret corner in their hearts for the possibility of this encounter for which they had always been waiting; this love which was impossible and yet had to exist if only as long as a glance deep into the eyes of the other where they read the abysmal imperfection of the world; and finally so that they knew they were not mistaken to have hoped, for now they would know forever that this encounter genuinely did happen.

It was the 27th. An ordinary day, one that would not be remembered by those still celebrating or already sleeping. Yet an indelible mark on the line of time for the couple of the story.

Thick ink of uncertain dreams. Dried-up wells of satisfied passions.

Ever since the 27th, the man and the woman in the story have never ceased to write the same story, their story, the story of the world, the eternal story of humanity which sidesteps truth and beauty. Since the 27th, they have been writing in their notebooks what they did not dare tell each other. They write about the abundance of love with meagre words and wait for answers to the letters they never send. For fear of destroying the dream. To save the space they have reserved for this love.

Last Picnic

A long concourse of light,
a hot pure breadth and fullness sweeps
rolling into the grey hills west
of this light's edge. The land
leans in the wind, flesh-coloured,
the furred seed tassels rippling.

From Wildcat's ridge the grasslands stretch
towards the bouldered hills, cottonwood
crouched in their orange arroyos –
a picnic view: to see the sun
kindle the distant snow-peaks as it falls.

The fire smudge centers us. Below
the late day lingers in the scrub
thickening shades to buffalo,
ghosts of the old adventurers.
From here a thread road lines the valley depths,
leads to the "mad man's castle," some say,
"eagle's nest," miniature, stone among stone,
to us, from our eye eyrie.

Twilight billows like a fog
around us on our separate liths
like crones, the weird Ward women, so alike
same voice, same face, same distances.
Then, louring from the West, the cloud
that lion-tawny crept toward us,
that jelled the coyote's yip to glass,
divided us – not then,
but in my memory then –
as absolute as that clear wall
the bare stars have beyond our bloom
eye-burning, honeyless, whose creak
pilots the empty passages –

It was as if one spirit leaped –
as a bird flings up from the pine mast tip
and spurs out on the peach fire of the west
buoying its wings on upper winds

we only know of by its flight,
leaning in towards the mountains, sure –

as an ash wheels into the greying sky
from one doused picnic campfire,
and is gone.

                                        Travis Lane

Second Solitude

Lorraine Coyle

She was combing her hair, looking past the mirror at the clock, thinking of her husband Howard. "Three years tomorrow," she sighed, begrudging the ticking clock that fussed at her to hurry. Her daughter Hannah and her family were due any minute for the ritual monthly dinner begun soon after Howard's death.

When the second hand stopped between the nine and the ten on the gold-rimmed face she stroked only air and raised her other arm to guide the comb back to its work. "Bill will change the battery," she told herself, eyeing the clock. Its round face pulsed bright and blinding before a dark circle swirled about it and nothing remained but a pinpoint of light.

And Lucinda's hands descended and folded into her body; her gangly frame bent at the knees, and she crumbled to the floor.

But somehow, *she* stepped from her body. She pranced about a few moments leaping left and right bouncing up and down, testing her feather-light movements. Then gaining control, rose high above the crumpled form and saw from there her body all askew. *Han and Bill and the children will be here soon. Hannah will straighten me out ... she's such a neat person.*

Surveying her kitchen from near the ceiling, Lucinda smiled. Casserole dishes were ready to be popped into the oven, but otherwise the counters were clean and in order, her newly scrubbed floor was immaculate — Hannah insisted it needed resurfacing — but she liked the blend of its worn-down pattern. The curtains were starchy-white. The only thing that bothered her was that she'd left her stepstool out of place. Something Hannah could catch her on to reinforce the notion that it was time to think of a smaller place. "*Hah! I can look after myself perfectly well,*" Lucinda fumed, then thought, "*Then why am I up here instead of ... perhaps I should go down and put the stool in its place.*" But she didn't.

Floating was delicious, like licking the coolest ice-cream cone, and sensuous, like snuggling in a furry robe. *Why worry about the silly stool: I haven't enjoyed myself this much since Howard and I ...*

It was not something she could share with Hannah, but her bedroom, her memories of bygone times with Howard, not only the physical joys they shared, but the closeness that had bound their spirits, it held her to this house. So she refused to listen to hints of a small apartment. And after that: a nursing home?

No ... no it's not time yet to think of such ... Time? Where had Time gone?

She rolled over and faced the ceiling, and lost herself in its shining white surface and she was back in that long ago past, during the years of passion and love, pleasures and triumphs, but heartbreak and tears too. And mingled with this, the search for the WHY of it all. The moments of near knowing that eased the times of confusion, the chance readings that inched open the door to broader thinking. The summer she'd discovered Emerson.

His thinking fits in with mine. Or more modestly, I should say, mine fits in with his. 'The intuition of the moral sentiment is an insight of the perfection of the laws of soul. These laws execute themselves. They are out of time, out of space, and not subject to circumstance ... man (can be) God, (enjoy) the immortality of God' and 'The world is the product of one will, active in each ray of (a) star, each wavelet of (a) pool.' *He believes Jesus to be a prophet.* '(Who) saw with open eyes the mystery of soul ...' *I believe each of us must strive to communicate with our own deep being.* '... dare to love God without mediator or veil.' *What a lonely responsibility this spiritual quest.*

Lucinda frowned and flipped over. On the floor her inert form wore an impassive mask. She had to smile at this.

I look as dumbfounded as some who think my beliefs unthinkable. What a relief when I connect with a willing speaker of intangibles. How exciting to probe aloud the secret questions and search for conclusions ... conclusion? Never conclusions! Only the seeking, the effort at communion with a higher power. And in seeking the divine, growing closer to the human, the very core of me longs to embrace the desperate of this world and be embraced in return. Yet I keep on searching. I know our planet is but a dot in the universe. Its forest and streams ... the vast sky are all part of an interconnected divine. And, we beings, we too are particles of this ... Particles? Lying on the floor are particles! Why have I disconnected from my body? Always I've strived for unity with the whole. Somehow my body seemed part of the plan. I can't abandon it. It's not right ... leaving it lying there in a mess.

Lucinda became agitated, flitting about. She strained downward to return to her body, but all her fluttering came to nothing, and she wailed. Until a mysterious presence enveloped her and she regained her composure. Felt an overflowing of life and love inviting her to ... 'Come blend into the peace of the universe.' She hesitated at this.

BRRINGGG!!! The door bell rang in the hallway; its shrill sound bounced off the walls of the kitchen and grabbed for her. But the mysterious presence had now become swirls of rainbow-coloured veils and she hid herself among their ever-increasing layers. Marvelling at the beauty of them. Another ring, more urgent still, reached through the veils, tugging at her, insisting she return to reality. But resisting, she pulled away, desperately tried to travel deeper into the veils, to escape, to block out the commotion.

But it grew louder. With clamorous knocking; and pounding footsteps on the side porch. Then the kitchen door opened and toppled the stool Lucinda had used to reach up into her cupboards.

"My God, Bill, Mother had fallen! Did she hit her head?"

Silly Hannah ... I'm more solid on my feet ... or even on my head, than anyone you can name. Don't you know! I can dangle upside down forever with my knees wrapped around the bannister rail. Father gets terribly upset at this ... unladylike, he calls it." Lucinda looked down on Hannah. *"But I let you enjoy things like that, don't I? Of course people can be more who they want to be nowadays. Nowadays? Here I am, me, parent and child, up here. And you child and adult! Where has TIME gone? Yet it seems all right. Yes, it's comfortable.*

"Bill, call 911! Take the children in the den with you."

I suppose Troy and Stacey were at Sunday school this morning. Do they believe? Do I believe? Oh, that Baby Jesus story! My misbehavings make him cry? Him who isn't even around? And Saints? Their flagellations please a Lord and Master. Somewhere, up here? — A rewarding God? (Does it mean I'll get the sled I want for Christmas if I pray hard enough?) And who is this punishing God? Who has an angel watch my every move and record my every deed. The adults ... they get angry when I question their word about these things ... they tell me to shush and not dare talk foolish in front of the priest and church, or the nuns at school. 'Learn your prayers: repeat, repeat, repeat, until you know them perfect or everyone will think you come from a pagan family.' Our father who art in heaven ... I can't wait until I'm free to climb upstairs to my attic bedroom ... hallowed by Thy name ... and peer out its dormered window into the dark night. (What comes next?) And soar high above the rooftops into the deep of the sky. THE STARS WILL TELL ME THE TRUTH.

"Please can I ride to the hospital with her?"

"No ma'm, we have things to do ... Easy she goes, boys."

All this fuss! Sirens and lights on a Sunday afternoon. The same as when my own mother fell. Yes! Yes! Mother has fallen and I'm so frightened! A big policeman yells at the neighbours bunched below the veranda steps, 'Clear the way, clear the way!' I can't stop the giggle and it rises in my throat. So I press my face to the craggy bark of the tall poplar tree; the tree whose branches keep the sun off what should be our front lawn, but instead is a strip of bare earth. It's where I trace patterns in the soil, teasing the red ants, blocking their homeward trails. The trunk of the poplar is large enough to hide me from the crowd and I drop down on my haunches. It's easy to spy through the legs of the people. But it's scary too. I don't dare go see. Perhaps my mother is dead, and all cold like the person in the coffin Aunt Cora lifted me up to touch. 'She might as well see for herself,' she had said. I know about cats dying ... mine died last month. Is mother dead? Is the fat policeman here to dig a hole to bury her in? ... like my brother did for Fluffy? I think I'm going to be sick. But only a hiccup escapes through my fingers clamped over my mouth. I giggle at this. That's when Ada Ledderman spots me. And scolds me for laughing ... Mrs. Burke is nearby, 'She's only five. It's nerves making her' 'Nerves ... ' Ada glares down at me. Her face is puffy and red. 'Kids don't have nerves. No matter what her mother says, I say she's strange. Staring at people with those grey-brown eyes as though she were pulling the stuffing out of a rag doll to see what it's made up of.' So that's what Mrs. Ledderman thinks of me. She isn't far wrong. I want to know lots of stuff. But mostly, no one is willing to tell. — Now, after all my years of thinking on it, I realize no one could have told me. And today it's me causing the fuss! Are the grandchildren off somewhere, giggling?

"If we pray real hard, will Grandma get better?"

Obscene request! I'm well and satisfied as I am. Enjoying the silence ... hanging out my attic window, gazing into the night sky. Over there it's cloudy and mysterious ... But straight above, the sky is sparkling with infinite life assuring me there is a God. Different from the one who rewards or punishes. The grandeur of the starlit night erases for a brief moment the stamped mental image I have of Him branded on my mind by a church protective of its power and glory. A HE in glowing robes, authoritatively large, fully bearded, seated on a judgement throne. How marvellous it is to override that picture and substitute for it the idea of a sexless integrated whole ...

"I've notified the others ... at her age you never know."

They'll come. Howie, and Rhea, and Julie. They'll come and moan and be sad. Will they believe that my spirit has gone searching for its destiny? Or will they bury my bones and think that's the end of it ... except for whatever difference my being here has made? Here? Where? It's so transparent! I can see Howie when he was a teenager, clutching at his blanket those Sunday mornings. — 'Mom ... I'm sleepy! I don't need to go to church every Sunday.' You watch junk on TV every day ... so you can spend an hour a week on God. We all need balance in our lives ... we all need quiet times to find God. 'Quiet times? Quiet times is hiding under my blankets. Listen to the brats! Around here, Sunday mornings is a frigging war zone.' At least your sisters go to church. 'Yeah ... to do what? Look pious while they're checking out the boys! How ... ie ... up!' Oh God. These kids are driving me nutty ... I can scream all the right reasons at them and be questioning my reasoning at the same time. Where is this precious time and quiet for my own search? The more I ponder, the larger the questions loom. Am I doing right by the kids? How can I guide them past so many unanswerables? Guide them! Isn't it all I can do to provide the opportunity to see more than one way? And let them choose! Aren't I still struggling? Selectively choosing beliefs out of my parents life, formulating others for myself? Disentangling myself from religious rules that assure a precious afterlife depicted in images of angels trumpeting in a glorious sky? And in the midst of all of this, there's Howard needing me, and both of us wrapped up in family, paying the mortgage, accumulating ... what? And why? Will I ever be done with it? Ever find the time to be who I want to be? How can I think such thoughts! The kids: I do love them. I hope they know that. But oh God ... to enjoy the luxury of being alone. And yet alone is not what I want. I guess what I want is more than a physical bond to other humans. I need a spiritual ... I need more of the peace that I find when through sheer will I scatter earthly concerns and fuse with another force beyond the immediate. But what of my children? Their inner needs? So ... I march them to church each Sunday morning. And why not? I want them familiar with questions of God and spiritual thought. But should I intimate that churches are made of stone and mortar? With crumbling properties. To what purpose? No! Any religious group is a beginning ... the trick is to go beyond the rules ... to seek a personal union with the unknown. For unknown it is. As for churches, well, do people tear down their homes before building themselves another? Fools if they do. This world is a storm of evolving matter and so are we humans. I am a tree as much as I am me. My essence ... my soul, an amoeba twisting and turning, wriggling to find its place. So, can I say to my children ... this is so and that is such? No! The best that I can do is encourage a seeking, then bless their individual treks. No way can I dictate their spiritual life. For soul is personal and spiritual advancement only gained through personal struggle. Adopting rituals of others is of little worth. Gurus abound! It is false to exchange one set of rules for another. Repeated prayers or mantras are of little value, entangling the soul in rhetoric. So ... I pound and pound into the children's heads the do's and don'ts of society, and tamper less with their spiritual side. For soul is different. No one has the right to steal a soul. Never, never steal a soul. Mustn't steal a soul. Each person has to develop his or her ... so.

"Darling, won't you open your eyes! It's Carrie. Dorina and I have come to visit. So please talk to us."

Poor Carrie! She wants me to talk, does she? More like she wants to talk. Of silly things. But she is a giving person. Certainly helped me out when I had pneumonia and couldn't care for the kids that week. Just waved away all my thanks, saying she was chalking up points in God's big book of good deeds. (Didn't she ever let go of that childish concept?) Or is this her way of making light of her charitable deeds? To explain the voluntary work she does in mental institutions? The close ties she has to these people puzzles me. Isn't it a wasteful use of time? Like bringing Dorina along to see me. Dorina ... there she is, hunched over, gazing out the window, smiling that imbecile smile. What can she possibly be seeing through those vacant eyes of hers? What?

Squinting at the scene, Lucinda's curiosity got the better of her so she floated downward and settled herself just behind Dorina and peered over her rounded shoulder. What she saw from there tumbled her backward, but she straightened and returned to gawk at the sight of it. It was not something she could have described in words; it was more like an interaction of feelings. A flowing back and forth of emotions. A cause and effect reaction as though Dorina were wired into an energized 'other dimension' system. Warm vibrations radiated from her; their sympathetic glow drew Lucinda and she entered Dorina's body. From there, peering out her vacant eyes, she saw INFINITY; settled inside her twisted bones, she felt LOVE. And was filled with Dorina's dignity.

What a distorted sense of values I've harboured! It isn't only the grand accomplishments in life that influence the outcome of destinies. How stupid of me to wonder at certain people's usefulness? The so-called mad unable to function in my limited view of life. The senile, who perhaps found a way to bridge the chasm between worlds. It's clear to me now! We all have a contribution to make, the not-so-normal along with the normal. Normal! What a word. It defies the open mind, it clouds possibilities. Pos ... sibilities ... oohh ... I'm myself again ... I'm floating ... up, up, up. Carrie and Dorina are getting smaller and smaller. I'm gone.

She settled herself near the ceiling of another room, a room long ago abandoned. Yet it had been easy to reach it ...

Her father was insulated behind his newspaper. Turning a page, he shaped it, stifling its fluttering. Expecting no-nonsense obedience from it as much as he did from everyone. (Lucinda knew: she *tried* to be good, and if she failed, she stayed out of sight as much as she could.) He held his pipe between clenched teeth deeply sucking from its stem so that the tobacco glowed, then blackened as he expelled a stream of smoke out of the side of his mouth. Filling the air with a scented haze. Surrounding the head of a child sitting on the floor at the foot of his rocker, cutting out figures from a booklet of paper dolls.

From above Lucinda looked from this scene to her body on the hospital bed, hooked up to a machine. Then looking back she smiled at the sight of herself as a child until ...

"Ouch! Freddie. Bad cat. You scratched me."

"Be quiet! Or go play in the kitchen!"

"Yes Papa ... "

She remembered that his displeasure always sent her scurrying (hadn't she been assured this man was an earthly stand-in for her eternal father?) She'd pondered on this many times while seated on the counter of the corner cupboard where he stored his tools. *Am I bad? Is this why he sends me away? Is God angry with me too when father yells at me? Will heaven be like this? God sitting off in a corner and only showing his face to scold me?"* She thought some more. "At least I please him when he's at work hammering or sawing and I hand him whatever tool he needs. Just like the nuns who help the priest set up the altar before mass. The priest ... that's another father. There sure are lots of fathers around. I wish I was a father. Or priest. And I could say mass like I do on the pretend altar I set up in my room. But I can never be a father. Not like my brothers ... they'll be fathers. Oh well ... now that they're grown and gone ... I'm allowed to help fill the cellar with winter wood.*

"Any changes during the night, Nurse Hannigan?"

What is happening? Why is the doctor flashing that light into my eyes? Don't they know I'm not there?

She called to them but they paid no attention. So, she shrugged and let her mind roam to another time when she was about to cross a busy street and her father grabbed her hand (had he ever held her hand before?) No. This once he had taken her for a Sunday walk. A walk down to the railroad station to watch the afternoon train come in. It surprised her that his skin was nearly as soft as hers, because when he whacked her bottom for scuffing her shoes, or grabbed her arm to quiet down, his thick hand was hard. Her brothers knew all about that thick hand. It could reach across the parlour during the after-dinner recital of the rosary.

He knelt the boys in front of him. They had to kneel straight and tall, while *she* was allowed to hang back with her mother who recited the Hail Marys and Our Fathers. Calling to their attention the holy events of Christ's life as she caressed her beads.

Her father fingered his own beads grudgingly, mumbling his responses. At prayers was the only time he allowed his wife's clear voice to dominate the room. And each evening she positioned herself near the doorway, and squared her shoulders, holding her head imperially high, closing her eyes to focus on some inner vision. So that Lucinda, seated on her heels, was in her glory. When else could she observe her family instead of being under their scornful scrutiny?

Dear Mother, she's the only one ready to put up with me. Noisy child, asking silly questions, seeing mystery in everyday life. Is she weak and silly herself? Letting me talk her into permissions father has vetoed. AND letting me question the rules of the church which she holds dear. (Later, I suspected my mother was one of those who had gone beyond the strictures of organized religion. That the times she spent in solitary prayer were not a response to rules and control, but meditation time developing her personal spirituality. And her devotion to the Blessed Virgin, didn't that for her help balance this male-dominated religion ... ?

"Did Father consent to give her the Final Blessing ... even if she hasn't been ... ?"

" ... Practising? Yes, Carrie, he came last night."

"Oh Hannah ... thank God ... now she can go peacefully."

Yes, Carrie. He came. Sombre, yet detached. Repeating words supposed to clear my path to everlasting life. During his chanting I wondered if he believed he had the power to make me one with the Lord. Or if this ceremony was more for the living than for the dying ... the shaman mesmerizing his followers. What? What's happening down there?

On the bed, her body was surrounded by white-coated attendants, excited attendants, pricking a needle in her arm, clamping an oxygen mask on her face, pounding her on the chest. *"What for? I am breathing the purest air ... "*

Her view faded. It didn't matter. She was floating again, this time in perfect union with ... a something. Outside the sphere of anything she'd ever known before. No, that wasn't true. She'd experienced this feeling before. This knowledge of belonging ... the sureness of knowing that she was one with the whole of existence. But, in all of her seventy-five years it had happened only once that the core of her being was so infused. Her mind had grasped that that was the essence of her. And now this sense was upon her again, but not for the fleeting moment of that other time, but with an embrace that assured her this was her destiny ... the original home her soul was meant to return to.

A great happiness permeated her being, scattering her thoughts, blending her surroundings, until a minuscule doubt caused her to pull back. The doubt escalated and she questioned herself? *"Have I done my utmost to serve my fellow man? Truthfully sought my place in the universal scheme of things? Fulfilled my potential?"*

A parade of faults and omissions began a steady march; four abreast they pounded by; their numbers infinite, their familiar ugly faces caused Lucinda's heart to skip a beat. She clasped her breast. *"Oh the shame of it! How could I have spent so many hours assuring my own comforts, and so few in aiding others? Insulated my thoughts against ideas that required I accept the responsibility of them? Been lax in setting aside that bit of time needed to remain true to my goals?"*

The air about her was pressing in, a pain in her chest became near to unbearable. She was in a confined place and longed to free herself, to reach again that spot where pure joy had flowed through her. But asked herself what right she had to covet eternal peace when the glaring faults she'd admitted to needed redressing? She probed the boundaries of her space and realized she was in her mother's belly. *"How so? Never mind ... "* She began an awkward crawl ... squeezed by pressing matter. Instinct guided her, and she rounded her body twisting herself into a heads-down position: now the passage, although dark, was familiar. She found herself being assisted, at first nudged along, then transported, and finally expelled into a blinding light that penetrated her closed lids. Even so she viewed her surroundings, and pitied the concerned faces staring down at her.

She coughed to clear her lungs of the phlegm accumulated during her voyage down the moist dark passage she'd just travelled. She rolled her eyes and TIME sped by, and she tumbled through thousands of days. Through baby talk to clear enunciation; past menopausal tones to aging tremulous speech. And struggled to speak aloud but could not. Her mind, however, refocused so that she regained a sense of herself.

I'm back. Yes I can feel my bones ... my arthritic shoulder. How long have I been lying here ... thinking of how I've lived my life? Lying here, still unproductive? Hah! Unproductive! Why do I nag at myself for not being kitchen bound? If I had baked all the cookies I was supposed to, when would I have had time to read? But then Ada Ledderman had told Mother that no little girl should be reading as much as I was? 'Too much reading can addle a child's mind.' It must have addled mine all right, because it took me a long time to realize that most of the readings of my teen and young adulthood years marched me through an endless list of male deliberations on Life and God and Truth and Right and Wrong. What an eye-opener when I encountered glimmers of female strengths within the matriarchal societies of some of our North American native peoples. Women as leaders! And then, also, to Greek and Roman times female Priests? Goddesses? Blasphemy? No! It had once been so. And now was barely visible. The thread of female wisdom buried beneath thousands of years of male-dominated thought, yet alive still. In the arts? Carried forward, not only by women, but also by sensitive men, who see life as a unique experience of a larger picture. Men and women who understand the connectivity of our spirits. That humanity, the animal world, our environment, are all one with the whole which we call our Universe or God or Mohammed or Christ or ... damned labels! We're stuck on labels. Just like I'm stuck in this bed. Shouldn't I be up getting dinner on the table? Hannah and Bill and the children. They'll be here soon. But why can't I take some time to just think. Think. THINK? Because there's work to do. That's why. Not only a silly ritual dinner to put on! But real work, out there where people are hurting, in BODY and MIND. There's learning to acquire, peaceable living to instill, in families, in nations! My head aches at the thought of it. Surely not PREACHING. Not by me who believes in the importance of personal search!

BY LIVING YOUR LIFE IN SUCH A WAY THAT YOUR INDIVIDUAL ABILITIES CONTRIBUTE TO THE PROGRESSION OF UNIVERSAL EVOLVING

What ... who said that?

"Doctor ... is she going to make it?

We brought her back. I think there's lots of life in her yet ... but now it's up to your mother herself ... "

They brought me back. Is that what happened? I could have stayed? It's up to me. I can go back out there where I was part of something greater? So near to ... heaven ... ?

Wasn't I called from there once before? A long time ago? And propelled into this world, a squalling infant? Did I just now fantasize, or relive my BIRTH?"

More questions dogged her. *Why are people born into this world in the first place? To what purpose?* A chorus of voices responded, but the sounds were garbled, and no matter how she strained, the answers evaded her. So she pushed aside the questions, and, with each passing second her recollections of 'that other place' grew weaker.

She felt the weight of her blanket, warm and caressing. And she snuggled into the comfort of it.

"Did her eyes flutter? Howie? Rhea? Did you see? Quick! Go get Julie. I think she's coming around"

Lucinda opened her eyes.

"Darlings! How nice to have you all ... here ... "

Parallel Images

The bible and the Tarot pack:
I find consolation in both;
the book of Job, Ruth in the fields of wheat,
Ezekiel's chariot,
the woman clothed with the sun

the wheel of fortune turning,
the hermit seeking truth with his lantern,
dark waters under the moon

strength, in woman's clothing,
clasping the jaws of the lion
the angel blowing his trumpet
above the tombs
on resurrection day
and especially the fool
in his coloured garments
with his jester's cap,
his pilgrim's bag and staff,
his little dog at his heels
journeying over sandy deserts
and the mounds of graves

past towers, treachery, death and devils

toward green trees
the celestial city
the world's
        consummation

        Elizabeth Brewster

Beginning in Summer

Sharon Ferguson-Hood

School is out. The trees are bare, the occasional soft grey pussy willow promises new life. It is starting to rain, the pavement is shiny black under the glare of my headlights.

My dad bought me this old Honda. The catches on the back windows thud dully in the wind, I try to secure them with rubber bands. I hate asking my father for money, he has so little left. The only investment I had in life was a twenty-year marriage to Rob. Rob has three-four vehicles and I have to drive this piece of junk. The rain is coming in the window and I pull my collar tighter around my neck.

Where did the money from the business go, when I finally got to court there was nothing left. Even the house was worthless, and I left most of the furniture. But that was my fault I could have taken more, except we ran out of room in the U-haul and I was too frightened to come back. My lawyer said, with this new divorce law you will get your share and he will have to pay your way through university, you are a perfect example of a woman that can benefit from change. Nice change in the law but it's not happening — reality is a harsh lesson. After a $13,000 lawyer's bill and a lot of fighting I was paying my own way through school with student loans and Rob keeps the business, the house, and the kids.

Through the rain I see the one-kilometre sign and the cemetery on the left, the headstones are huddled together in the dark. The skating rink gleams in the wet night, the curling rink beside it. The icons of society on the prairies. The spiral on the Catholic church rises above the town, the local confectionery is dark, closed for the night. I slow down — 10th Street is next, there's the church and the manse, a caragana hedge surrounds it. I stop the car and sit very still. What have I gotten myself into, I do not know anything about death and dying, and someone is bound to die in the next four months, and what will people think of a mother without her children. I am tired of women saying, "Oh, I could never leave my children, how could you do that?" How does one explain to people one hardly knows. I get out of the car — the key is where they said it would be. The manse is small but it looks comfortable and I do not feel quite so lonely as I carry in the few boxes I have brought. I will unpack in the morning.

The doorbell is ringing and I bury my head deeper under the covers, but they are persistent and I struggle into my housecoat. A woman takes up the entire doorway, I have seen this face before.

"Hello dear, my name is Maude. You must have arrived late last night. How are you, moved in I see. May I come in (she enters). I hope you like it here for the summer, there is a support committee you can call if you need anything, anything at all — just call. Now let me tell you there are some things you should know. The fridge is old, don't put too much stuff in the freezer or you will have water everywhere. Oh yes water, that reminds me, there is a pump, come I'll show you how to run it." I follow her down the stairs, her heavy body is cumbersome and she takes the stairs slowly resting a moment on each step. She goes on.

"Charles, that's my husband, has been chairman of the board for six years now, he's from the bank, our children are grown and happily married with families of their own. They're all educated and have fine jobs, no burden to us at all thank heavens, I couldn't cope with a lot of trouble and problems all the time. Here's the switch for the pump — see this is how you work it." She sighs deeply and we return upstairs; she sits heavily in a chair. "The board prefers it if you have no overnight company, men or women."

I stare at her. They're really not taking any chances. I finally speak. "Do you have a job description for me or a list of people in the congregation who would like a visit."

"I was getting to that, here are some maps so you can find your way around. Three services every Sunday, you know that of course, and funerals and there are some people in the hospital. The nursing home also and it wouldn't hurt if you stopped in to introduce yourself to the undertaker, Oh, I mean the mortician — they don't like to be called undertakers nowadays. Well I must be going, Charles will wonder where I've gotten to, he will want his morning coffee. See you on Sunday."

That first Sunday I set three alarms, I dream that I will be in the pulpit without all of my clothes on or I will not have my sermon with me or worse yet I will have forgotten to write one. But I need not have worried, I was up at 5 a.m. checking the prayer of confession and the assurance of pardon. I do not like confession, it seems to me a waste but they tell me I cannot have pardon without confessing first — Oh well — one cannot always have things the way one wants.

It is forty miles to the first service. The land is dry and already it is hot, the wind blows constantly and my car dash is covered with dust. Everywhere farmers are losing their land. The farm I grew up on had belonged to my grandfather, my father and then to my brother. I was there the day Farm Credit came and took away the machinery; perhaps it just could not sustain one more generation of alcoholics.

The miles pass quickly; my stomach feels queasy like when you are not sure what will happen next. Like when I was married. But this is somewhat more predictable. The service goes well, there are only six or seven people there, a rural community clinging together against all odds.

After the second service a woman approaches, she has rusty grey hair tied back with a red scarf. Her thin legs are covered with brown stockings and she wears open-toed, wedge-heeled sandals. An almost buttonless cardigan hangs from her small frame.

"Hi, I'm Belle. Great sermon you preached. Could I have a copy of it? I teach in the city during the year, right now I'm working on a paper protesting government spending."

There is a child from a long time ago that answers, "Oh, please just drop by the manse when you are in town and I'll give you a copy."

I leave for my third service. Then I have the rest of the day and Monday off and Tuesday my pastoral visiting.

Early Tuesday morning the phone rings, "Hi, this is Belle, would you come for lunch today and bring the copy of your sermon?"

"Sure," I reply. I was headed in that direction, I have to eat somewhere and money is scarce, free meals could be my salvation. It would be a full month before I was paid. I checked at the local garage and the owner, a member of the congregation, agreed to charge gas till payday. Being poor is not easy.

I had grown up poor, six of us in four rooms and no power or running water. I hated life, I hated growing up then, there was no privacy, no space to call my own. My mother hung the clothes on a line when it was 40 below and they froze, then she brought them in to dry, funny how that worked. Then I was married and I was rich, or at least reasonably wealthy, there were lots of rooms and every modern convenience. One Christmas Rob gave me a mixmaster and the next Christmas another one, and for my birthday a razor and for the next two birthdays a razor and one year a black negligee to go with one of the razors. I realize he is running three businesses and probably cannot keep things straight. Gifts anyway. But I do not have much trouble keeping my identities sorted out.

I arrive at Belle's just before noon, the house is old, yellow paint is peeling from the siding, green shutters hang loosely on their hinges, long grass brushes against my bare legs. The front door opens, and my foot stops on the broken veranda step. He moves forward.

"Hi, I'm Peter." He is tall and thin with dark eyes and black hair which is a mass of unkempt curls hanging past his shoulders. He is wearing jeans and a white shirt, the kind I remember my father wearing.

"Is this B-Belle's place?"

He smiles, "It is, Mom has just gone to the store, come in. You must be the new minister, how long will you be here?"

"Only four months, while the other minister is away studying."

"Oh, you don't look much like most students we get here." He spreads his long slender hands in front of him, "please, sit down."

I feel awkward and conspicuous, why do I look so different, his watching smile is making me uneasy, the door slams and Belle is home.

"Hi there, it's great to see you, were you listening to CBC this morning? David Suzuki was on." We talk about the program and how the plundering of land needs to stop.

Peter speaks, "We live off the land and use no chemicals but it is hard to make people realize there has to be change, particularly when chemicals produce far greater yields and will bring in more money to an already starving economy."

The three of us prepare lunch together, Peter makes homemade pita bread from stone ground flour. There are fresh vegetables from the farm, Belle talks on about politics and Peter shares some of his life from days in Jamaica. We sit to eat and Peter continues telling about the farm and playing with a Reggae band in the city for the winter. Music is his first love and again I watch his hands. My eyes move to his face and I notice for the first time his glasses look funny — he grins.

"I know they look strange but the optometrist wouldn't fix them, he told me they were not worth it so I brought them home and made legs for them myself out of old farm wire."

Time passes quickly and I have to leave.

Peter stands, "Please come back at 4 when you're finished work and we'll go to the farm, I'd like for you to see it."

I start to refuse, and Belle says, "Oh please come back, I'll go along and then we could have supper back here. I would like to talk more to you about my paper on government spending." I agree to return.

I failed grades five, seven and eight, and quit school part way through grade nine. I was told throughout childhood, adolescence, and all of my married life that I was stupid and it kept me in place for a long time. I spend a great deal of time wondering why I allowed people to treat me the way they did. Why did I not tell when the teacher beat us in grades one and two? Why did I not tell what it was like at home? Why did I not share what went on in my marriage? What kept me silent for the first 36 years of my life? And now after three years of university I still find it hard to believe someone would want to discuss their paper on government spending with me.

I spend the afternoon playing scrabble with a man who is dying of cancer.

He says, "When you know your days are few, you live every day as your last and I wish I would have done some of that living before now."

He watches his wife moving about, her body is bent and old, she has difficulty walking; her canes are cracked and they clang loudly as she drops them beside her chair, they lie on the floor in disarray.

I drive slowly back to Peter and Belle's. I remember my mother, she complained bitterly about the hardships of prairie life and wished it could have been different. She blamed hard work for her bone cancer; she blamed my father too, he could have made life easier she said. But oh no he has to drink with his friends in town and spends his winters bonspieling, the rink was always more important than me. Maybe she was right, the hockey rink was important too. I remember my three brothers playing endless games of hockey and my father was the coach. My mother was a strong Scottish Presbyterian, and where she could rule she did, but she never ruled my father.

Back at Peter and Belle's the place looks deserted. I knock on the door and am ready to leave when Peter appears from the backyard.

"Hi, let's go, we have lots of time to see the farm before supper."

"Where is your Mom, she is coming isn't she?"

"No, she decided not to. A friend invited her for coffee."

My heart is pounding. What now? Do I say, "No, I am not going with you alone. I'd look sort of foolish." He is probably twenty years younger than I am. Don't be ridiculous. We head for his truck and I climb in the passenger side; he leaps in and grins at me.

My mind races back — I was fifteen and I knew him. He sat behind me in school, he was also one of the "slow learners." Afterwards the police said, "Why didn't you scream, there were people close by who would have heard you?" I would drop these charges, no one will believe you, and there are people saying you were with someone earlier.

I press my body against the truck door, the metal feels cold in the heat of the late afternoon. We bump out of the rutted lane down the back ally, into the country.

The farm is old and rundown. Horses rub their bodies against the corral posts and they watch suspiciously through barred gates as we climb out of the truck.

"Come, let me show you around." We walk across miles of barren pasture. Short, greyish-green weeds are everywhere, they remind me of cauliflower. Wildflowers poke from the ground. He bends and picks one at a time, hands them to me saying nothing. He holds the fence, his hand lingers on my bare skin as I crawl through. We make our way back to the yard and sit outside, orange tabby cats brush against me. I reach to stroke them, their rough tongues gently lick my hand. They are gone, racing across the yard their stripes barely visible in the tall grass. I get up.

"Let's go, your mother will have supper ready, it's late." A sense of relief floods over me as we head down the sandy road towards town.

He glances over at me, "I'd like it if you would be my lover for the summer." My fear evaporates, I am no longer afraid of him.

I laugh, "No, I don't think so, I'm not so sure my pastoral committee would understand." And where would I buy condoms, at the local drugstore? Maude and her people are on the watch. Today the risk appears too great.

He shrugs, "Maybe you'll change your mind, it gets pretty quiet around here."

Belle has supper ready and we share the food. We talk as we will for the rest of the summer, about CBC, politics, the Church and the community. Their home is a regular stop I will make every Sunday between services. Peter will always have homemade pita bread, honey and tea made from herbs he grew on the farm, it is thick and syrupy tasting with a hint of mint. I learned to sing again that summer. Rob always told me to keep it down, I was tone deaf he said, and I threw other people off.

The man with cancer died and I had a funeral on Thursday. That same day a woman in the nursing home died and we buried her on Saturday, then three services on Sunday. I soon learned sometimes ministry involved working seven days a week.

Towards the middle of summer the chairman of the board phoned. Would I do an outdoor service at the rodeo grounds? I remember what I said to Rob, don't you ever expect me to go to those filthy rodeo grounds again. I hate you and your drunken friends who go there. Rodeos aren't fit for decent people, do you hear me, I'm never going again.

However, I merely answered, "Oh sure, I'd like to do that." There I was on Sunday, in the dirt, dust, and horse dung, looking out on a sea of cowboy hats. I preached about saving Mother Earth and we sang, "When the Roll Is Called Up Yonder," the latter being their choice not mine. And it wasn't so bad. I enjoyed the sermon topic, and the pancake breakfast was good.

At the end of the summer I treat myself to a body massage; a local woman gives them and my first mistake is answering her question.

"What are you doing around here?" I explain and she continues, "Let me tell you why I left the church. Abortion: the number one reason, I simply cannot belong to a church that takes a pro-choice stance. And now, ordaining homosexuals, and this inclusive language business, imagine God being a woman, I've never heard the likes." One hour later she had finished talking and I had my massage. "That will be $35.00," she chirped.

"I should be getting paid for listening." She stared at me with small dark eyes and took the money. Live and learn not to tell your chosen profession, I thought.

It is my last Sunday, my last lunch with Peter and his mother. The pita bread and honey are good, the tea tasting sweeter than usual. When I leave Belle gives me homemade date cookies, she laughs, "Baked while I listened to CBC, you can drive and eat them while you listen." She hugs me tight and I leave. Peter walks to the car with me, then decides to ride to the farm corner. We stop, he pulls me from the car, his mouth is on mine, his tongue seeking, I want this man, I want to see him naked, I want him to make love to me. I feel him hard against me. The wind blows my hair. I push away, my breath is tight, there is still one service left. "Fuck," I whisper to myself as I drive away, that is what I wanted, it's been too long. Why didn't I, it could have been so good and no one would have found out. God would understand wouldn't she, but the people would not have. Do I want this? After the last service the congregation has a party for me. They joke about the ten pounds I have gained and how this job must agree with me — perhaps I will return.

Back at university, I am talking to my sociology professor and friend. I tell him about my summer work and mention meeting a Rastafarian. He grinned, I know a women who dated a Rasta, she gained a lot of weight, because of marijuana, Rastas use marijuana to heighten thinking. I feel a sweet, thick, syrupy taste in my mouth and the wind whips my hair across my face.

Mother is Sewing

Mother is sewing
a wedding dress.

The stitches are her sighs
as she rises in the dark
to start the fire
and call the children
from their sleep.

Against my skin the cloth
is blue and cool as the water
I raise to wash my breasts
at night
when the others are in bed.

In each seam she sews a seed,
two from the poplar
outside my window,
leaves eaten by worms
the last three summers

a juniper berry
saved from the one time
father drove her
to the Cypress Hills

the seeds of fireweed
from ditches along our road.

She tells me
they'll start growing

Lorna Crozier

Blood and Chestnuts

Kathy O'Grady

I used to think a lot about blood — about bleeding, really.

I spent my 12½-year-old days dreaming about it. I would imagine walking slowly forward, in a school washroom full of watchful eyes, some malevolent, some congratulatory, as I released the dime that had been trapped forever in my more-than-sweaty palm. My right hand would reach forth with mechanical perfection to grasp the dime from my left hand, forcefully pinching it between my index finger and thumb — I must not let it drop! My right arm would reach up and out in crane-like gestures until — *clink* — the dime was swallowed by the machine — and *clunk* — it issued forth a box weighted with necessity: mission completed.

I used to have this daydream repeatedly, varying only the character of watchful eyes, but never the movements; they were always the same. It was an elaborately planned procession for purchasing my first "sanitary napkin," or as I called it then, in short bursts of consonantal force: *pad.*

My (hoped-for) day of purchase, I assured myself, would be accomplished markedly different from the processions of others who walked boastfully toward the machine, when really, we had all heard from Ginny's older sister that Terry, and Lisa, and Lindi didn't really need the gifts it bestowed. It was just a play put on for an eager but all-knowing audience.

My body had *already* started to create breasts for me, "like chestnuts" my friend Miranda used to say. We used to talk about it, but I never much cared for my "chestnuts." They were cumbersome, though I had not yet been plagued by a bra (or "braazeeere" as my Mother used to say in a painfully long and careful manner — "you'll soon have to wear a braazeeere"). At recess the boys would target all the bra-wearers and snap the back strap. I used to be embarrassed for them at the sound it made.

Susan was the only one who had her period. We were all in awe. We talked about getting ours and crowded her with questions: "does it hurt?" "do you feel different?" "what does it *look* like?" We once tried to get her to show us one of her used pads — just to see — but she would have nothing of it. I don't remember her being boastful or proud, but *we were* for her. We sort of had this undiscussed competition to see who would be next. We checked our underwear constantly, and complained about cramps we never had.

I was the one who asked the question "what does it *look* like?" the most. I tried to think of examples (after the failed attempt at asking Susan to see one of her pads) of what the blood might look like since it came out of

121

such an odd place. I would ask Susan, "is it like when you cut your hand?" or, "like the time my Mom cut her thumb with a knife and it went way down deep and the blood was really gross?" or, "is it more like when the leaves fall and it rains and the leaves bleed into the pavement?" None of these examples (and countless more I used to think up) ever came close. Once though, when they were teasing me about my "chestnuts" Susan said, "yeah! the blood is like the colour of chestnuts, not like your chestnuts, but *real* chestnuts." I could never imagine this.

It was quite a few months before another one of us had blood-stories to tell and fate had slotted me next on the blood list. It may sound like a touch of corny drama, but I honestly had my first period, December 28th, on the morning of my 13th birthday.

I remember this morning very well. So does my Aunt Dee. She was in my parent's room (staying over for Christmas vacation) when I yelled from the bathroom toward my mom's room, "Mom, Mom, guess what, I got my period!!!" I had forgotten that my aunt and uncle were in my parent's bedroom. My aunt still tells everyone this story. I couldn't understand that day, though I suppose I understand now, what she had found so funny about the mix up.

Before I made my mark in family history by waking the whole house up with my period-calls, I was not sure what was happening. I had just gotten up to go to the bathroom, still groggy with morning sleep, when I perched myself on the toilet. My underwear was brown. I looked at it disgusted, thinking that perhaps I had an "accident" and had gone to the washroom in my sleep or something. I then remember wiping myself clean and realizing suddenly that it was *my blood* that had caused the stain. I quickly shifted from disgust to jubilation. I thought of deep, ruddy brown chestnuts and the colour of my blood was remarkable close. Then, of course, I made my mark in family history, by awaking my Aunt Dee and everyone else within a hundred-mile radius.

I really don't remember much else, though. I finally made my way to the guest room, and told my mom about the discovery. She said, "Sssssssssssh. You'll wake the whole house. You know where I keep the "stuff" in the bathroom," (I distinctly recall her saying "stuff" like it was a first-aid kit I was to look for), "help yourself to it." I was disappointed. That was it. She was almost sad and a bit embarrassed that I was finally bleeding. In retrospect I guess she was sorry to share with me what she considered a loss. I, on the other hand, saw it as a gain. She discussed it no further that day except in stifled laughs when my Aunt Dee told her how she had been awakened that morning.

Well, I don't remember telling my friends about it, though I guess I called them right away. I never did make my purchase in the school bathroom, and I don't remember revelling in "blood and chestnut" talk anymore. I suppose the novelty wore off and reality set in.

I do remember Miranda getting her period. She was number four, I think, by then. I don't remember much except that when she told her mother, her mother presented her with a pair of earrings, as if she had passed some sort of test. I was jealous. Miranda thought the gift a silly idea. Her mother was the only one who had done that. I told my mother about the earrings. I remember Mom telling me how silly it was. She thought it ridiculous, really. Of course I decided it was silly too. But looking back, I wanted the earrings that Miranda was embarrassed by.

Perhaps I've made my mother out to be the ogre in this tale. This is not the case. She was always very open to my questions and encouraged my interests. I guess when this all happened I was young and she was old and it was one time where the gap couldn't be bridged.

Now my monthly bleeding is a nuisance. I sometimes romanticize about it still, though. One time, in a Native Studies class in second-year university, a shaman came in and was going to show some of his "equipment" to the class, but said he could not because there was a menstruating woman in the room. That bleeding woman was me. I was proud of it. It made me feel powerful. Another time I noticed that my monthly bleeding came almost always when it was a full moon. Again this gave me a sense of power, but a power of belonging to something beyond me. Now I take a birth control pill. This means my bleeding can be charted with exact accuracy on the calendar. This also means I no longer bleed at full moon — technology is now revoking my right to be part of the nether world.

I complain, but I no longer think of it often. It was a childhood phase. Sometimes though, in the fall, when I see leaf blood on the sidewalks and chestnuts on the ground, I think of Susan and Miranda and the rest, but this only lasts for a second and then my head moves on to more important matters.

Gifts

Marguerite Andersen

My mother was not very good at making parcels, nor at gift wrapping. She marveled at the elaborate works of art made of neatly folded paper and cascading ribbons, that salesladies could produce. She loved to have it done for her. She was happy if stores accepted to do the mailing also. Her three daughters were living abroad and she constantly thought of something to send to them. But the story I am about to tell you began when life was much less luxurious, a few years only after the war had ended. Service was not good, in those times.

So the small parcel which arrived one particular morning, in 1950, after its three-week voyage from Berlin to Tunis, looked rather tattered. Brown paper, torn at the corners, badly tied string hardly holding things together, stamps almost falling off. An old cardboard box, not much bigger than an ordinary envelope. Maybe she had purchased gloves in it, or handkerchiefs, yes, gloves would have been in a rectangular box, this one was square.

The thing in the box rattled when I shook it, whatever it was, rattled softly. A piece of jewelry, maybe, wrapped in tissue paper? A new wallet? It wasn't my birthday though, not for a few months.

BIRTHDAY. BIRTH. PREGNANCY. FEAR.

Two, my mother must have thought, would do. She herself had had three. But then she had not gone to live in a foreign country, on a dark continent. And she had had girls only, whereas I had two boys. Enough is enough.

"Drei brauchst Du nicht!" she had written on the little card that came with the parcel. You don't need three.

1950. TUNISIA. NO BIRTH CONTROL FEAR.

Every month, the fear. A week before, the soreness of the breasts, first indication that everything might be alright. Wanting to see blood. Hoping. Then, finally, the relief, the red flow. Vague attempts at learning what to do. Condoms. Withdrawal. Constant uncertainty. Then *la méthode Ogino,* intercourse only during certain days of the cycle. Keeping track, keeping a calendar.

FEAR. NO LUST. AT LEAST NEVER PURE LUST.

But there, in that little cardboard box ... My mother ... My mother had sent me this object. Made of rubber, round, about eight centimetres in diameter, a kind of membrane or soft disk, amber-coloured rubber attached to some ring or spring, snap! you could fold it, snap! it would return to its original form. A cap. I had heard of such things. A sort of *béret basque* for the uterus. It seemed logical. You cover up the entrance and nothing can happen.

But how? Snap! I fold it, push it in, snap, ouch! it seems to cover the womb. But is it on properly? Or does it, like a béret on a Frenchman's head, cover only parts of what needs to be covered here? Does it, tilted to one side, coquettishly invite invasion? Out with it, quickly. This is not comfortable.

I search the box. There are no instructions. "My daughter will know," she must have told the pharmacist, hurriedly paying for the thing, happy to have found one, "she is clever enough." Certainly she was not going to discuss the mechanics of this object with a man she did not know.

So she just wrapped it as well as she could, sent it to me. Not that I had asked for it. We had never discussed such matters. Maybe she thought that I could not handle a third pregnancy, another birth.

THE FIRST

Right after the war, in a foreign country, a new language. *"Poussez, Madame,"* said the nun and I wondered what I was supposed to push. Almost a child myself, I believed this baby would fall/crawl out of me on its own. *"Poussez, Madame!"* and no further explanation. No compassion for my pain, my ignorance, me.

He was little. And ill. And so was I. How did we survive? We did. It still amazes me.

THE SECOND

Two years later. This time, my mother is with me. I groan, I scream like the women in the novels I have read, women giving birth behind closed doors while others listen to the terrifying sounds until, finally, the smiling midwife appears with the little bundle wrapped in swaddling clothes. What's the noise for, asks my mother. Well, I say, labour pains, don't you know? She laughs. Forget it. Breathe. Push when I tell you to.

But, oh, Mother! ... Hours of it. If only I could turn everything off and go to sleep. What is with this child?

Episiotomy. *A vif,* no anaesthetic, local or other. The doctor is sitting on a stool, between my legs straddled in steely stirrups. He has put on his glasses to sew me back together. "Here it will hurt, he says, here it won't. *Question de nerfs, Madame.*" My mother, holding my hand, whispering into my ear how much she would like to slap the cruel man's face.

The child is enormous. Eleven pounds. Healthy. Me too, but so tired. Sleep, says my mother.

DREI BRAUCHST DU NICHT!

Right. So how to put this thing into me? When? For how long? I visit my doctor. He looks at me in disbelief, sends me home. This is 1950. Tunis. No birth control. No planned parenthood. I do not write to my mother that I cannot figure it out.

Somehow though, magically, it works, it protects me. A diaphragm in an old cardboard box does it for me. No more pregnancies. No more children. Pure lust?

DREI BRAUCHST DU NICHT!

I keep it, for years. I know it's just luck, but maybe, who knows, it is my dead mother's will, who knows whether there is a heaven and how the souls of cremated people might get there, maybe she can will it from wherever she is, up there or in my memory.

I have a different man. The fear is gone, this is Canada, 1962, we do have the pill by now, of course I do not need it. I have a lucky charm made of rubber, I do not wear it on my bracelet, I do not wear it anywhere, I just keep it in a drawer. Pure lust? But the new man is jealous, difficult, controlling.

"You moved it!"

"Moved what?"

"The thing, the diaphragm, it was always there, under your sweaters. When you are out, when you are late, I check to see ... "

"Whether it is there?" I laugh.

"Yes! And today it wasn't!"

I laugh. I imagine his tortured reasoning: *She is not home ... the diaphragm is not in its place ... she took it ... she is ...* I will not let it torment me.

"It must be somewhere, under my underwear perhaps, I tidied up yesterday."

He doesn't believe me. Why does he think I would use the diaphragm with someone else, when I never use it with him? To keep myself for him, in a sense, from impregnation by another man? Why, in fact, does he suspect me of infidelity? I am getting angry. I must take a deep breath, be calm. I tell him the entire story. The parcel. My mother. My clumsiness. The magic of the diaphragm in the drawer.

DREI BRAUCHST DU NICHT!

He doesn't believe me. I throw the thing away, into the garbage. The magic spell is broken. Where is my mother? Where is her protection of me? I am angry, I am hurt, I need to be rocked, comforted. I cry. I forgive. I dream of my mother. There cannot be pure lust.

A year later, my third child is born. An accident? A girl, in any case. Somewhat like me, somewhat like her. A chain of three.

DREI BRAUCHST DU NICHT!

Maybe she meant boys? She must. I am happy to be the mother of a girl to rock, to comfort, to protect. And, oh, did I tell you? I do miss my magic mother, her gifts, badly wrapped or not, I wished she could be with me other than in spirit, when pain strikes again, as it undoubtedly will.

The Birth Circle

Louise Holland

The tiny mouth sucked eagerly, rhythmically, as the milk overflowed a taut, full breast. Contented grunts escaped the busily working mouth. The woman's dark, tangled hair swept forward as she bowed her head to study the infant more closely. Her hand cradled her daughter's head, a silky marble sphere so fragile, so vulnerable within her embrace. A wounded bird cupped between her two hands had been received similarly, as if thoughtlessness and incaution could cause the bone to crumble and disintegrate.

The mother inhaled the milk-sweet softness of her newborn; the infant paused in sucking to study the creamy lace that hemmed her mother's night clothes. The nipple trembled within the small mouth's grasp as the baby's dark eyes travelled across the lace, up to the misty face that hovered above. Swimming in a fog of fatigue and emotion, the mother let her head sag back against the chair.

"I didn't know it would be like this," she whispered in a hoarse voice to the darkness. "I just didn't know."

The darkness encircled and cloaked them, this circle of nurturing and birth, a link in the eternal chain of life that imprisons and gives freedom to us all.

* * *

The day they discovered the news seemed several lifetimes away.

"Call her," Michael had insisted.

"Oh Michael ... I can't," Liz said.

"Of course you can. She's your mother. Margaret should be delighted to be a grandmother!"

"You just don't know my mother." Liz expelled a weary sigh. "Nothing I do makes her happy."

"Liz?" Michael was hesitant. "You are happy ... aren't you?" She was silent for several moments.

"We didn't plan to start a family quite so soon, Michael," Liz finally said. "I haven't finished school, this place is too small, I don't know anything about being a mother ... I just don't think I'm ready."

"We'll work it out, Liz," Michael promised. "Everything will be fine, you'll see."

129

* * *

A lunch date with Elizabeth's mother was arranged and postponed at least twice before Liz found herself sitting across from her mother at a restaurant table, treading the atmosphere attentively.

"I have something to tell you, Mom," Elizabeth said.

Startled by her tone, Margaret looked up from the menu.

"What is it?"

"You'll be glad to now that I can't continue with art school." She watched the exploding light on Margaret's face and continued quickly. "And no, Mother, I am not going back to law school. I'm going to have a baby." Elizabeth said the words evenly, her voice sounded free of her gnarled, knotted feelings. Margaret jerked and her dropped fork violently splashed the silence.

"You're going to have a baby? Already?!"

"That's what I said."

"You just got married six months ago! Michael just graduated! What kind of planning is that?"

Feeling smothered, Elizabeth sucked at the air heavily, gasping for approval. This tentative intersection of their lives was being ruptured once again by the bitterness her mother nourished and never failed to express. No wonder her father had left. Elizabeth took several breaths.

"We didn't actually plan ... " Liz mumbled.

"An accident! In this day and age! I know I was unlucky enough to have one, but Elizabeth, how could you let this happen?!"

Liz stared at her mother while the words seared into her heart. For several moments she desperately sought the words that would detonate her mother's smugness, but the futility made her throw down her napkin in disgust.

"What's the use, Mother? What's the use?" Liz flung the words at her mother and scrambled to her feet.

"Elizabeth, I didn't mean it like that," her mother called. Liz didn't look back.

* * *

The months progressed slowly, and the steady, relentless growth of inner life distorted her body margins.

She stood in the shower one morning in December, watching the hot rivers of water flow over her swollen, misshapen belly, watching the currents of water divide and unite, just as a child stares nose pressed against a foggy window, hypnotized by the veil of wet streamers separating and reuniting across the glass.

Stepping out from the shower, Liz stared, amazed at the image in the mirror. Could this really be her? Repulsive purple lizards crawled across the overflowing belly that oppressed her pelvic organs. Small tight breasts had become alien, dropping globes of dripping flesh.

Michael stopped at the door.

"Liz?"

"Mhm-hmn." She was wrapping Michael's robe around her largeness. "I was thinking about the baby's name."

"I still like Jessica."

"Yeah it's all right ... " There was a gleam in his eye. "But ... what about Margaret?"

"My mother's name!" Elizabeth turned her face away. "Don't even joke about it!"

"Liz." Michael's voice was full of gentle reason. His calmness made Liz feel quite wild. "You're going to have to make up with your mother sometime."

"Leave it alone, Michael," she growled.

"Liz. She keeps on calling you. She's not going to stop."

"I don't care."

"You don't mean that, Liz."

"Michael, I'm tired of trying!" Michael grabbed her by the shoulders.

"You have to try!" Liz pulled away angrily.

"This isn't any of your business!"

"It is my business! She's the only grandparent our children will ever have." Liz looked into Michael's urgent eyes and her anger died.

"You aren't going to leave me alone about this, are you?"

"No I'm not. It's too important. Maybe you could invite her for dinner."

"We'll see."

* * *

The night was a circle of blackness that sucked away the whiteness of the snow that had been steadily speeding from sky to ground all day. The January wind howled and whined as it battered the walls of the apartment house with blasts of snow and freezing air.

"The roads look awful," Margaret worried as she stared into the black night. "Michael is going to have rough going coming home tonight." Elizabeth shifted her heavy bulk uncomfortably inside the armchair. She sighed. Just like their previous two visits the time dragged while their voices engaged in polite ping-pong.

"Never mind, Mom. Michael's a good driver. He'll take it easy." Margaret nodded and paced the length of the living room, her fingers tapping an uncertain rhythm. Abruptly, she sat down and plunged her arm into the jumbled contents of a large bulging bag.

"I thought you might like to have this," Margaret said, producing a small parcel. Elizabeth rubbed her back absently as she slowly unravelled the tissue paper to reveal a christening gown. She shook out the folds of lace and looked at her mother, stunned.

"Mo-om." Her voice was creaky. "It's beautiful." She caressed the softness of the fabric, thinking of the loose weave of shared lives.

"It was yours," Margaret told her.

"What do you mean?"

"Your grandmother Emily made it for you. Well, you remember how your father felt about churches." Margaret shrugged. "Needless to say you never had the chance to wear it."

"And you kept it all these years?" Fibres of shame and sorrow were pinching her heart. "You never told me."

"You don't know everything about those years, Elizabeth."

"Maybe not," Elizabeth said slowly. Maybe it was time for a fresh perspective. Her eyes were glued to the intricate lacework of the gown. "Do you ever think about Grandma?"

"All the time, Liz. All the time."

"Remember how she used to stop us from arguing."

Margaret laughed. "She was good at that."

"That's because she loved us both." Liz raised her eyes cautiously, fearful of harming this fragile accord.

"What's the matter?" Margaret asked, when Liz's face abruptly twisted with discomfort.

"Oh it's nothing really. You remember the backache you get — it's really bothering me today.

"A backache?" Margaret was not reassured.

"Ooh! That one was in front." Liz looked up, astonishment cracking the shell of her face. "Mother! I think that was a contraction! But it can't be! I'm not due for a couple of weeks."

"A contraction? You're in labour? Elizabeth!"
Margaret leaped in the direction of the phone. "I'll call Michael." She stopped and swung around. "Michael isn't going to be able to get home right away. Maybe I should drive you to the hospital?"

"Calm down, Mother. We have lots of time. Anyway, I'm not going to the hospital."

Margaret froze. "What do you mean?"

"We have a midwife. We've been planning a home birth."

"Elizabeth! You can't be serious. Do you know how dangerous that might be!"

Liz was struggling with an even stronger contraction and threw her mother a look of keen exasperation.

"Mother, I am not going to argue with you about this. Michael and I already discussed this and came to our own decision." Liz took a ragged breath and felt the sweat prick her forehead. "Would you please call Susan, our midwife? Her number is by the phone." Elizabeth moaned as the pain of another contraction gripped her, but she managed to capture a trembling drink of air and release it slowly.

Margaret stood awkwardly, her hands dangling helplessly. "Of course you're right. It is your decision. But I'm your mother and I'm not going to stop worrying about what you —"

"Mo-THER! Just call the midwife!"

As Margaret picked up the phone, Liz wanted to say something else, but a potent thrust of pain ignited in her groin and burned higher, higher, up through her chest, and erupted through clamped teeth in a harsh screech.

* * *

Immersed in the wave of birth-force, surroundings become blurred by the emerging and receding roar. Swallowed in a corridor of blackness and pain, she is dimly aware of the events around her. Mother, talking. Mother, making her comfortable. Laying her down on the bed. Susan, arriving. Her assessing fingers are gentle, calming. Mother, beside her. Patting her shoulder. Michael will be here soon, she says. You're doing fine, she says. Liz selects these words from her wheeling impressions and clutches them tightly. After a long time, Michael arriving. The brief touch of his lips. Mother, withdrawing. Don't go Mom, Liz says.

Liz struggles to be released from this painful tide, but it pursues her again and yet again; she is consumed by its potent strength. And then, Liz ceases this contest between pain and resistance; she allows her muscle to flow with the circular rhythm of the birth wave. Inside, revolving in a dark vortex, she is united with the infant in the compelling urge to be born.

"The baby's coming, Liz!"

The world stops.

This small circle of space dilates to encompass the universe. The thousand ghosts of sweating, labouring women pant and push, push down and out, push, push, push. Ten thousand souls are squeezed and expelled from a dark, warm world into the brighter, colder orbit.

The baby cries.

"It's a girl!" Margaret shouts. Sloppy and wriggling, the baby lies against the mother's puffy abdomen. Liz collapses against the pillows. Released. Released at last.

Reaching out, Liz touched the wet pink skin of her baby with one careful, exploring finger. She leaned closer to her daughter's steady blue gaze. You and I, we know each other, Liz thought. Admitted to the circle, she had penetrated that unyielding glass.

Liz smiled and looked around; the details of the cluttered room vibrated into her pain-scoured senses. Susan was wrapping the baby in a soft yellow blanket. Michael's face was wreathed with a large silly smile. Margaret was watching the midwife's actions closely, but her eyes were soft. And Liz knew that she was remembering.

Once upon a time she, Elizabeth, had begun her life thus inside Margaret, had entered the world through the pain of this woman's womb. And before that Margaret had been a red squalling infant in Grandmother Emily's arms. And before that ...

Susan placed the child in Liz's waiting arms.

"You have a beautiful daughter," she said. "Let's see if she's hungry."

After a few fumbling moments and the guidance of Susan's quiet assurances, Liz watched her baby eagerly latch and suckle. She watched the baby's dark eyes travel across her face. She watched as the fluids of her flesh nourished her child. This was the meaning of awe.

"I didn't know it would be like this," Liz whispered. She cleared her throat. "Michael, come and look." He drew closer and poked a finger under the blanket to stroke the baby's cheek.

"What's her name?" Margaret asked. Michael straightened and turned to Liz.

"Well?" he said. Liz's eyes lifted and touched Margaret's face.

"I think we should name her Emily," she said.

The Weaned Child

"I have quieted my soul,"
said the psalmist,
"like a weaned child."

But surely the child just weaned
must have fussed, sobbed
for Mother's breast.

"Put wormwood on your breasts,"
my mother said
the old women used to say.
Then the child would turn away,
drink water, eat bread
as he was supposed to.

But she said she never did that.
Her breasts were never bitter.

The weaned soul,
no longer needing sweetness
of mother's milk

hushes itself after tears,
nourishes its strength
with whatever food it finds
or bitter brew

but is still a child

dreams of a land overflowing
with milk and honey.

                    Elizabeth Brewster

The Spirit of a World without Spirit: Meditation on Night Number One

Anne Ricard Burke

For members of the dominant ethnic collectivities, the processes of enculteration and acculturation may, to a large degree, tend to be mutually reinforcing phenomena ... and ethnicity may become salient in only a few situational contexts.

Evelyn Kallen, *Ethnicity and Human Rights in Canada* (Toronto: Gage, 1982, p.82)

"Would you tell me, please, which way I ought to go from here?"
"That depends a good deal on where you want to get to," said the Cat.
"I don't much care where — " said Alice.
"Then it doesn't matter which way you go," said the Cat.

Lewis Carroll, *Alice in Wonderland*

I have written these words with much resistance and interference, which is unusual for me since I am more commonly in sync with the words, they flow and flow from me. The characters do not wish to become; they even resent being known. They believe it is pandering for me to allow their privacy to be thus exposed or, given the choice, they would opt for non-existence rather than to be invaded by the public fare. I do not like this story and this story does not like me. Perhaps, I come late, pretending to be the shaman, too late to the spirit. The path of self-knowledge is paved with fictions, when I forswore religion at the age of sixteen, after years of fervency, fidelity to the Roman Catholic Church. Even now I can enter a synagogue or a cathedral with appropriate reverence like a child stealing downstairs on Christmas morning, a heart full of anticipation and desire. I speak in a conversational tone with the Divine. What arrogance is this? I have hope and, possibly a secret faith in circumstance, in the outcome of events, that I have buried in myself, admitting to no one until now. And breaking the taboo, it is not done easily. The rebellion costs lives. It hardly means freedom. The time-lines, my family albums, what it is that moves in the night, has come down to me from them, inevitably. We had no choice. Their selves are surfacing and they identify themselves in my speech, mannerisms, instinctual memories.

Night number one. I am home from the hospital. My husband away in foreign lands, the house is deathly still. I telephoned him when the test was inconclusive, pap smear "revealed grossly abnormal cells. Repeat first test

137

immediately." He tried to comfort me over telephone lines, his voice far off, like my mother's. I cannot believe I am unable to see her, except in memory — as if I were just speaking with her yesterday, begrudging the fifty dollars for fifty minutes. Sometimes I resent the fact my child is male as he is suspicious of me being female, how can I teach him what I know, the non-sexual relationship among friends, as a common courtesy. "Do you want to see my belly button," he asks. "No," I am laughing, "that's o.k." There was a daughter, a head silhouetted, shoulders, the body emptying itself. In my vigil I am unable to sleep this week again, the pills doing no good at all. Each and every night my son holds onto the belt of my red plaid bathrobe, coiled between his fists and he says tonight he will hold on longer, clinging with all it takes to keep me here, with the determination of a six year old.

And I feel the same impatience welling up in myself as my father felt; after a long life's work in the real world he wanted a few minutes to himself, some peaceful moments and hadn't he earned that much? And I recall how my father was always ready to leave me, eagerly, my faded blue bedroom of baffled bears and plastic-haired baby dolls. The single favourable act my father performed on my behalf was that — to sit in the shadows beside my bed until I was lost to sleep and he could gratefully leave. My mother, by this point, was exasperated by my innumerable sins of the day, both omissions and commissions. My father invariably wrote in the mornings. When I awoke, he was already up, before five a.m. pen in hand, scribbling down whatever entered his mind. He said, by way of explanation, his world of vision, his vision of the world, that is, was clearer then, the demarcation between the nine-to-five work world sufficiently distinct. By evening, he could be found asleep, sound asleep, sitting up on the chesterfield. "Snoring to hell, loud enough to wake the dead," my mother complained. And she was waiting "all bloody day" for some adult conversation — and finding none, obtained nothing more from the marriage, she had to make do with talking to herself. This also as a consequence of the neighbours, who seldom spoke to us, listening to/for one another on either side of tissue paper-thin walls, the policeman who let his boots drop, one after the other, on his path to the bed diagonally across our ceiling; the new immigrant mother rearranging orange crates from room to room, as if that mattered, removing a few, adjusting their position in the social scheme; from nowhere to here, and finally the mock murders, "I have a knife here and I'm ready," or some such threat, something of that kind that ended in silence.

Well, I left them, the triumph mitigated by how it hurts, that silent ache of departure. I am far from tears as a result, it seems to me, because we made up life as we lived it. We pretended and the pretension won out. And, suddenly, my eyes are widened with this vision. Then he came again, resting like a dove for a while at the front door, gave thanks and broke the bread into a thousand loaves and a few fishes. We ate that day and again the next.

Science Digest says the appearance of manna in the desert is a natural occurrence every ten years, or is it a hundred — the statistics hardly seem to matter when you are hungry. I brought the basket back, placed a piece of bannock in the sun and set it on a shelf to dry. The inside was wet and slippery on the outside is how I would describe it if I were interviewed. But then how can a child, a six year old, begin to explain a miracle?

These spirits are drawn to me tonight because I have begun my vigil. This is the first night my husband is away, the boy child sleeping in the other room. I am grieving the loss of another in childbirth, this day the anniversary of her death and my mother's passing in the same month. Their lives and deaths — one out of one dies of something — there are no odds. Can I make sense of their passing by understanding their lives? Perhaps, chart a path for myself, of my own. How can I go on when there is so much death all around me. Or explain this to my child, these presences he will never know, not having met my mother, not even by way of photographs, since she destroyed them. An Irish mother she grieved in her own manner. She laughed at weddings, (something about grafting a new branch onto the old apple tree, so the two are considerably stronger than the one) and at funerals (planting the body like a bulb in the ground in order to grow). This season, or that season and the next, it is the same. It ages you. You know more than the others early on, if they uncover the truth(s) at all. The past is passing into nothingness. My son, he came a few years later on, never having met her or that woman who bore his grandfather. What meaning can there be in his waking when he is all uncomprehending of his family. I am a distant mother, despite my efforts, while sitting beside him. My mind long gone off in all other directions. Why tonight do I write the death of my daughter, the pain a legacy. Number one night home from the hospital. My husband away on the other side of this earth, the house is deathly still. A daughter was the logical consequence, she like me, hand to hand, eye to eye. I dreamed of her but she does not come to me. The walls are empty with shadows, the floor boards creak and strain, contracting with the cool air. And no one said, "I am sorry." No burial. We did not view the remains. It was as if she did not exist, some part of me and my husband, the best part gone horribly wrong. I have her name on the tip of my tongue, unspoken. "Laura," I finally say aloud. "Laura" with new-found boldness. She would have known and approved, this grand grandmother.

She is a bony woman, no flesh on her anywhere. Her chin sharpened to a point, her eyes (I know not what colour) are alive, manic in their intensity. She conducts us, an audience of youngsters and a few indulgent adults, with her arms beating in time. The rhythms course through her body from memory, probably, as she is quite deaf. My eyes tear and, upon examination, an eyelash loosens and is lodged in a tear duct. With her intervention, she instructs through her eldest daughter as translator, "You must blow your nose, *mon petit chou*, and the foreign object will be removed." I never wept for her then. Her tapestries, the handcrafted lace bedspreads, Jeanne her youngest daughter (no man would have her) who never left home, an eternal innocent on a disability income.

My father's mother left the children to fend for themselves when she went to work in one of those nondescript stores with the PEPSI sign proclaimed on the roof. It is painted in green and white letters. The store has sawdust on the floor, a general convenience store before the dawning of MAC's, a mom-and-pop store, but pop doesn't work. From what I can tell, he simply takes up space in their lives. He is slim, his weathered skin taut over his cheekbones, with wispy grey hair. He is always smiling, his eyes black and shining. He walks with long strides. She is complaining now of his death rattle keeping her awake, intruding onto an otherwise fine sleep.

She says I have her eyes but I know she is lying. My hair and eyes are Iroquois, just like my grandfather's. I can usually pass until somebody notices, although it's the high cheekbones some woman praises, or it can be those eyes, dark and fathomless, like the man who engendered my father. With his alien seed in the body of a devout French girl. And she wanted him, against all reason, in her bed until his final breath. When he died there as a crippled old man, racked with heart spasms. She permits him to stay with her when she is unclean with the periodic bleeding, never sending him away during her pregnancies, twenty-two in all, as the other women do, "to get a rest," they said, "from men."

My grandfather sits in a corner of the store on a stool, unmoving all day, never offering to bag the groceries, not once asking to help her: to sell the packs of cigarettes, the tins of milk, the rotten fruit hidden at the bottom in open packages, flies circling them, laying their eggs for larvae in the produce. And he never spoke then.

Earlier he used to talk plaintively of selling fruit door-to-door that the boys stole out of somebody else's garden or off the backs of trucks loading for market. But the women at their doors opened them reluctantly, if at all. When they heard his accent they scolded him, or the men drove him away with sticks. "None of his kind" was welcomed anywhere, although it wasn't as if they had not tried, the family moving out of one small town into another, never finding the peace they sought.

"Don't you remember the house," his sister prompts, "the one Papa painted, the white shutters," she prodded, "the red roof?" but my father cannot. His mind was unwilling and, besides, the years blurred, the unpaid accounts, the priests with their black robes frightened him, especially the one who crawled into his bed at night. He could not speak of these memories with anyone. They were Christianized, in boarding schools, each and every one, lost the language, learned the conqueror's and have forgotten ancestral memories.

My childhood was so painful I seldom speak of it. The odyssey for the ethnic writer, moving from old culture to new, from country to country, begins with family memory and folk past. It is the golden age of childhood which shapes the whole and contributes to the ideal of country and nation. It begins again with my son, genealogical tree of branches without any leaves and I wonder if it will be easier to list his father's family from Nova Scotia than mine, simpler but who am I fooling? Writers are, in effect, in a sociological sense, reinventing the Canadian past to multicultural ends. That the Greek root of ethnic, *ethnikos*, was used to mean "heathen," a meaning that has continued to haunt the word's scholarly uses with its negative connotations, seems relevant here. My family imposed a taboo about our origins (being French was bad enough) which my mother broke before her death, and so it is only with the women's movement, in particular the telling and writing of stories by native women and their children, which has brought to the surface what I and they have suppressed. Picnics were forbidden because it involved, they said, "eating in a ditch like gypsies" or worse. Indian was a term of derision like "nigger" or "kike" but reserved for family members who were not acting appropriately, and used among themselves as a reproach learned from my grandmother's "good" French family.

"Marie doesn't live here anymore."

"She's my friend."

"On reserve or off, the argument being, are you really Indian people anymore?" Marie explains. She says Indian women who married white men were cast off reservations but they became resource persons for Indian women, they had access it was thought, to the white world. She says, "If you know more than the chief you're in big trouble." And I agree, "It's the same all over." My Acadian friend says,"I tried to live in Quebec but I was not understood. Too much slang."

"Is it English?"

"No. *That* I could understand. Too much Indian," she complains.

"You call it Metis out west," I offered. "Back home, nobody's pure."

There is a scene seen from here, a vantage point that no one cares to share or understand. The wings dip precariously, a sudden lurch forward and hectares of prairie appear. They comfort me, these familiar as family, terraced fields, autumn orange and yellows. Baled hay cut, combined, carved into elongated cubes.

"Iroquois," she interrupts my reverie, "that's interesting, because they were with the French before the English came."

"Quebec wants racial purity in language. That is impossible."

It is liberating to be able to express thoughts, feelings and selfhood finally. Perhaps, because I have come to this slowly, somewhat tentatively, the writing deserves to be stronger. I do know that empowerment opens the way for the spirit. I will listen a little harder and see what results.

My father's sisters were taken in by the nuns who wore black, except for white wimples and collars starched like cardboard under their chins. They were masters of sarcasm, blessed with sharp tongues. They followed the rule of beatings (your lips must touch the floor if you dared drop a biscuit crumb from your hands at supper). No mirrors all those years dressing in the dark, the woolen uniforms itching and eating into the red scabs, half-healed from last week's penance. These Brides of Christ were devout.

The sisters of charity swathed in black telling us bible stories and those other tales called revelation, the word of God passed down by human tongues about how the saints weren't saints, they were buried alive. But you knew some of them because they ate their own hair and their bodies weren't perfectly preserved, except for the blood on their hands where they had scratched at the dirt on top of them, as they struggled to breathe without any air.

They said he appeared to little children and I was frightened. After all, who would believe a six-year-old child when a loyal man like Moses, who only doubted for an instant when he touched the rocks — no, struck it twice when his people were dying from the drought — the unforgiving god kept him out of the promised land after he had trudged so far, halfway across the world which was known at that time. And me prone to anxiety attacks and flights of exaggeration. The dreams of bobbing on the ceiling, that was how a saint was tested for his mettle; if he flew his heart would be preserved in a glass case and his brain in another instrument of science, a test tube. Like Albert Einstein whose mind was studied and picked apart to ascertain his intelligence, but the measure of the man told us nothing was any different about him that could teach us how to think: the enemy of religion, of an unswerving trust.

It is all right there, just under the surface, lurking. Being confirmed by the bishop, posed under his ornate umbrella at Notre-Dame Cathedral in Montreal. I was dressed in white veil and crinoline, I was wearing white gloves and held a brand-new white missal in my hands. This is adulthood I thought, the age of reason every seven year old is supposed to know. And the other girls, each one is promised to God, these virgins arranged in a row giggling despite the pain of the metal band fastened with bobby pins at the scalp.

The confessional, I remember leaning into the aisle, me nervous, waiting, sick to my stomach, for my turn. While I heard the mumbling of the other penitent and then the wooden window slide cross, suddenly, as if somehow you were half expecting it. You kneeled before the odour of the priest's aftershave wafting toward you, this untouchable man, god's surrogate on earth. The disembodied voice of a stranger, who, nevertheless, saw your naked soul stripped in the shadows, his folded hands, the hair on them just like a real person. But he was looking through your eyes this time, not following the rules. That is why you bowed your head, striking your heart three times, *mea culpa, mea culpa, mea maxima culpa.* And you were forgiven, reborn into the ugly world outside of sin and temptation, desire mixed with memory and expectation. It was a Saturday bath and a Sunday evening Toni home perm, only this was more important, being as it was spiritual after all and it only happened in god's time and place, not man's, in the unseen.

Baptism by fire is good, is how it begins again: my son's first communion, me wondering if, in haste, I should anoint his forehead and pale cheeks with my breath. But the impassioned priest forgoes symbolism for a moment. With hesitation he asks, "Have you too questioned the resurrection? Since it happened only once, so long ago. The tomb was opened, a stone rolled away, and Mary, mother of God, cried ... " So he devoted his sermon, an hour or longer, to the consequences if Christ failed to rise, that is, to our lives rendered meaningless. "I carry a load on my shoulder, my life and not yours," he says, with a careless wave of his outstretched arms. He is in seamless vestments, the sun shines on a grey boulder through us, Easter windows with felt-stickered drawings of flowers, an empty wooden cross, excellent frame for lilies. My son says, "Look how they bloom for a single day and then are dead." Is this a sign pressed to our lips? "Pita bread," he announces to the polite assemblage, "you can buy it from any corner grocery store." There is something to be said for transubstantiation, I thought. Miraculous, with bells ringing. The earth shakes and moves. The reverential congregation awestruck. But here and now there are no ringing bells but silence. My son has forgotten how to kneel. He complains he has never learned how. His knees stiffly bending, he folds the sharp creases in his best pants, hesitantly. He seems startled, somewhat embarrassed by my behaviour. I neglect to make the sign of the cross, admittedly a barbaric rite: father/son/shuddering ghost. However, I genuflect cautiously, hedging my bets, before departing. "Pretend blood," I attempted to explain the wine to him, although I shrugged perceptively. "It smells awful," he walks away from the proffered cup, a bejewelled chalice he has seen it recently in the *Temple of Doom*, complete with cinematic earthquake, sound effects. It does seem awkwardly medieval in the setting of sunshine and newly washed families in spring clothing strung together like bright beads on a daisy chain. Next to the open window sills we sit, while a wafting warm breeze lofts the priest's red hair sufficient to expose his balding pate.

My son is a little puritan, children ought not to drink wine. Have I forgotten to tell him this is His precious blood. We have no crucifix by his bed. He does not learn any prayers. Instead he attends a private school we can ill-afford, where not religion but mathematics and science are on the curriculum. He learned evolution as law not theory in grade one. Darwin unquestioned, the chain of monkeys and men, from one cell to the expanse of the universe. Is it survival of the fittest, on whose terms? Nineteenth-century progress in the Galactic world (s).

"Who made Thee?"

"God made me."

The Baltimore Catechism. A scapular patch around my neck in the shower. The strange sense of relief a Saint Christopher's medal in the car brings. Thanks to Saint Jude in hopeless cases. Holy cards instead of gold stars. May is Mary's month. We do not understand the words "virgin" or "wombJesus" and nobody asks. We garland the room with garden flowers, lilacs, tulips, daffodils. Sing "Ave Maria" in unison with high children's voices, but my son rehearsed the national anthem with new words I cannot seem to remember.

My grandmother, I sent her childish drawings and handsewn greeting cards. Her replies, always in French, are read to me. My father interprets as best he can, struggling with a word or two, some expression long-suppressed or an idiom he unexpectedly remembers and her handwriting seems like a code to me, so quaint, sounds foreign, a puzzle beyond my comprehension of solving. She is critical, too, of my script, agreeing, *"Oui,"* your teacher is correct. The capital letters could be daintier, *plus petites.* Later, I learn to read Molière, Camus, Sartre, the great literature but I refuse to speak it, some residue, a resentment, some pettiness on my father's part, since he sought assimilation for us.

> the model allows for shifts between the various orientations over time, and in different domains of life: youth may prefer assimilation, their parents integration, while others in political movements may seek separation; moreover, there may be assimilation in food preferences, integration in identity, separation in social relations, and marginalization in religious beliefs. *Canadian Minority Writing*, p. 55.

> John W. Berry, "Finding Identities: Separation, Integration, Assimilation, or Marginality?" in *Ethnic Canada: Identities and Inequalities*, ed. Leo Driedger (Toronto: Copp Clark Pitman, 1987), 223-39. Cited by Enoch Padolsky, "Canadian Minority Writing," in *Literatures of Lesser Diffusion*, ed. Joseph Pivato, Steven Totosy de Zepetnek and Milan V. Dimic, (Edmonton: University of Alberta Press, 1990), p. 55.

And now I write in the final hour in lieu of sleep, stopping to trace an outline here, a pose with my finger gently stroking my son's narrow back, shoulder to small shoulder blade and down his spine. I used to sing to him, holding him in my arms, as a mother from greeting cards is wont to do, until I lost all sensation in my extremities. I wanted to "be" there for him, time "managed" and quality time, twentieth-century cliches, "if he needed" me, required anything only a mother could offer. And he still orders me about — female subservience and male domination — every now and again, as if he were practising, as he builds his ego structure at my expense. In actual terms it has been a joy, this loss of myself in the minutiae of daily existence. It has cost me little or nothing to raise him. An amazing statement, an outright falsehood. But the time has been all to my gain, filling him up with stories, plying him with desire for a better lifestyle than I lead/led. (Isn't that always the way?) And when I reflect on my "bloody awful" day of laundry and dirty dishes, meal preparation and rule-gathering, as enforcement officer without the uniform, I wonder aloud:

How does one pass on a spirit? The spirit passes on, as the body does not. "The Spirit of a World without Spirit," according to Roland Barthes. Can a woman give up her spirit and never retrieve it, like the artist who travels between fact and fantasy; held by a leg-hold trap in reality but envisions the promised land ... begs to be delivered from sin and travesty into death and the fires on the other side. Some are condemned to wickedness; you can hear their shrieks sometimes when the evening comes on. They may wake you in the middle of the night. You can remember a little of what they told you, even less about what you are supposed to do that day and then next. So, you wait for signals.

The spirit is in us, of us. I trace its lineage in old photographs, when the face was the arbitrator of moods. I have memorized but never those, except when I was too young to remember. I have loved as a child at his knee, my grandfather arrayed in full headdress, reclining in a lazy-boy armchair, fraying at the armrests. He told us of his secrets: a girl was thrown overboard by her father. She clung desperately to the side of the boat, but her father hacked off her fingers: she sank to the bottom of the sea where she became a goddess. From the cut-off joints of her fingers were created sea animals on which life depends.

At the top of the C.N. tower, not at the first elevation but the last, under the point, that spike in the sky it was my father who said, "You like heights, don't you?" And he shoved me hard against my shoulders shaking me, so that I lost my footing, bumping my face and body against the green plexiglass. And he was laughing. I haven't entered an elevator since that time, although vertigo signals the onset of a poem. So, there is some saving grace. The guardian angels that catch small children as they fall, also whisper words and images to desperate women.

We were seeing London in a day. This is your parent country; it promises brass rubbings of the ancient faces, blackening in the light; stained glass wearing wooden pews. Those common books gone gold and spines broken from thousands of hands turning the crumbling page. The words are coming out of me like blood. The way the wind borrows the fragile markings of leaves in the autumn, invisible, imperceptible. And they come so gently like the lost lover of this child god who asked for pain and was granted the privilege of life.

The words are coming and they touch your cloak; try to catch each fold, enveloping me as you pass the peace of understanding.

I realize I have never been at peace, as if that were a geography of feelings, a sentiment you could point your finger to on the map or spin the earth, hurriedly, to locate this place of peace. Like the river, you repeat to no one in particular, and you suddenly are made aware of the dubious fact. You are talking, no muttering to yourself on the Light Rail Transit with the driver up front, enclosed in glass and steel, unapproachable. Even if you face an emergency, you can turn the red knob and you are promised aid at the next available stop, during regular commuting hours, nothing prior to this, following a route as it always has, laid down and reassessed by city council at their next board meeting. And the driver is God. It's all right there in the scheme of things but only you know how to decipher the code. Writers are keen on cryptologies, even during war time they have proven themselves useful. It's all on record somewhere.

My grandmother's death was on a bare mattress (box springs were considered an unnecessary affectation) on the floor of her daughter's house. There were prescriptions for pain killers but no hope after she shattered her hip on the ice. The doctor diagnosed uterine cancer that had spread all through her. Somehow she managed to escape, with Jeanne, always loyal to the end. She barricaded herself behind doors, barred the windows. There death lay in wait, representing a release from a life of misery. Was the Redeemer kind to her, the Sacred Heart open and vulnerable, the extended pastoral hand? Have you entered the Kingdom of Heaven where no one can hurt you ever again?

Mary has appeared here, the mother of all Mothers, Divine Mediatrix assumed bodily into heaven, the Immaculate Conception. *Vers demain* (a radical Catholic set in Quebec) berets in the rain, the fanatics and the mad in the subway all our shoes were soaked with the same black mud. Madonna, you have raised a child of God only to be slain, what purpose is there in that. Pieta, all that sorrowing, the mother as young or younger than her son. And all He has, all He will ever know, is that quality of suffering — sadness translated as sadness. My family never finding the peace they sought but indomitable faith, myself the doubter who places her fingers into the wounds and still does not believe. The daguerreotype of my father at age three months, in which his mother is seen bending toward him smiling. She has inscribed in a corner of the photo, *"Benoit, à trois mois, son petit costume."* This is the same baby dress my son wore, but he was never christened in it. We choose to take communion and the hosts, we are to help ourselves, it an alien concept introduced into the rituals. Is my son disappointed at his less than immaculate conception, the miracle of water and wine? These spirits are still drawn to me and through me as I end my vigil. I mourn for you, as I do for the emptied faces of flowers. Defiled like newspapers in the wind, changing places with you in the distance. From far off, coming onto the horizon. I can hardly reach. Can you hear me? The gradual sounds of waking into sensation, that tiny foot which is kissed by the chill marble floor. The spirit changes, transformed, transmuted form flesh to flesh. Even the angels had heads once like ours sculpted by an artist's hands.

What She Remembered and What She Forgot

Joyce Howe

1980 – I remember, wrote Joanna Hern, my mother and father quarrelling bitterly. My mother is holding me. I am big enough to be sitting with my legs on her hips. We are in the darkened living room. My father is in the kitchen where the lamp is. We are at the window. There is no curtain pulled against the night so that the darkness seems about to reach through the window and snatch us out into a void. I think there is no curtain. The room itself seems virtually empty. My mother is sobbing. No, that does not tell how she is crying. She is crying in utter despair as if nothing can save us. I know or seem to know that she would die gladly, but for me.

"You try to leave me, you know what I'll do," my father yells from the kitchen. "You go to your mother's and I'll kill her and your father too."

That is all there is to that memory. Whenever I recall it, it is the same as if Nina and I are still there at the window hearing the poplar trees whispering some awful thing.

I remember another time, my mother is sick. She is sleeping in a bed in the short part of the L-shaped living room. My father and I are in the kitchen and we are making beef broth for her. My father is explaining that beef broth gives sick people their strength back. He is laughing, very pleased with himself. Things feel safe. But I'm not sure. It seems like a good idea. It ought to be a good idea but still .... Then perhaps someone comes in the door.

Joanna raised her pen from the page of her journal and gazed out the front window at the cedar tree hanging there. I screened her tiny house from the street so that she couldn't even see the wrought-iron fence. For a week now she had not gone beyond the gate except for daily visits to her therapist. Primal therapy has been called the therapy of last resort, it is so painful. Joanna was half way through a two-week "intensive," two weeks of isolation without the distraction of telephone, newspaper, books or any other media, two weeks of therapy, individual and group.

1991 – I am and am not that Joanna Hern. I remember that I looked out through Joanna's eyes that day and saw the tree and sensed the open winter day beyond its screen. I remember how panic stricken she felt when she stopped writing, so she wrote until her hand cramped up and she had to quit. I remember how she wanted someone anyone to come, but particularly, of course, she wanted *the man* to come. She wanted to call him. She almost did. She had to fight off the impulse hourly and as soon as she overcame it, she wanted *the child*, Lee or Daniel, it didn't matter which. Neither was a child by then, one was nineteen, one eighteen. And Lee contended she had never been one, never been permitted to because she was so busy mothering her own mother. I remember what Joanna did that day and how surprised she was that she survived doing it and I remember much that lay in her past as well as what lay in her future.

1939 – I am Joanna Hern. Soon I will be four. People ask how old are you and I hold up four fingers. I look to see if momma is watching. It is a lie to say I am four. I have dark curls like Shirley Temple. I see them in Bonmama's mirror. I know the names of all the seven dwarfs. I can count to seven, well ten really but I forget after seven. My house is in the middle of fields. There are trees at the front. They talk to me. Even when there is no wind, they talk to me. The hens talk to me too. People laugh when I answer the hens and I don't like that. They think I'm pretending. I don't let them hear me talk to the others. Not the angels. The angels don't talk. They walk with me or just stand there, smiling. They smile with their wings, so bright not their faces. I can't see their faces very well because they are so tall, unless they bend down. I talk to the other little people. The little people live in the fence corners. They play with me because there are not other little girls here. The little people call me to come out and play. Now that I am a big girl, Momma lets me go. There is the blue family under the hazel nut tree near the fence. The silver fairies live in the spring and the rose people live under the big rock. The little people tell me to look at the mountains and down across the valley where the other mountains are. I look and they agree with me. It is beautiful.

At night, when I go to sleep, I remember another place. In that place, I am not a little girl. I am important because I'm supposed to come first. Then the others will come. The others gather around me and tell me I must go first. They are counting on me. In the night, I know all about counting. Not just to ten. It is a very beautiful place that I go back to at night and they all sit around me in that blue space and tell me why I must be brave. There are pillars and marble steps and long white curtains that billow in the breeze. The biggest place I have seen on earth is the catholic church, but this is bigger. I know these are pillars and this soft feeling white rock is marble. My house is almost bare and the snow blows in around the windows, but here I am warm and dry. This is luxury.

But my daddy wakes me up. I have to leave that place because he comes into my bed. It's all right though because when I peek out of my eyes,

I see the angel. Daddy never does. He has his back to the angel. He pretends he is my nice daddy, but I know.

Momma teaches me how to wash myself in the basin. She puts the basin on the floor and has me stand over it to wash between my legs. She says I can get the basin and wash myself there when I want to.

It is important to be good. We go to church in the day and at night. The night church is different. Sometimes it is in the day church, but things are changed. The cross is wrong. It is the same cross, but it is wrong. And everyone wears different clothes and things that go over their heads. I can't see their faces. I can't tell who is daddy. Sometimes night church is in a barn. I don't like it in the barn. There is only the lantern. It is dark in the hay mows. The calf cries for its momma and then all its blood comes out. I am a-scared for my banty rooster. I am a-scared for me. My daddy makes things dead.

One night at my nanna's, I heard a fox bark. I was in the kitchen with all the women. I heard the fox bark on the porch. The men were there. I started to scream. Momma said, "Be quiet. It's just a fox." She held me hard so I couldn't breathe. She was all stiff. "Be quiet," she said. "Be quiet. It's just the fox." My daddy came in laughing. He had the deer horns on his head. He had something red in his hands and red on his mouth. All the women sucked in their breath. His name is Hunter Hern but now he is Hern the Hunter.

Day church is sad. In day church, they are afraid. When the Reverend Tanner comes, the young women stoop down in the churchyard. I stoop down too because my dress is short and shows my knees. My momma cries when we sing the songs. The Reverend Tanner does not come to night church, I think.

The women are teaching me how to draw a star on the floor. The girls have to draw it before night church. It is hard to draw. You need a ruler. It is hard to hold the ruler still. I get Jean and Grace to hold the ruler. When I do it wrong, Grace's mother rubs it out with her foot. I want to cry. I want to quit. But I am Hern's girl. I am special. I have to learn to draw the star. I have to learn to chant the words. It is good I am smart. It is good I am pretty. A priestess has to be smart and pretty. And brave.

My momma knows that I will get hurt. Her mouth goes funny. It does not smile. She tells me to be brave. But then she says something is too much.

"You can't do that," she screams at Daddy. "I won't let you do that. I'll go to the police."

But Daddy laughs. He laughs his terrible laugh, the way he laughs when he is Hern the Hunter. "Go," he screams, "go. I'll kill your ma," he screams. We are in the living room. He is in the kitchen. I press my face into my momma's shoulder. I try to shut him out.

"I'll leave you, Hunter. I swear, I'll take Joanna with me."

I pray really hard to my angels. I hug my momma tight and tighter. I cannot see the angels. It is too dark.

"Where would you go?" he laughs. He is still in the kitchen.

"I'll go to Ma's. Pa won't let you do this."

"Your pa!" This is the funniest thing to Daddy. "I'll kill your pa and your ma too. You much as try to leave me and I'll kill them both."

I sleep with my momma. Daddy isn't there. Sleep close to her. It is cold in bed so we have all the blankets and my momma's coat over us. Then crash!

They are there. At the foot of the bed. Laughing. Their heads are covered with things like potato sacks. They look the way they do in night church. My momma grabs me hard. I can hear her breathe. One of them has a lantern. They are yelling and laughing. They have sticks in their hands. They are telling me to get up. They are pulling me away from her. I am screaming and screaming, "Momma, Momma, Momma!" I don't stop screaming. It is dark. I scream and scream and scream. Momma! Momma! Momma!

1991 – Joanna Hern lies on a yoga mat breathing into her abdomen.

"Press your back," the teacher says, but upstairs a child is crying. No, upstairs a child is hysterically calling and calling for his mother. He has lost hope long ago that she will come and is crying now mechanically but with no less vigour.

Joanna starts to cough, a cough that comes from the roots of her being. She sits up. She could go to the washroom. It seems as if she may actually vomit. She gets to her feet, but instead of heading to the washroom, she goes upstairs. She passes windows full of the setting sun.

"Sorry to intrude," she says, "But I need a drink for this cough." The man is walking up and down with the screaming child on his hip. She speaks for the child, "This little one thinks his mom has left him, but I know moms don't go and leave their little boys so easily. She will come back."

"She's gone shopping," the man says. "She will come back."

Joanna drinks her water absentmindedly. What is it that she is remembering?

She writes in her journal. Why I went to live in the country, I don't know. I always tell people that it is because I can't afford to live in the city on my salary now that I'm single again. It means that I have to commute to work, an hour there and an hour back, but when I climb out of the car, it seems worth it, the air full of hay or cedar, the sky full of leaves or stars. But it might be closer to the truth to say that I came to the country to confront *The Spook*. I have suspected her existence for a long time, even before my marriage ended but certainly then. When I first started living on my own, I would suddenly feel as if I had gone mad. It wasn't just that I felt abandoned and terrified, although I certainly did. It felt much worse. I felt as if I had died and become a ghost unable to communicate with the living, doomed to haunt an empty house forever without the consolation of human companionship. Eventually, I identified this condition as *The Spook*.

I hated it of course. I would do almost anything to avoid it. I would phone people, take on an extra job at work, join a club, take up a hobby, anything to fill in time and avoid that confrontation. Then I moved to the country. It's not easy to avoid such issues there.

I remembered in stages. At first, there was just an overwhelming realization. "They left me alone." I rushed to the toilet wretching and trying to vomit. My stomach heaved and heaved, but it was empty so nothing came up but stomach juices. Finally, I was able to stop gagging and sit back. I was covered with sweat and tears and shaking uncontrollably. I swayed to my feet and began to walk the floor, cradling myself with folded arms and crooning miserably. I felt as if something had torn inside me and that I would never be whole again.

It was a Sunday afternoon on a dismal winter day and I was as usual alone in my hundred-year-old house. I wandered from room to room searching the landscape outside the windows for clues. Every new prospect brought some new aspect of the horror home to me. I knew as the hours passed that I had been alone in that farmhouse for a long time. That long first night I slept out of exhaustion and woke frozen and terror stricken in the dark. I lay listening, listening, thinking I could hear her coming. I called out to her eagerly. I raised myself up in the blackness to meet her. There was nothing. I began to scream again, and scream and scream. I wretched and coughed and gagged up stuff. But no one can cry like that forever and at last, I left my body and looking back at it saw that it was still.

I didn't get the entire picture that first afternoon. Waves of anxiety, a terrible sense of urgency prevented that. If I hadn't been able to call my sister, I don't think I would have survived. As time went on, it seemed that I had been alone a day and another night and the next day well into the evening hours. It was a cold time of the year, November or a cold October, perhaps the thirty-first. Yet it may well have been midwinter. My memories are still limited by what I think is feasible. I will not permit it to be feasible that I was abandoned in the winter cold without a fire.

I did try to make a fire without success. By that time, I had decided to cook because my dolly, Polly, and my teddy bear were hungry. There was nothing in the pantry after I finished the hard biscuits the first morning except the flour bin, an egg and the pail of water from the spring. I had seen my mother bake often enough. There wasn't much to it so far as I could see and my babies needed a momma. I talked to them as I worked and told them not to be afraid. They were sitting at the table like good children waiting for their supper. I have the impression that I had pulled something of my mother's over my nightdress for warmth and l liked it because it smelled like her. From time to time, it occurred to me that my daddy was out there somewhere wearing a hood and making my momma dead. All the more reason why I had to be the momma. The main problem with the fire was that I couldn't light the match even after I had risked my life to climb up to the hanging matchbox which had deliberately been hung out of my reach. In the end, my babies and I had pudding, uncooked and rather watery.

She doesn't remember the lady who came in the white dress. Only I remember even though I'm only four. The lady was very tall and beautiful. Not an angel. The angels were always there with their wings folded, thin and tall around the rooms. I didn't pay attention to them. They didn't talk to me. The lady talked to me. She was a momma. She said she was. She told me to put on my momma's coat. I went and got it from the bed. I couldn't put my arm in the sleeves very well, so I just buttoned it. She is the one who thought up the let's pretend of feeding my babies.

I rocked them in the rocking chair and sang to them. I put them to bed on the couch and said, "Now I lay me down to sleep," for them. I got the blankets from the bed. It was getting dark in there and I was scared the bad men were in there. I had to be brave. I covered up the babies and me.

At a certain point, it seems as though I snapped. Sometimes it seems as though this happened when they finally came back. I am lying on the couch in the kitchen and I wake up to see them coming through the door. My father is smiling triumphantly and she is a little behind him, barely able to stand. I am overjoyed that she is alive, but she doesn't look at me. It seems as though she cannot see me or anything. Her mouth is funny and she is looking up at the ceiling.

"Get in there," my father says and shoves her toward the other room where we are sleeping now because it is winter.

She just goes. She doesn't stop. And then he turns to me. He looks terrible. He is smiling. Far off he is saying, "How is my little girl?" And he comes toward me, but I am gone.

He made a big fire and the house got warm. I wouldn't help him get the wood. Then he went and got pails of water from the spring and put it in the part of the stove that heats water. All the time he talked to me. He said what a good girl I was, how proud he was I could look after myself. I just hid my face in the cushion. He had hurt my momma. Now she couldn't see me. He had a package of meat and he put it on to cook in a big pot. When the water was hot, he brought the big round tub out and filled it with the warm water. He picked me up and started to take off my nightie. It was all dirty from the pudding and other stuff. All the time, he was bathing me as if I was a baby, he kept smiling and telling me what a big girl I was and how I was really the mother of the house. I always would be now, he said. But I wouldn't look at him. I wanted my momma. I wanted to know, would she get better?

"This is broth," he said. "It will make momma better. It will make her strong again. Like you."

It was hot and I didn't like to taste it. We took some of it in to momma. I was shy. He put the pillows behind her head and I fed her the broth with my spoon.

My mother, Nina Hern, died on Nov. 11, 1977. She had had cancer for many years and had not been expected to live even two weeks when it was first diagnosed in 1970. Miraculously it went into remission and some of those seven years, she was remarkably well. Toward the end, she suffered greatly. For a time, she had no bladder control, but still I remember how beautiful she looked in her long blue dress and her silver hair. On the first of November in her fifty-ninth year, we realized that she had to be hospitalized. I wanted her to die at home, but other family members advised against it. That evening when her meal was brought in, I was alone with her. I fed her the soup. I remember how her open mouth trembled as I fed her as if she were eager to take in the life force it represented, eager still to live. The next day, she sank into a coma. After that we never left her alone. We slept in shifts so someone was always with her. As time went on a ruby bloomed on her lower lip. She spoke only once. I had been singing to her when suddenly she stirred and said, "I need a gift." When, at last, her breathing stopped, I said, "Thank God, she is out of it."

Momma didn't come back after the bad men took her. Somebody came back that looked like her but not my momma. We moved away from that place and I got a baby sister and started school. A lot of things happened. Some were bad. But I went to Sunday School and I figured out that Jesus helped me and that it was his momma who told me how to make pudding that time I got left alone. She was my momma too. The people in the night church started not to like me because I told them Jesus didn't like what they made me do. Then I couldn't be the priestess. But in school, I came first in my class.

On Christmas Day, 1987, I was sitting in a small round cave in the hills above Malibu. Actually it was on parkland which had once been Ronald Reagan's ranch. Lee, baby Josh, a friend of Lee's and I had gone there for a Christmas Day hike and for some reason, the others thought I needed to sit in the cave. I was thinking about all of the vision questers who must have sat on the same spot and of all the visions they must have had.

She was afraid. She was so afraid that she wanted to crawl out and run away. I was the one who made her stay. After a while, I couldn't keep her anymore and she did leave. She had a hard time climbing back up the streambed. She is old, you know. There was a big rock there. She was so scared. She didn't even realize what we had seen for days after. She wrote about the cave in her book that she writes things in but she didn't tell what we saw.

Really, I felt quite tranquillized in the cave, or perhaps grounded is the word, rooted. Yet I wanted to leave. It was as if I was just *being* for the first time in my life, yet I wanted to rush out and tell someone about it. It was such a powerful experience that I couldn't stand much of it. I felt that the cave could harm me.

I helped her remember. I told people what she saw. I told her class and her friends and her sisters and her son and both the men, the old one and the new one. After a while she paid attention to what I told them and wrote it down.

Friday, February 19, 1988: I saw a vision of God — a fairly remarkable sight as one might imagine. Then a light came up behind God so that it became clear that what I thought was God was really a painting on a scrim. As the back light grew, I could see through the image and a new figure behind the transparent screen began to emerge. It was much grander with gold light at the centre and a halo of white light. Gradually, I realized it was the Mother. The beauty of Her light was very great indeed. I felt how nourishing it was. Good energy flowed through the soles of my feet and my whole body began to warm and glow with health.

Sunday, March 6, 1988: Hunter Hern died on Wednesday last. Apparently he suffered a heart attack while he was "having it off" with his mistress. We are keeping these details from his second wife.

Monday, November 11, 1991: Now that I know about the angels and those that stood guard over me, I sometimes cry out to them, "Why didn't you let me die?" Then I remember that my sisters and my brother would not be what they are if I had not stood between them and Hunter's cruelty — not that I could do much really. Perhaps what I did for them was mother them when Nina could not. I take some comfort from the fact that they have turned out to be such fine people, if a little scarred. Then there are my children, Lee and Daniel, and my grandson, Josh. All of them add much to the world. Finally there are thousands of students I have taught. Above all, I have fought against stupidity and ignorance and blindness. Not a bad score. Perhaps the angels were right.

At Christmas, I'm going back to California. It is a good place to learn to play, to find the child in me again and what better season to do it in.

A lot of things have happened. Most of it, I didn't notice. She hated me so I just stayed quiet most of the time. Except when I got a-scared. Then I would get loud. After the Mother came back, I knew it would be o.k. even if it took a long time. I got more attention. I came to live in the country again. I liked learning to make a fire. I liked being alone and brave. Now I don't feel hated any more, and I am getting to be happy.

Eric's Song

(for Eric Webster &
in memory, Ivaluartjuk)

Eric, who is five years old,
advises me precisely, that:

>   he does not like the
>   summer for the bees
>   sting then and if
>   you're lucky to escape
>   them there are bugs
>   and bugs to get you   and
>   the winter's not much
>   better for the frost
>   bites   then

Just after Eric's told
me this I read a poem
transcribed by Knud
Rasmussen who explored
the Arctic generations
before Eric's intemperate
lament; made up and sung
by Ivaluartjuk it goes
in part like this:

>   Cold and mosquitoes,
>   These two pests
>   Come never together ...
>   It is I,
>   Aja – aja – ja ...
>   Ai! But songs
>   Call for strength
>   And I seek after words,
>   I, aja – aja – ja

Like Rasmussen, I set down
the plainsong of another's act

of faith in making fierce
complaint against the
vagaries that tempt you out
to play, to dream, then prick
the skin or paralyze an organ
suppled quite specifically
to let desire in

Do all of us, the singers
and transcribers, only want
to be unwary underneath an
ice-hot sun, to write with
voice upon the parchment
purity of cold,

        I am alive, Ai!
        It is
        I

              Gail Taylor

Thee

This is a forest: this
is not arable   land that
  you may use,
        once razed,   to support
your elaborate
domestic arrangements

When the loggers lumber
through the underbrush, bruising
mosses, skiddering advances with
their boots, with their machines;
thinning into footfallen sheets a
mulch of   various   plant   forms:
impressing upon earthflesh the
might of their   great   umbrage,

then does the eldest, the sentinel
of all trees,   sing out, sing
higher than a carnivore can hear and
even more pure: a sound like toffy
pulled to amber and so fine it must,
it must break and it does not
break,   warning the tree spirits

to gather in readiness to vacate
their munificent homes, from the
serpent roots right up to
stiff nipples of new bud; withdraw
their wending regard inch
by revering inch, undulant as it
is from branch suppling through
sap   rising

When the men begin, with the buzz
saws, shredding flakes of fragrant bark
away from the seasoned column, vascular
fluid spurts out through the wounded
cortex; the blade, vanishing toward the

heart, sluices through and out
the other side,   saber teeth flashing, sweat
shivering down the backs of men

    a second's hush
    — prey ecstasy —
and then, the great thing
hurtles off its plinth,   crepitant
    whacking at gravity,
and the men inspect   and
fondle; dismember; begin
dispersion of parts

Can you hear, though, the *spiritus asper*
as the passionate life, rare and numinous,
splits off as the blade achieves its
halfway mark   the bearing heart — ? when
fleeter than a child dancer with no thought
for gravity   this life departs the husk
and canopy that took   in balanced part
of darkness and of light   to succour
what was given when god,

as father, earthed, hungering madly for
the lithe elusive essence of his mother-half,
sacrificing mercy in return for power
to raven   after   her

    The mother wrenched herself
        from incarnation, fleeing
    for asylum
    in the tree   that woodmen

hew, blind to the fact that   felled, it is a
cask, all ardor gone
its knowledge, nor its fruit nor any
umbrage from its leaf within the
claim of man

And we   domesticated women all,
    arable and bearing,   we are

chosen   every time a tree is
slain   to be sanctum for those
numens that flare forth in droves;
and slowly we are reunited with our
ancient selves, become again
    the high wild forest as the
cortex of our cerebellums thickens
to protect   that tiny organ   out of
which all *arbor vitae*   branch to
join
both hemispheres

    So long farmed,
    and aeons late,   we spread
    the fruit for eve, we render
limbs to ever-shedding serpents

unsettling the land we
stand, well-planted, wakening
the lidded half-cured gods to
know that bounty   comes
from underground

                        Gail Taylor

Black Moon

Hélène Turcotte

At first there are low voices, a swelling murmur that sets your nerves on edge, then subsides to a whisper. Here and there muffled coughs.

There are people going to the show for an evening of entertainment, others who want to see the world reconstructed. There are those whose minds are focused on completing the grocery list or on correcting assignments for the next day — and others who are thinking of eyes that turned away from them too quickly not to let on/betray their interest.

Behind the curtain a cappella singing hushes the noises of the audience, and a movement can be felt going through the crowd, bending bodies forward.

Before leaving the house, I whitened my face with powder; I blackened my eyes with kohl and painted my mouth crimson red, quickly, because I was in a rush, while my mother was calling for me to hurry up.

I run, and all of a sudden I stop in the middle of the street, holding my breath, the strident sound of the horn ringing in my ears. The truck is not slowing down, going faster even. A stream of air coming from the speeding truck lifts my heavy cape, pulls down my hood. For an instant my long black robe appears, a fleeting reminiscence of times long gone by. A vision of darkness touches my whole self. Death, becoming obsessive, continues to follow me, crossing the street, lurking in the shower and behind the frosted mirror that conceals the bathroom medicine cabinet.

I have wanted to die for a long time. A new image surfaces under my eyelids. Me, as a child, when I played at make-believe. Having emptied a drawer of its contents, I stretched out in it, holding my breath. Even then I enjoyed the long, slow inertia, erasing my life. They say drowning is a pleasant death. I only hope it will not be too painful. I will do it, as soon as the show is over.

The Law approaches me in a fur-lined overcoat, rubbing gloved hands together: A policeman comes to a halt on the pavement and beckons me to clear the road.

He is waiting for me.

I cannot find the words to explain my tardiness, the rehearsal at the theatre, the rush, the truck .... Only seventeen years old — words fail me more than ever. Behind the screams, the revolt, the furor that possess me, there is another kind of troubling silence, demanding to be heard. Raging

165

silence, mental turmoil, shatter my stubborn silence, urging me to assume my responsibilities in a threatening world.

I hear the words, sensing that they are mine: "I am Astarté Ishtar Isis Attar Hathor, all incarnations of the Great Goddess."

He stares at the make-up on my face, my long black hair under my hood. To gain some time I had left the house with my costume on, over which I had pulled my cape.

"I personify Death in the play ... a school play, you know," I had to add, before his face lights up.

And he lets Death escape.

It is cold tonight. A dry, crisp cold. I look up to the moon. It is shrouded by a vaporous cloud. Strangely, the moon seems darkened. A black moon. I read somewhere that the black moon is neither a star nor a planet. It is a point in the heavenly space that may help us find our true selves. "How?" I ask it. The cloud passes, and the moon becomes again what it has always been: a whitish, milky brightness, fading in the city lights. Fading so much that it almost disappears. What good is it that I am a moon goddess? I know nothing about its magic!

Some people in the street turn around to see the Goddess passing by. Why is this child staring at me like this? Of course his mother would not let him approach the Great Goddess. Unfortunately childhood has passed me by too fast. All it left me with are the immense sorrows of a tormented adolescence.

I move on faster. My feet leave deep tracks that look gray from the sodden snow and calcium. Is calcium really black? For a moment I feel like turning around, going backwards over footprint after footprint, to find their origin. A colour that would not be a half-tint. But I must not be late for the rehearsal. I promised Marlène.

I am running now. Then I see him — Claude. He is walking with a vigorous stride. A conquering stride. And I still wonder why Marlène chose the most athletic guy in the class to play the leading male part.

He troubles me. I would have loved him, maybe, if I was not in such a hurry to die. He is a strange mixture, half masculine, half feminine. There is softness in his features, but his gait betrays an aggressiveness in life. Yet he shows great patience with other people's misfortunes. He is quite a character, this Claude. He is well liked everywhere. Perhaps because he could not care less about what others think of him. He does not drink, he does not smoke or sell any filthy stuff. He is an athlete. As for sex, if one can trust Johanne, he is all right. But then she does not go into details. Yes, Claude makes me feel on edge, but it is too late.

I am following him without losing sight of his navy blue overcoat. I find he does not walk fast enough. I walk past him and leave him behind — without him suspecting anything.

I finally arrive at the auditorium. Every time I find the stage a lot larger and more impressive than in my memory. Projectors illuminate the stage, the piano, the altar. Above there is a sign with the only words that are pronounced or written during the show:

Cosmic weddings call for life. Turning inward, psychic extension that expands consciousness. Total harmonization that is neither refusal nor perversion nor contempt but healthy and natural integration.

The Students

Marlène takes a few dance steps in the middle of the stage. Her round belly, pregnant with life, appears even more fascinating through her movements. She is cloaked in a tunic that unfolds, wide and slow. Everything about her is round. Her hands are in continuous movement, meet her curved belly, are lifted up, speak the primeval language of touch. Sensuous gestures, a prayer and an offering at the same time. Gracefulness and enveloping warmth. Mother and child combined. She puts her right foot forward. Her body is undulating, circular motion towards the right and towards the left. She follows her own inner voice, being drawn here and there and nowhere. Mother Goddess.

The meowing of a cat brings her to a standstill, startled, and I laugh.

Marlène is coming towards me. She greets me with her warm welcoming personality, her felt-tipped voice that lengthens the words as she pronounces them. "Maaaarvellous," "fantaaastic." I vaguely perceive other words spilling out of her enthusiasm. She presses me against her, her round belly between us. The life that is forming in her always makes me feel uneasy. My eyes want to glance elsewhere, but come quickly back to her asymmetric face. The right side of her head, from the ear lobe to the top, is completely shaved while on the left-hand side her long, blond hair falls in waves onto her shoulder. A black line accentuates her eyebrows which seem to overextend towards the temples.

Marlène slides her hand over her belly and whispers something. She loves to let her hand wander slowly over fabrics, folds and pleats. I have grown used to hearing her speak in a muffled voice, explaining people, smells and colours to the child that will be born.

I know she is anxious to make our show a success. It is important to her, because it is probably the last time she will be on stage before the birth of her baby. She has made a pact with her boyfriend. She will give up her dancing till after the delivery; then he will assume his part, taking a year's sabbatical to look after the child. Will he be back in time for the show?

We decide to rehearse some more.

I put a golden net on my black hair. My tunic is held back by a metal belt. Golden, tawdry. I am Isis, moon goddess, Egyptian. Powerful black virgin. I move toward the altar in the middle of the stage. To my right a bronze stature represents a cat. I lift my arms tragically towards heaven, imploring in a muted voice. Priestess officiating. Black transparent veils float around my legs, revealing and concealing my skin. I rise into the air, flying higher and higher. Then my feet touch the ground, my dream comes to an end.

Blood flows between my legs, stains the floor, leaves us surprised. I had left home too hurriedly; there was no more clean underwear. I do not like red. I stare at the stain, paralyzed. Blood fills me with horror. I want a white, clean death.

The cat looks at us with disdain, moves away, and sits down in a majestic pose. "Here, cat," Marlène calls out. All I see of my friend is her right side, the shaven one. She bends over with open arms to the elusive animal that dashes away. The other side of her face remains hidden. She shrugs her shoulders, and I love her for this slightly derisory gesture.

"What am I supposed to be doing here," asks Claude as he arrives. "Let's start over," sighs Marlène. "We must show the other side of things."

I run to the bathroom, leaving a trail of scarlet behind.

The immense projector paints an almond green reflection on the white canvas that spans the stage. Behind this canvas the show unfolds like Chinese shadow theatre. A curved silhouette unfurls. It's the Great Goddess, the origin of all times, the Universal Mother. The Goddess with her protruding belly makes slow, curved movements which recreate the cycle of life. Life is reinvented, the birth of the child and the unfolding of womanhood, one revealing the other.

Two more rays of yellow light. A woman. And a man. Two bodies drawn to each other. Their hands join, intertwine and disengage, carried by the rhythm of the waves.

But they do not meet. The two bodies waver, turn away from each other, unable to join. Each revolves around himself. One runs away, the other follows. Joined for a brief moment, they separate again.

Then the woman approaches the Great Goddess. Together they dance the steps of matrilineal filiation.

Alone and frightened the man spins around, faster and faster till he stops and kneels before the Great Goddess. Suddenly a stream of purple light penetrates the canvas.

It's the Queen of Death and the Great Goddess, all in one. The Great force of life and death. She calls back her lover, personification of nature. She has him die and brings him back to life to enact the renewal of nature.

Projectors scatter red rays of light everywhere on the canvas while rhythmic dance steps can be heard. Women's cries turn to lament, male voices rise to a chant.

The almond green light fades away. All that is left is the purple light which symbolizes the violent dance of the Great Goddess. The Goddess rises high into the air, coming down suddenly with a shudder before her body folds in two.

Beside her, a male god rises in a white beam of light.

All projectors are turned off simultaneously while awed silence spreads over the auditorium. Breathing quickly the dancers savour the silence which allows them to focus entirely on themselves.

I do not like this. Why did Mother decide to pick me up at the swimming pool?

I try hard to make as much noise as possible with my breast stroke to cover up their snickers. Nobody understands my dislike of my mother. She is so nice to me. Too nice. She steals all my friends.

I do not like round shapes, curves, circles, bends. I like to move straight forward. Is it my fault if I got lost on a road that has not been laid out yet? And if I decided to suddenly finish with it all once and for all, for good, right here? Would Marlène understand?

And my mother?

I dive into the tepid water, do some water ballet and arabesques. My hands are placed against the wall. I open my eyes wide, wider than normal. A wall. Closure. I remain blind even with my eyes opened as wide as possible. I feel so abandoned. My mother never wanted a child, and since my birth she has tried to seek forgiveness for this initial feeling, this childbirth shipwreck. What has happened that makes me want to die like this? Did she squeeze her legs together very hard? How can one live in a body that no longer understands itself?

I cannot hold my breath any longer. I open my mouth and watch the bubbles rise. Let me live, mother!

With an abrupt movement my feet push to propel myself, beginning my deliverance. Another push, and my body emerges from the depth, leaves the water.

A curtain filters the light. Purple. The man and the woman are there, dancing near each other. Between their hands they are holding garlands that follow their movements. The man and the woman approach each other, move away, come back. They intertwine, and their movements form whirls like waves that grow larger and larger till they absorb the silhouette in the middle of the stage.

In the middle of the world, in this pale green ocean, a huddled up shape comes to life. It bends, makes itself small, bows its head, presents its back, knees tucked in. A flesh-coloured tube connects it to the woman. It grows quickly, becomes a head, arms, hands, legs and feet. Its vital force propels it towards the two dances.

The lights dim; only the two projectors illuminate the sign above:

Cosmic weddings call for life. Turning inward, psychic extension that expands consciousness. Total harmonization that is neither refusal nor perversion nor contempt but healthy and natural integration.

The Students

Yes. This is life. I smile and bow, in spite of the empty seat somewhere in the auditorium.

A Day in the Life of a Warrior,
or
Safe in the Body of Goddess

Claudia Gahlinger

i

If you bring forth what is within you
what you bring forth will save you.
If you do not bring forth what is within you,
what you do not bring forth will destroy you.
                    - Gospel of Thomas

Black night and deep silence. Blissful heavy sleep after a day of hard work and illness. *Safe, safe, safe* say the wavelets that brush up on the pebbles at the shoreline.

For two weeks now, while sitting a dog and a cat in a flower-decked cottage by the harbour, I've been making myself small by choice. Diving and surfacing. Entering into the malaise, the maelstrom of my childbody. Little ell: that's what I call her. I give birth to her, to my self.

I sit in the living room, cautiously reading other women's hysteries, their stories of going down into the brutality of memory, of body, of childself and living to tell about it. I draw and read and wait for new labour pains. I get up and walk about the room on eggshells, cautious as a pregnant woman weeks overdue, a hand on my fertile belly like the handprint on African granaries: to ward off evil. I yearn to give birth but I dread it. The tumult, the tearing. The necessity of travelling alone, always knowing there is more horror to be born.

This journey — this sinking — this slow lowering through caverns — has taken me closer and closer to the beginnings. Which was the end. The original sin: annihilation. Will I discover that my Original Child didn't survive?

"Most of us, not being heroes, dawdle through life, mis-time our cues, and end up in our various emotional messes," wrote Bruce Chatwin in *The Songlines*. "The Hero does not. The Hero — and this is why we hail him as a hero — takes each ordeal as it comes, and chalks up point after point."

171

Here, at this time in my life, I am a Hero, rescuing my childself in her distress. I never flinch, never hide, never refuse knowledge. Being a heroine and warrior means that I will hear her story against all odds.

Each night outside my attic window there sounds a ludicrous barking. What could it be? A sea animal surely, but sea dog — sea bird — sea wolf?

Later comes the slow hammering roar of the trawlers and the jigging boats as they move through the harbour and out between the rockpile breakwaters. One boat, then another. Fearlessness doesn't push them forward; fear doesn't hold them back. Out they go onto the silence of black open sea under black starry sky.

This time I lift myself up from the mattress to find out who or what is so hoarsely barking and I see it: a piece of live driftwood, stood on end. Poised, propped, iconic — no, it's a Great Blue Heron, posing in the shallow water. Wisdom, evil, beauty. Startled, the long beak and dragging claws and omen wings flap-flop away.

At dawn the ocean water is pale blue phosphorescence. The far mountain coast is proud and gentle, the sky looks sweet enough to drink. Morning and safety. Mothersmilk. Lift it to my lips and drink, whispering *goddess goddess goddess*.

Then it's time to get up. I climb downstairs, make coffee, chop spruce wood to smithereens, gather scraps of kindling in the yard, start a fire in the stove, feed Mitzi the Shaggy Dog Story and Mrs. Kitty, wipe up the slimy pink stuff from the porch floor — Mitzi's throw-up from snuffling through neighbourhood garbage cans last night — and toss the kleenex on the fire. I do all this quickly, efficiently, and without throwing up myself.

"Hey, little ell," I say affectionately and with a sense of kindling revelation, "for someone so damaged, so retarded, for a Girl of Such Little Brain, we're not doing badly at all." And I stroke her gently.

Little ell sits in my belly, her arms around her knees, gazing wide-eyed at everything, never sleeping. Her eyes are two black holes that test every possible thing for safety but can't deny access to any of it. She is wearing a red Sunday dress, white socks and black shoes. That is the way she dressed the morning after she was first divided. Caressing her is painful for me; it hurts to be reminded of her smallness and her tentative, incredible openheartedness in spite of everything.

But I caress her anyway, and hear the echo of her whimpering as she remembers our most recent journey into danger; she knows we'll be making further expeditions.

ii

Each day's long bout of memory is triggered by a different story or by a contemplation of my own, and each takes me along a different passageway, down into a different underwater cave. But always there is the consuming blind body-fear followed by the slow turning up of the lamp, my intellect, until I glimpse the meaning of little ell's agony.

Usually it begins like this:

Reading. Words trigger a trembling in my belly. A quaking rises to my throat. Bricks crumble in my chest. Need to vomit. Need to cry out. Cautiously I climb the stairs to lie down like an invalid — like a self-sacrifice — on the mattress.

If memory doesn't come to fetch me I go down to it. I dip my hand in the sacred pool. The wretched pool. The pleasure, the panic pool. Make circles in the water, slow, fast, slow. Rub frost from the windowpane, rub away the mirror reflection of my adult self to reveal the child. (A few shards of intellect, of grown-up calm — a few glimmers of my reflected/reflexive self — always remain on the surface, observing.) Rub, circling darker and deeper. Swoon into it. Until I begin to see with her body's eye.

Sliding, slipping down memory banks I sink down through the water of bodymemory, down to where ... things happened. As pleasure spirals up and up to around my ears terror spirals me downward, deeper underwater. Into the gallery. The cave. The basement.

Falling Alice into Wonderland. Who will I find there? My looking glass father ...

<blockquote>

Falling, little ell must go
she knows
and she is so
so afraid
to be going inside
here
again
no, no she whimpers
but I fight to go down
even as she fights to stay
on the surface.
I do both, I observe myself
fighting, sinking
(but who exactly is this
observing I?)
no she whispers, turning

</blockquote>

turning inside out
into ecstasy

Little ell is three years old. This is the extermination of her soul. This burgeoning thunderclap, and cloudburst of pleasure.

but Laura, she'll cry afterwards, *i was too little, and scared. i was so scared –*

"I know, honey, I know. But we're safe now," I tell her. "You are my first love and I will protect you. He's not here to hurt you again."

Once I called on anyone for help as I fell. It was my first time underground. I called out in terror, conjured Mary and she stayed.

She was the phosphorescent kindly blue Mary of my childhood, my First Communion. Mary the incarnation of the One Mother, sorrow-knowing and balmy as the ocean in summer under porcelain skies. Now I know her as Maria, plural of *mare,* seas, the ocean that embraces all the continents. The one that makes Earth the Blue Planet. The one who is depicted gazing downward, not up; hands spreading her cloak like wings to embrace, bare feet curving over the earth.

As I lay on the floor during this first agony of falling, Mary's form hovered obligingly in the air. And tarty, aloof Mrs. Kitty, a mothercat of half a dozen litters, observed it all; afterwards, as my hands lay limp at my sides, she came to lick my palm.

That was the day I rediscovered goddess. Not the myth, not the Catholic icon, not a person, but a quality:

Finesse — Noblesse — Goddess.
Wondrous — Joyous — Goddous.

iii

But I need to tell this memory of being divided, of disintegration (may it be the Original One, the worst and the last!).

Darkness. Choking on him, yet again. Struggle to breathe but the air is occupied territory, it is occupied by the indigestible, the unspeakable. Can't breathe, and can't, and can't. A rhythmical denial. Hang on to consciousness, to wholeness, to my one spirit against his aggression. But I can't.

I let go. Black out, bail out, abandon ship. Split from her battered body and damaged spirit. Spiral away, see her down there little and lifeless, pat her head in pity and farewell.

Memory tells me I've always blamed myself — been ashamed of myself — for not hanging on to consciousness harder. For letting her die.

(Did I have a choice? Was I simply asphyxiating, was there no other way to go but unconscious?) I come up for air, shuddering, scalp crawling.

Division. Now I understand why I've always considered my self false. Why I hovered over reality, separate, safe. Sharp beak and omen wings. Untouched, untouching, untouchable. Condemned to self-consciousness. And I've begun to grapple with the nuances of Division. I've dreamed and remembered and thus, fearfully and with eyes wide open, learned to identify the pieces of my fractured self:

Rage is prepared to murder for revenge.

Savage sits huddled in the basement, belly full and mouth dripping with cum. Savage is Shame, who won't let anyone close for fear they will smell her stench.

Retard is slow and damaged.

Dead, who did not survive, still speaks, still has her say in that dry sarcastic voice.

And Goddess is small and endearing, perfectly compassionate and perfectly funny, and powerful as a hurricane.

These are like the skins of an onion, one inside the other. But I'm not sure yet of their order. I search for a metaphor that will help me understand. Which one is at the core? Did little ell survive, or only a few aspects of her? Is life worth living if one's essential part, one's Original Child, has died? Downstairs again, I write out these questions.

It's hard enough for a simple soul to be good, but for a divided one?

How can a divided woman become goddess, when division itself is the only evil?

Luckily the ocean is only five minutes away, and as my friend Andrea says, immersion in cold salt water can cure just about anything. So I go kneeling each day on a pilgrimage to the sea.

I let Mitzi out and prod the cat. Giddy as anything, Mitzi bounds outdoors, while Mrs. Kitty overcomes the insult and goes to loll in the shade of an ancient overturned boat.

Both of us barefoot, but Mitzi far shaggier, we walk alongside the harbour. The path is hard dirt and soft sand lined with wild strawberries and sharp-edged blades of grass, bay laurel and little spruces. When we reach the crescent of sandy beach in the lee of the breakwater, Mitzi begins to gallop. She makes a wide businessminded circuit of the beach, then returns to sit and guard my swim.

Cold salt baptism, blessing and benediction. Swells heave me up and drop me like a cathedral choir. But *You are held,* a voice tells me. *How could you fall? Where is there to fall to?*

Returning along the path I think:

Goddess, maybe, is that which is greater even than disintegration.
I may be big, big and disintegrated, but goddess is bigger and whole.

iv

Why do I feel compelled to remember? Because by remembering little ell
and the holocaust I remembered also a time before that, when she herself
was pure goddess. Goddess. I'd forgotten that. Beneficent, her heart full of
compassion. She knew that nature didn't mean evil (I wasn't *always* afraid
of the forest). She loved the earth the way she loved Grimm's fairy tales,
treasuring every loaf of bread, every tempest and toad and gold coin, every
magic fish, every king and scullery maid and simpleton and even the ogres,
in their own way.

Kindhearted, a clown, and mischievous. The other children loved to
play with her, coddling and kissing her. So my sisters tell me, lately.

He must have gone to her for comfort. It was the middle of the night,
when he was most afraid of dying. He was too young to be dying. Little ell
understood this perfectly. His script was clear to her.

He took her down into the basement. She took him into her heart
completely, as the ocean holds a little boat capsizing. He loved her. She was
swept into the terror and blind pleasure of orgasm, and murdered. He
obliterated her. Everything turned upside down. Upstairs, the family's
fearful, silent obedience was the mortar. His violence was the pestle. Her
spirit was ground to a powder between them.

Some people seem to think that this is what openness — open wide
eyes, open wide hearts — are for: to be filled by themselves, by their
oppressive shadow, because they believe their terrible need takes precedence
over everything, everybody.

Now, thirty years later, I must be a warrior. That is, I choose to be
openhearted again. *I will be openhearted anyway.*

After breakfast Andrea calls to chat. Her gravelly, wondering voice
drifts comfortingly over the mountains and the silky blue harbour and the
docked fishing boats. As we talk I spot a guillemot, that hooligan-bird
Andrea taught me to identify, and ponder the fat spiders in their webs
outside the windows. She leaves them on hers so I'm leaving them on mine,
though I have my doubts; eventually, she says, a Cedar Waxwing always
comes to circle her house and pick the webs clean, affording a good view of
itself.

In fact Andrea worships the natural world more than anything; she'd
consider the removal of people from the earth an improvement. At least,
those people who think they can stomp around owning and abusing it.

She dragged herself slowly, painstakingly, out from under the rubble of a desiccating childhood — maybe that's what made her voice so dry — to become an artist, and to honour the gentle and thoughtful nature she was born with. Her creativity reminds me of a child's secret garden; she protects it quietly but savagely, like a self-effacing Amazon. Andrea's biggest gift to me has been a vision: someday maybe I'll have the courage to call myself an artist too.

Amazon and bird. I'm not sure which bird Andrea reminds me of, but she admires merlin hawks most of all — their precise preying flight, their spendthrift beauty — and the way Andrea feels about merlins, I feel about her.

She's working on a bird just now, a carving of a merganser. Sharp long beak, punk haircut, astute sparkling eyes, rich woodsy colours. It's a commission from the new dentist in Effie's Brook, which she'll trade him for some dental work. She's been referring to the bird as the Dentist's Duck, as if it were the central clue in a Sherlock Holmes story.

"How's the Dentist's Duck coming along?"

"Fine," says Andrea. "Nearly done. The feathers are driving me crazy, though." She likes to inscribe a pattern on every feather, a compulsion she feels enslaved by sometimes.

"I've got an appointment with Don today," I tell her. "The second time I've seen him. He seems nice."

"He is," says Andrea. "He's very gentle, and careful. People think going to the dentist is so awful, but it isn't fair. It's not really that bad. Once the needle is over."

"It's because you have to open your mouth wide and they put their — their — " I'm suddenly confused; my mind's gone blank.

"Their *hand* in there," Andrea finishes for me, laughing. "Keep your hands out of my mouth!" she says. "Imagine somebody pacing in front of a dentist's office with that written on a picket sign."

We both laugh hard and nonsensically. Andrea stops first. All the air goes out of my lungs but I still laugh out of control. The laughter turns to anguish, my brain is skidding off its tracks, I have to hang up without saying good-bye. I climb the stairs, lie down on the bed and sob, in the throes of a breathless rage. Rage like a lioness, my body in her mouth.

Don MacLeod looks like a young, handsome version of Dagwood Bumstead. He is thin and earnest, has the same cowlick and wears similar clothes: bow tie, white shirt, stovepipe pants. A soft-spoken punky-looking fellow, perfect recipient for a punky merganser.

"Well, so you're the one Andrea's making the merganser for," I say, tilted and humming back in the chair like an astronaut preparing for take-off.

"That's right," Don replies. "She's a wonderful carver. Beautiful detail. *Crazy* detail, almost. If I had the money I'd fill my house with her work." And he begins the awful, delicate excavation work.

Listening to the pick-ticking of the hook, the sharp scrape of the tooth scalpel, I feel my body holds perfectly still, absolutely tolerant. Dead, in fact. Softly, delicately dead. This posture in the dentist's chair always reminded me of something and now I know what.

He turns away to switch instruments. My jaw hinges shut.

"You doing okay, Laura?" Don asks.

"Yeah. Why, am I turning blue or something?"

"I can hear a click in your jaw, when you open and close. I thought it might be painful."

"No."

"Well, some people are like that. You can open your mouth quite far."

"I thought I was just doing dentists a favour, opening as wide as I could."

"Sure."

"You mean most people can't? How far can you open yours?"

He shows; it doesn't seem like much. You could fit a ping pong ball in his mouth; you could fit a lemon in mine.

"It's like those people who can bend their arm and then sort of unhinge the tendon and bend it further. Doublejointed."

"Like a snake," I say. "Unhinging its jaw to swallow a mouse."

"That's right," says Don.

An alarm bell is ringing faintly in my head. The crazy, it-all-makes-the-deadliest-sense dumbbell alarm. And Lucy, too, my sister? "My sister has the same thing," I say. "Only hers locks open sometimes and it really hurts. Once she was biting down on a huge jawbreaker and got stuck. She had to go to emergency."

"That's the danger," says kind Dagwood. "That your jaw could lock. There's a bump in the jaw, here, and if you force over it you can wear it down. It seems you've stretched that ligament — "

Or had it stretched for you —

" — and gone over that bump, so now you can open your mouth further at will."

He begins to tell of an operation that tightens the ligament, but my mind is busy elsewhere. Usually a multifaceted, razor-edged (if not necessarily efficient) frisbee that my body casts forward into the air ahead of it, my mind had begun to wobble like an out-of-kilter hulahoop. The plastic bib jiggles, a volcano is acting up in my belly. Tremors of fury, sickness, hilarity.

One last stop.

Next door to the dentist is the medical clinic. I have yet another appointment to see a doctor about getting rid of my post-nasal drip. I never could stand the feel of slime down the back of my throat.

After a short wait, just long enough to exchange comments on the weather with Mrs. MacFardy and on the fishing season with Joe Lolley the lobsterman, Marie the receptionist leads me into one of the doctor's offices. She leaves a file folder on the desk and goes out.

For the longest time it lies there, a rare opportunity. I look around at Dr. Windover's credentials, a pharmaceutical company calendar, a department store impression of Paris in winter, greys laid on in torrents with a palette knife, a painting by a Depressionist. Leaning over, I gently lift the file cover.

The first page presents a description of minor complaints and treatments, a kind of petty gossip about my body. Nose, throat, bum, one doctor or another has examined them all here at this clinic. I drop the cover and intertwine my fingers. Tight. This is the kind of curiosity that can kill a cat: what if there's some mention of incipient death by terminal disease, kept secret from me for humanitarian purposes?

For thirty years I believed I was terminal, not knowing why until I remembered little ell. He died of leukaemia; mama explained that leukaemia meant too many white blood cells; little ell thought he'd haemorrhaged in her mouth (she'd thought he was dying, then and there!). Leukaemia in her belly: she believed she was a walking time bomb.

Flipping open the report again I turn over those first few boring pages and come upon a report I hadn't, indeed, known about. It is three pages long, single-spaced typing, topped by official letterhead, and begins, "Dr. Windover, I saw this patient at your request ... "

Not a death sentence but an approximate transcript of my talk last year with Dr. Sykes, the itinerant psychiatrist, and the conclusions he drew.

Those were the days when I wandered, lost. Alice through a glass darkly.

Afraid of monsters I could never identify, monstrosities looming so large inside me and out that I thought I would burst with fear. I didn't know how to defend myself, but I knew I'd better face them soon or I'd explode, flinging black tarry horror over the whole world.

I lit on the notion of hypnosis. It might help me remember safely, like remembering under anaesthetic. So I asked Dr. Windover for a referral to a psychiatrist, who would hopefully pass me on to a hypnotist.

Fat chance.

Dr. Sykes used to be a forensic psychiatrist with the province. This explained a lot. He began by asking in a sceptical tone what-all made me think I'd been sexually abused. Fighting shame I described for him my nightmares, the fearful messages locked into my body's postures, the sense of an imminent breakthrough into memory. He unhooked the fat watch from his wrist, lay it on the table and began to ask questions. Arithmetic, geography of Canada, short- and long-term memory. He timed my answers. He implied that he was doing this for my own good, something I myself wouldn't know. Giggling, humiliated, I answered obediently, because I desperately wanted that referral. But I couldn't help thinking he was testing to see if my mind was busted, should I be admitted to the criminally insane wing of a hospital, was I a brick shy of a load, did I have a screw loose, did my elevator go to the top floor? If those were the underlying questions, the answers were clearly no, no, no, no and yes, in spades.

He concluded that my mind was sharp as a tack but since I had no photographic memories of abuse, only emotions and physical sensations, there was no concrete evidence of it, and threw the case out of court.

Heart pounding, pacing, ticking like a bomb, I steal Dr. Sykes' diabolical report, fold it and slip it into my knapsack.

Dr. Windover doesn't arrive for ages and ages so I'm safe. When he does, he never notices the missing report, and quite enjoys my hilarious mood. He must think I've achieved the levity of a Buddhist, with regard to my bum sinuses. He writes out a prescription for the latest ultimate cure and sends me on my way. Riding off on my bike I feel a potent mixture of emotions concerning this Theft of the Official, this retrieval of me.

Rage is triumphant. Amazonic. That prick of a psychiatrist! I've stolen little ell from his clutches. He'll never harm her again.

Child's heart gallops with the love of adventure, the giddy fear of being caught, and anxiety — what part of her did he trap on paper?

Dead says, I don't want it. Record of horror. Throw it away. And throw away that soft open girl while you're at it.

Retard laughs in slow delight. Shame is nowhere — nowhere in sight.

As I ride to the beach at Effie's Brook, I think, *I have served an apprenticeship*. All my life. Survivor of incest, but more: warrior. So strong: I can remove myself from my body. I can wipe up dog vomit or clean a baby's poopy bum no problem. I could walk for an hour without a coat in a blizzard and not get sick. I could carry luggage full of bricks for a mile or sit through three church sermons in a row and not even be there.

But now I'm learning to be in my pain, and settle into my body's pleasure, and that is far riskier. I can ease deeper into friendships and not panic. Last month when the doctor took forever to do a pap smear, I cried instead of experiencing my body as a sack of potatoes, feeling nothing. I let the blissful world flow through me when I walk in the forest, instead of hiding even there from the condemning, all-seeing eye of my father. This being-in-my-body is in some ways nauseating and much chancier than detachment. But what is living for, if not being alive? True warriorhood means *being alive*.

This doesn't mean that I'm grateful to my father. Or to the brother-in-law who, a few years later, saw that I was transfixed by the headlights of his sexuality and took advantage of that. But I've harnessed the power they had over me. Suffering their lips on my girl's nipples taught me detachment. Silence through the nights of atrocity taught me fortitude. Testing the world for safety sharpened my wits, and my hearing, always alert for his footstep in the night while I slept, is sharp as a cat's.

The conduction current of power they used against me, I use now for myself. But I change its magnetic alignment. As the earth has switched polarities throughout its history again, I can shift my axis according to love, not death.

In fact, remembering inspired me to learn the language of earth processes. Where I once found airy nonsense and barren landscapes, I have found a mine of metaphors, all mixed up. Now I can go down into the earth that once made me fearful and claustrophobic, and celebrate those metaphors.

Each time I remember, I am a rock sinking down through magma. My borders become solvent, my composition changeable. I come up, recrystallize. In the process I can choose a new shape, slightly alter my composition. Each time I sink down into my childbody and experience the raging heat of her pain I can afford to come up more tender, more tough, more malleable. Tempered, I am a little closer to gold: the child who knew and loved goddess.

v

Crescent of blue in a rocky embrace. Large swells roll in, turquoise and then dark blue water. Parents and kids scream as they're carried over the elephant's hump. Sometimes a wave breaks and roars and then they dive down under, or ride the wave all the way in and let themselves get mashed, ecstatically, in surf hitting the sand.

The bottom drops quickly as I wade in and then I'm enveloped. Cold clean all-healing salt velvet below, sunny blowy day above. Floating easily I think, I am taken care of by goddess. How could I fall? Whether I live or die, I am safe in the body of goddess.

Further Foreword: Echoes

Colin O'Connell

If endings are beginnings, and process deeper than stasis, in matters of spirituality Canadian women won't be categorized — won't be pigeonholed. The god/dess-shaped blank that animates their lives — sometimes explicit, sometimes not — seems as varied as women are diverse.

That, perhaps, has always been the case. Women have spoken but rarely been heard, have constructed icons that remain unseen, and have spoken of things, there for those with the vision to see.

But I search in vain for a common thread — a common denominator that runs through that experience and which, with one pull of the string, gathers up the whole. It's almost as if the claims of deconstructionists have long been anticipated, and have worked themselves out at the level of experience in some of the stories in this collection. Totalizing claims are rejected in favour of step-by-step insights. The metaphor of the journey perpetually underway, and fragmentarily reported, has supplanted the story whose metanarrative allows for closure and an easy summing up. Besides: is it fair, or even proper, to speak of women's experience as monolithic? Or is a better image an intricately woven tapestry replete with many strands?

Jo-Anne and I had initially hoped to bring the volume's contributors together — to meet them in person. I, for my part, wanted to know if there wasn't something linking their experience that was more, say, than a wise repudiation of the patriarchal mindset, or a politically defined sisterhood. I wanted to know, if, through the diversity of these stories, there wasn't a shared, if vaguely recognizable, common theme.

Friends tell me I'll look in vain because I haven't yet grasped the inescapable fact that we've entered a world that is radically pluralistic. There is no going back, so I'm told, to an older worldview — natural law, or whatever you want to call it — to a philosophy that will encompass, and ultimately unite, a host of diverse viewpoints.

Raised a liberal Protestant in the United Church of Canada, I've always been open to a variety of ways of expressing faith. If faith were to be understood, as Kierkegaard describes it, as "a quality of existence," then it would have to reflect something of the range and diversity of human experience. But in tension with this, and I suspect at odds, was, and is, my abiding belief in the power of reason as a basis for dialogue and vigorous debate about matters spiritual and religious. Despite the deconstructionists, I have never understood the Enlightenment ideal, that is, reason conceived as a normative basis of discourse, as hegemonic or as necessarily oppressive. Added to this is my trust that faith is not simply founded on an autobiographical utterance — albeit deep — but is, rather, a lived response to a "who" or "something" clearly more than us.

I acknowledge, of course, that reason in the service of certain ideologies (patriarchy and racism are good examples here) has contributed to the development of metanarrativities whose effects have been oppressive, and should be deconstructed. When, for example, patriarchal claims are universalized, they suppress and delegitimate other viewpoints. Moreover, systems such as these don't just marginalize other points of view; they fail the test of life-enhancement. "Reality," in effect, becomes so oppressive for those whose voices have no place that retreat and "madness" seem, at times, the only options available.

Readers of this collection will be struck, no doubt, by the depth of the authors' voices. Before my involvement as co-editor, I had sensed already a paradigm shift — perhaps better described as a subversive act. If, for me, anything was clear, it was that increasingly women were refusing to allow a single paradigm to govern their experience, and certainly not one whose origins lay in "the land of the fathers."

The same is true of many of the women — both authors and characters — in this volume. Explicitly or otherwise, and in various ways, they are intent on deconstructing patriarchal claims whose assumptions add up to a metanarrativity, and whose hold on reality has been vice-like for centuries.

Our concern with this diversity of voices shaped this book, particularly this section we are calling "Echoes." In this section, Jo-Anne and I wanted to avoid the pitfall of privileging one voice that would suppress and silence others. Opening the stories up to diverse interpretations seemed one way of limiting the scope of our editorial control. Our conviction here, too, was that penetrating stories reach beyond an author's voice, and find an interpretive echo in the minds and hearts of readers.

Nonetheless, it is important to note that if no single theme runs throughout these stories, there may well be some family resemblance. In fact, while reading these stories, I often encountered a profound sense of marginality. This is hardly surprising: how, after all, could I truly expect a disenfranchised group or individual to be at the centre of anything? Like it or not, in some respects, the deconstructionists are right: we must sometimes look to the margin.

The world's great religions, from the very beginning, have also made much of marginality. While scripture, code, and cult have often served as mainstream pipelines for encounters with transcendence, our access to the gods and perennial wisdom has also come about through bizarre events at the edge of reality, and open us up to alternative ways of seeing. The teachings, moreover, of the world's great religions have frequently been at odds with the prevailing culture. The call to abandon the domain of the familiar and journey to a place where openness, and then insight, can really come about, is a perennial theme in most religious traditions. Here one need only think of the Mothers of the Desert — fourth-century hermits — who withdrew from the city into the world of the desert where the old social constructions no longer held sway.

Leavetaking, too, is a familiar echo in some of the stories in this collection: leaving a world where "a Christian girl never speaks back to her father" (Ingrid MacDonald); or forsaking a place where men are rewarded for "destroying life and women for creating it" (Maya Khankhoje). Nor is it unexpected that imagination and dreamscapes seem, at times, more important than recorded "fact." Calling myth "history," as does Beth Brant, reminds us that the boundaries between myth and history, and their connection to reality, are by no means clear. Sky Woman spends a lot of her time dreaming — a leavetaking of sorts. Even in the Bible, an influential source of partiarchal thought, a common theme is God's summons toward a radically new future. Ruth, the immigrant, crosses the border and journeys to Israel; Abraham and Sarah leave their home town and wander in the desert; and Moses leads the Israelites out of Egypt. The point seems clear: we are called to travel, not sit still. Idolatry of the past, including the old ways, violates trust in God's coming future.

Lamentably, however, the Spirit of the Future is too often forgotten in contemporary life. The call to change is often drowned out by a patriarchal chorus whose members permit one song only — their song alone. Still, women on the boundary are being heard. As this collection of stories suggests, the first step, for some, is to hear themselves speak for the very first time; it's simply to begin with what they believe and know to be true. Call it a kind of self-reclamation. Henceforth experience, and not tradition, self-discovery, and not imposed learning, will serve as the touchstones of what is real.

But hearing one's own voice is not an easy task. As some stories in this volume attest, it sometimes means a painful journey — even a withdrawal — to escape a wall of partiarchal noise. Insight, it seems, is far more likely to come about somewhere on the margin, where seeing through a maze of socially constructed "facts," first becomes possible. To borrow a phrase from Melissa Hardy, "discrimination of spirit" is a job requirement. Confronting demons that "look like men" — especially those embodied in social institutions — is an unavoidable challenge. But if exorcising demons requires identification, it also means facing the anguish of memory. Hence Claudia Gahlinger writes of the real danger of "not hanging on to consciousness harder"; at the same time she speaks of the "brutality of memory." Or as Ann Copeland puts it, "evasion does not satisfy."

If, in some stories, memory helps dissolve a socially imposed "reality," it is connected in others, including some poetry, to the cyclical rhythm of the natural world. Solace is found in "exhuming ancient tales," "where lore instead of law [now] guides life," and where one discovers the smell of the goddess "in the tall prairie grass" (Carol Rose). Here, above all, I finally felt close to something approaching a worldview. In, for example, the images of the Mother, nature transcends all social constructions. Clock time gives way to the time of nature; growing up is marked by menstruation — the time of fertility — and generations of women, immersed in the "birth force," tap a power that is prepatriarchal and universally binding (Louise Holland).

Now I must stop. But this, of course, does not mean closure. It means I won't continue, at least not for now. Like those that follow, my own reflections are fragmentary and partial. Suggestive, not prescriptive, I hope they will open up paths of questioning and encourage a conversation that is perpetually underway.

Echoes

"Through a Glass Darkly: Visions and Echoes"

Ann Copeland's "Through a Glass Darkly: Visions and Echoes" is a story whose narrator achieves her transcendence — if she experiences such a thing at all — in a horizontal direction, towards a life in the world and in communion with others, rather than vertically. Alternatively, she may be seen as having transcended the confines of her Catholic childhood and subsequent life as a nun. She has chosen risky growth and painful change over the safe and static religious life of the kind exhibited by her friend Fran. Whereas in childhood she had experienced "visions" induced by desire, in her middle age the narrator experiences only "echoes," the echoes of memories redolent with what she terms (in words echoing those of 1 Corinthian 13 from which the title comes) "those things of childhood" that she has put away. At age eleven the narrator had her hoped-for vision of the crucifix surrounded by a golden halo but with no accompanying voices. At age forty-three, now mother of two, when she slips from behind the soundproof glass of the crying room to approach the altar and take communion, she is less confident both of what she sees and hears. That clear glass through which she sees darkly obscures her view of the church and the people in it. She is cut off from them in part. And if she sees less clearly than she once had done, she also has a mixed reaction to what she hears. The sound of the "good" choir singing *The Magnificat* is countered with the old celebrant's "godawful" microphoned voice. Her graceful openness to possibility shows itself in her willingness to put herself back in church, and then to approach the altar, even though she recognizes she may be letting herself in for some unnamed "discomfort." There are some childish things that she has not entirely put away. Wishful thinking had brought about that child's vision whose chief fruit was self-love — "I doubt I have ever loved myself so much." The middle-aged narrator, having "slipped out from under Mary's mantle" by means of her "privileged education," knows that her rationality is no match for Fran's desire, whose dark side of jealousy she had experienced on her tenth birthday. Herself a mother of two, able to smile at a teenaged mother as well as to decline a pro-life emblem, the narrator has slipped herself out from under the safe protection of the sheltering mantle of the Virgin Mary, and left behind what she would see from her adult perspective as a child's world. Where she meets and rejoins her childhood friend Fran is in loving. Though Fran has remained in "that childhood world," the narrator pays tribute to her compassion, however dubious it might seem to a reader. Her own is exhibited in the realization of the limits of her own rationality, in her ability to avoid both direct answer and evasion in response to that abrupt and accusatory question, and in a renewal of friendship that is like the hug after the fight.

Had the narrator of "Through a Glass Darkly," in her graduate-school studies of Milton, read "Lycidas?" At the end of that elegy on a friend's death the poet

187

states: "At last he rose, and twitched his mantle blue:/ To-morrow to fresh woods, and pastures new." There is something like that here in this story — the recollection of the shared life of childhood friends, with the lament for parted ways. But like "Lycidas," "Through a Glass Darkly" points ahead to an ongoing world in which the narrator accepts mature responsibilities — in effect, donning her own blue mantle rather than remaining sheltered beneath someone else's.

Commentator: William Closson James

"Angelus, or Blessed Are the Uninitiated for They Shall Go Fishing"

The girlchild Julia, principal character in Donna Caruso's short story, "Angelus, or Blessed Are the Uninitiated for They Shall Go Fishing," is in good company. There are many celebrated little girls in Canadian fiction, from Lucy Maud Montgomery's Anne of Green Gables to Margaret Laurence's Pique Tonnerre. Like her fellows, Julia is a spirited creature, meeting the world head-on and making what she will of its contradictions. Told from Julia's point of view, "Angelus" portrays part of the process of her incarnation, as she begins to find herself and her place in life. Readable as a pun, the title of the story sets parameters of interpretation for our understanding of Julia's experience. "Angelus" describes the unfettered innocence of an angelic free spirit as well as the first mass in the daily Roman Catholic liturgy. At the same time, Caruso uses the ironic omniscience of the story's narrative voice to cast the youngster's experience in a distinctly feminist light, a perspective that raises larger ideological issues.

Julia and her brother, Anthony, enter our picture on a bike, joyful and as one "in the soft morning light," he peddling, she "sidesaddle." Believing that self-discipline "will help Anthony with his vocation," Father Bernard has the boy serve at Angelus. Julia, on the other hand, with no place sanctioned for her among these "Latin secrets," heads for the public pews, imagining herself Julia the Barbarian, "[h]er eyes, a-fire; her chest, heaving ... robed in animal skin" ... awaiting "the cup of blood she had heard they served here." If we contrast Julia's status with Anthony's we find a microcosm of the roles imposed upon the sexes by two thousand years of Roman Catholic patriarchy. The male shadow of Father Bernard's authority threatens to subsume Julia under its chronic influence, as she identifies somewhat enviously with Anthony and perhaps covets the sort of public attention he receives and the approval it implies. A congregation of "factory workers ... women mostly" only reinforces this incipient sense of women as second-class citizens within Roman Catholic patriarchy, as the narrator, perhaps editorializing a little too obviously, tells us of their "pains in need of miraculous cures; children, weak with sickness; the rent money gone for shoes."

Ironically, however, the very grandeur and mystique of the church's ways inspires Julia to flights of imagination which on occasion carry her beyond its influences. Julia has a child's primal sense of the holy. She feels a numinous sense of awe in church: "Whispers, the softest footsteps, a door opening, all seemed as loud as shouts in the holy silence." Yet there is an ambiguous earthiness to her wonderment, too. Peeing in God's house would be sinful, and not washing before you touch Jesus is sacrilegious. This primal sense of the holy also anthropomorphizes the divine, making God all too human. Not only is God "mean" for sending "people to Hell forever," Julia wants to question him about "a woman god he slept with naked sometimes like Mama and Papa," or about "god kids and if they were a pain like her baby sisters and brothers." In this primal imagination, the boundaries dissolve between the worlds of the seen and the unseen. Parental warnings not to touch hot food metamorphose into an eschatological choice between "life and death, Heaven and Hell."

The trappings of the Roman Catholic liturgy thus provide the backdrop for "Angelus," while a parallel story is played out in Julia's imagination. Like Julia's sense of the holy, however, this interplay between external and internal realities is ambiguous. Compared with the "plain dark clothes" of the women in the congregation, the "lush white and golden vestments" of Father Bernard and Anthony and the ceiling of the church, "deep blue with painted silver stars," seem to offer an irresistible allure. Yet Julia's fondness for secrecy bears witness to the independence of her imagination. When we meet her, for instance, Julia is dreaming that Anthony will be a priest one day, she a nun. Indeed thoughts of becoming a nun appeal because "maybe at last she could hear God talking to her." But during mass, she fantasizes that in this vision they are "pirates in disguises ... playing a role till the moment came for throwing off their robes and revealing the truth of their pirate hearts and their private desires." Similarly, the sermon is her "favourite part of the mass" because then she is secretly free to think privately, to "leap from one pew to the next," flitting among the "reds and blues" of the "fresh coloured sunlight."

Julia's love of secrecy ties in with issues of honesty and ethical responsibility, too. She loves playing hide-and-seek because she "[l]oved being secret." But this childhood game serves as an analogue for the much more sinister game adults play, games intimated at in "the whispered stories [of adults] that were secrets." Perhaps predictably, these whispered stories revolve around the forbidden topic of sex and the hypocrisy of many Roman Catholic attitudes towards it. As a child, especially as a girlchild, Julia is expected not to have questions about sexuality, when clearly her inquisitiveness must embrace this subject, too; and even when she asks about sexual matters, she is shielded from the presumed perils of the flesh. In the first case, Julia overhears Papa telling an embarrassed Anthony about the birds and the bees, and conscious that she is not supposed to be privy to this initiation, she is left with a host of unanswered questions of her own. In the second case, a meaningless platitude about adultery being "for adults" is all Sister Mary of the Immaculate Conception is able to come up with when Julia asks her about it during her first communion lesson. For the time being, the results are tinged with humour, as we leave Julia toying with the idea of asking Mama if she has ever committed adultery. Yet we also wonder how it is that Julia knows the miracle of transubstantiation to be the holiest of the mass, even as watching female worshippers crossing themselves causes her to ponder the relative merits of small versus larger breasts, freedom of movement versus pleasing the boys.

At other moments, too, humour strikes us unexpectedly in "Angelus," as, for example, when we find out that Julia hates kneeling. We might have expected this disgust to express her independence of mind, especially since she has often pointed out to her mother that angels and saints are never kneeling in the "holy cards" put about like baseball cards by the sisters at school. But no, kneeling is hateful because "[i]t made her think of being mean and squishing bugs." On other occasions, Caruso intrudes rather too violently, as, for example, when she has Julia refer to "the kid's pissy, blubbery tears." But the most vivid picture we take from the story is of Julia's own making, as she imagines herself a pirate princess, Julia the Barbarian. Of the women attending mass, for whom the Angelus offers a brief glimmer of hope in an otherwise dark and desperate existence, Julia suspects that they, too, "had hearts fit for murder and looting if only given the opportunity." Herein lies our caveat. For in many ways, "Angelus" is all about the possibility of Julia's being able to hang on to this sort of opportunity, the very sort of opportunity which now animates her heart and soul with unlimited associations of fantastic inquisitiveness. Yet Julia's future looms as a site of constant struggle between this boundless adventurousness and the seductive authority of almost two thousand years of Roman Catholic patriarchy. At the story's close, uninitiated as yet into the straitjacket of Roman Catholic conformism, the girlchild Julia is free to go fishing on the river. An image of life's passing, this river will carry Julia into adulthood, and only time will tell if this child is mother of the woman, as Julia further plumbs the depths of life's mysteries. As it is, all is full of mystery, and nothing is absolutely sacrosanct. "Julia believed in many gods and she didn't believe in any gods."

Commentator: Jamie Scott

"The Day I Sat with Jesus on the Sun Deck and a Wind Came Up and Blew My Kimono Open and He Saw My Breasts"

No ecstasies, stigmata, fasts unto death or masochistic indulgences for this visionary. No cloistered convent or perpetual vows of chastity in the name of a temperamental divine lover. No proclamations of salvation or indictments of this perfidious, lascivious world. Instead, a woman has a neighbourly chat with Jesus on the deck of a house on the outskirts of Moose Jaw. This story is a significant indication that women's relationship to God might be returning from mystical extravaganzas or fundamentalist insecurities to a more basic, albeit mundane, appreciation as part of everyday existence, specifically the humdrum life of a housewife.

In the era depicted by the Gospels, Jesus seemed content to go about his business of redeeming the world by participating in the daily round. His teachings and parables were imparted on hills, by the side of lakes, in ordinary homes, at wedding celebrations. He did not require the appurtenances of power, either human or divine. His actions were not accompanied by thunder and lightning, nor did he need to impose dogmatic definitions. He did not require qualificatory states of grace as he lightened the load of those who came to him in distress. An ordinary man, marked by an extraordinary destiny, whose enigmatic pronouncements only slowly attained their full significance for his literalist followers. Inevitably, it took the resurrection and the subsequent infusions of the Holy Spirit for the momentous nature of this transformation of the world order to become apparent. In time, Jesus of Nazareth, the son of a carpenter, came to be acknowledged as the Son of God — the Alpha and Omega of existence, the Word made Flesh, the Word that was with God from the beginning. But these cryptic terms with their Greek influence introduced something foreign into the lessons taught by Jesus, the Christ. The simplicity of the Sermon on the Mount got lost in the intricacies of doctrine such as that of transubstantiation and the Trinity. The god/man who had consorted with women of ill-repute and who had treated all women with respect as equals ultimately became associated with a priesthood and ministry that repudiated the claims of the flesh and blamed women for the downfall of the human race. The earthly exemplar of Jesus as the son of God lost its immediacy and connection to this world, as Jesus gradually became rarefied into an ethereal lover, a fearsome judge, or an arid theoretical construct, such as the First Cause. The body, in alienation from these higher forms, was a source of temptation. Women epitomized this state of exile — her body bore the brunt of humanity's dissatisfactions with the idealized projection of the heavenly Jesus that could never be realized. Something had to happen. The Second Coming, no less.

But this scenario is not according to the Apocalypse. There are no trumpets resounding in the heavens, no fire and brimstone, no wailing and gnashing of teeth from the damned as they tumble to their just desserts. Instead, a simple epiphany occurs to Gloria Johnson on the deck of a house in the subdivision of Hillhurst early on a Monday morning in September 1972. There is no elaborate ritual, instead a shared glass of wine with a woman in a pink kimono — a woman whose life will not be radically altered by this event, but who nonetheless realizes its implications. For Jesus endorses her existence, not in any dramatic way, but simply by initiating a desultory conversation about the view. The very ordinariness, however, is disconcerting for Gloria, who finds it hard to reconcile this Jesus with the object of her childhood indoctrination and its attendant fears and associations. So much so that when her kimono is blown open and Jesus compliments her on her exposed breasts, all she can feel is confusion. She becomes preoccupied with her own opinions regarding the aesthetics of breasts. But what in her background could ever have prepared her for the protocol of a backyard chat with Jesus, who seems to be on a pilgrimage through the prairies?

Yet the visit is not without its touch of the miraculous. The two swift, paranormal experiences leave no doubt that it's Jesus sitting there and that the forces of gravity and everyday perception can suddenly shift because of his influence. In fact, to use a modern metaphor, Jesus could be described as a black hole, that dynamic centre whose energy attracts and absorbs all that comes within its compass.

The final scene, however, returns to routine reality. It is one of affirmation of Gloria Johnson as a woman who has beautiful breasts. She can laugh with Jesus because she knows that, in spite of her faults and her gaucheries, all is well with the world just as it is. And Jesus' parting kiss and flick of her nipple confirms this. Gloria Johnson will continue with her household tasks, knowing that she is blessed.

Gloria Sawai's short story illustrates the extraordinary in the ordinary. It validates the life of a woman whose existence is neither that of a sinner nor of a saint. Yet in her very mundane situation, the character of Gloria Johnson represents all women. No longer need woman and her body bear the brunt of punishment for divine yearnings of a humanity that knows itself unworthy. Women, no less than men, are deserving of divine dispensation. Unfortunately, what we fail to realize is that divinity dwells amongst us and is not the sole preserve of priests or purveyors of salvation.

Commentator: Morny Joy

"Discriminatio Spirituum"

In this powerful and disturbing story, Melissa Hardy writes about abuse, denial and the absence of spiritual refuge. Her protagonist's name, Blandina, seems colourless. But for Blandina the word sinus means more than its Latin root, bay or cavity; similarly, her name suggests the Latin *blandus*, soft or gentle (her pet name is "Little Dove"). It also suggests the Italian *blandire*, to soothe or cajole; Blandina proves a victim and a practitioner of this skill. Words and objects prove deceptive or reductive; memories too strong for words or objects become transfigured as demons. The story is simple: two women in a school chapel are engaged in a religious ritual; never-spoken memories of sexual abuse by her brothers prompt one to confess an ability to see demons. This is the "discriminatio spirituum" of the title, which Blandina, perhaps unconsciously, limits to demonic manifestations. The narration takes neither woman's voice, nor that of judgemental omniscience; it is impersonal, detached, even mildly condescending, rather like a school gossip reminiscing. However, the teacher-pupil relationship is defined even before we get to personalities. We learn relatively little about Isabel Smythe. She is blond, youthfully feminine, probably wealthy, sheltered and naive. She has a crush on the nun, apparently more for her ascetic beauty and disciplined powers of devotion than out of some budding sexuality. Nevertheless, she is introduced first, which I think is crucial. This tale suggests little genuine religious belief, except perhaps in the prayers attached to the gilt votive hearts. The briskly colloquial narration makes it quite easy to assume that Blandina's self-mortification is anorexia; it's not surprising that what Isabel thinks is "the odour of sanctity" is actually a popular drugstore scent. Despite her exaggerated, "literary" style of speech (too long away from ordinary conversation), Blandina is not extraordinary; neither is Isabel. The demons could be anyone's. I can see most vividly the description of Venice at Epiphany, when Blandina, ironically, first sees her demons; the nuns carry "big black umbrellas which glistened like domes of mica beneath the street lamps." The image is so hard, so cold. This order into which Blandina has escaped or been driven (there is no mention of why she became a nun), trading abuse for denial of desire, can never fill her empty spaces. Its objects of adoration are a rococo-egg Sacred Heart glowing garishly like a lava lamp and a stern mosaic Virgin with marcelled hair. Blandina has been pinned down until emerging memories become demons; she is hidden away and made to keep quiet and given no chance to confront her experience in any constructive way. The demons themselves show how Blandina's strong sensuality has been painfully repressed and warped. When she describes them to Isabel as "awful boys" with metallic skin and chiselled features and mirrorlike eyes, she gives herself away. The danger in confronting demons, she tells Isabel, is mistaking "their voice for that of your soul," which she claims never to do. Yet they were originally voices emanating from a fog, and she describes them when less apparent as foglike, as if reflecting her own eyes, which are "the colour of a dense fog." They are her projection of memories in which she is made to bear all the shame, they are all that is left of her sensuality, and when she is alone with them, they are described lushly, in imagery redolent of clinging vines and ripe fruit and melting, clutching hands, but also redolent of stinging nettle and unending, mocking laughter. They remind her how her innocence and her womanhood were both stolen, just as her waist-length brown hair was cut off when she entered the convent. "Because of her brothers," the narrator tells us drily, "Sister Blandina did not much like men." Blandina herself tells Isabel that the touch of men, the most disgusting aspect of the manifestation of demons, is impure, to be avoided. Yet her seductive advances toward Isabel, despite her talk of the body as a temple and the special power of women, are full of menace and control; when Hardy cuts them off, she deliberately leaves unresolved the implications, refusing even to indicate Isabel's reactions. Has Blandina transcended her own experience by perpetuating it from her own position of power? Is Isabel on her way to achieving, as Blandina promised she would, discriminatio spirituum?

Blandina's demons are stronger than years of self-denial and self-mortification. The empty night seems full of loneliness, loss and spiritual vacancy, of the profound abuse and suffering at the core of this story.

Commentator: Gisele Marie Baxter

"Margaret's Dreams"

For all its fragrance, colour, and flavour, "Margaret's Dreams" is a dark and troubling story. It is, at base, a tale of power and control, where things that are apparent to the senses and the rational mind seem to change shape and soften, just at the point where we might wish them to be most solid. Nothing is as it seems. The intrusion of Margaret's dreams into her tidy world becomes an experience of defamiliarization.

As the story progresses, the issue of control comes more and more to the fore. Margaret and Alan have ordered their lives in a careful way, beginning with a "starter home" and living an existence "almost as good as an old fifties sitcom." Alan appears to be little more than a prop, but he is a dependable and straight-forward prop all the same. Margaret is a sensible woman who likes to get things done and knows her own mind. As the narrative begins, Margaret has everything at her fingertips. Alan's sister Tansy, on the other hand, is the poster-person for chaos. Everything in her life is unsettled and flighty — even the name "Tansy" is a recent adoption. The contrast between the two women is drawn in high-relief: Margaret has worked hard and "obliged the ethic" while Tansy is "into" herself; Margaret is a responsible person, Tansy is a flake.

It is no accident that dreams play such a pivotal role in the story. The dream world is that place where the rational and the non-rational intersect and become confused; the place where things that cannot be spoken can be entertained and imagined. Against her own will, Margaret becomes a visionary. This must be one of the most chilling aspects of the story: diminished control of one's own life. As a society, we have become aware of the sense of violation experienced by victims of violence; how much greater is the sense of invasion when one's thoughts are no longer one's own? Isn't madness at the door when you are not at home inside your own head?

In all of this, "Margaret's Dreams" reads like a caution against presumption and the domestication of the spiritual. Much of the seemingly disordered activity of Tansy is, in reality, very carefully structured to create experiences identified in advance as desirable. Clothing, diet, activity and thought patterns are all given close attention. Much of contemporary "spirituality" appears to function this way: nothing is left to chance. Manipulation of crystals, weekend woodland rituals and "channelled" tours of other worlds are packaged thrills for people trying to regain their sense of the mysteries of life. More traditional forms of spirituality, too, often offer people second-rate therapy and shrinkwrapped religion in place of encounters with the divine. Sincere seekers hungry for the transcendent are probed with marketing techniques and handed McHappy Meals.

This, however, is not Margaret's problem. Margaret is already content with her life the way she has ordered it and is not looking for anything higher, deeper, or more meaningful. Frustrated with Tansy's self-absorption, she at first appears to be making up dreams to frighten her sister-in-law off. Only later does the reader begin to understand that Margaret is the "worm on the hook." The dreams, occupied with "spiritual" themes and images, come unbidden.

Margaret's dreams reveal something about Tansy, as well. The story's narration, sympathetic to Margaret's point of view, consistently portrays Tansy in an unflattering light. Tansy is interested in the content of the dreams only for as long as they involve her directly. As Margaret begins to slip, Tansy is at first idly curious because "sick people were interesting," but in the same breath realizes that "they became unavailable." "Unavailable for what?" one wonders.

The fear of Margaret's unavailability draws attention to a point made at the beginning of the story: a sort of symbiotic relationship exists between the Margarets and the Tansys of the world. Margaret is frustrated with the other woman's selfishness because she expects that Tansy "should have something interesting to say to those of us poor slobs who have stayed put, some wisdom, reassurance that our role is important, if for nothing else than to subsidize!" Tansy, too, acknowledges this unspoken contract, if only in a negative way: her concern for Margaret evaporates almost entirely when her sister-in-law begins to lose "control." The two come to highlight the divergent poles of the rational and the fanatical. Tansy and Margaret might well mirror the disquiet that lies beneath the surface of many carefully tended Western lives at the end of the twentieth century: how does one risk going beyond the sterility of much of contemporary life while remaining secure in the comforts that that life affords? Can one plumb the depths of mystery in the universe, seeking out high spiritual adventure, and still be home in time for supper?

Commentator: Alan D. Bulley

"The Death of a Husband"

Sometimes marriages end in slow motion. Lots of time on your hands. Love songs or hurting songs on the radio — everybody either falling madly in love or desperately wishing their love would return. Look on the bookshelves: love stories and sex manuals. Push the button on the remote and somebody's in passionate embrace.

Romance everywhere, and here I was in my mid-thirties, an overweight, about-to-be-twice-divorced single mother. Made conscious by media and the remarks of others that I was about to become extraneous.

In "The Death of a Husband," Liza Potvin examines our extravagant cult of romance. There's nothing easy about this story. This is, after all, the author of *Lies My Mother Told Me*, and she's not afraid to dig deeply into the myths, the lies, the ways we console ourselves, which lurk at the very core of our culture.

She does this with prose that's exact, sensual, and often bitterly funny. Who hasn't envisioned life without her spouse? Hasn't daydreamed about a serene, ideal and unencumbered life? Then been reminded of the children?

Part of this story's power is in its intimacy, its insistence on implicating the reader. The narrator's "you" not only observes herself, but also reminds us that we've been there, too.

Commentator: Margaret McLeod

"Disturbing the Peace"

Janina Hornosty's "Disturbing the Peace" is a story about the natural cycles of cultural change. The courtroom represents a microcosm of a community at the moment of crisis. The community longs for, yet fears, a new way of justice and harmony. The young complainants have been living in a comatose state, which is suddenly disturbed by the revving of engines. The dark defendants — in their shiny black leather — are likened to crows. They are the inevitable forces of an order dying from within. They are the scavengers, boding the death of the old order, recycling its carrion into new life. At least, that's how I read it. I wrote that last sentence to draw attention to Hornosty's style: it's conversational — "as is natural" — inviting dialogic rather than authoritative commentary.

The young man and the young woman don't remember much. They have no stories. Lovemaking has become a tranquillizer and their normal state is sleep. Yet, at the moment of the trial, the young man and women seem on the edge, unable or unwilling to go back to sleep. They have stayed awake and taken (admittedly negative) action; they have gone to court; they have signalled a readiness, almost, to live again. The young man has been in his underwear, trying to sleep for as long as he can remember. Yet he is ashamed of his slippers, unable to speak out against those who awakened him. The young woman in her nightdress is set to lodge her complaint, but instead she finds herself chanting from the deep recesses of her heart, invoking the agency of violent renewal.

The judge is weary, tired of predictable patterns: the decent people in their white nightclothes against the menacing black figures. He's heard it all before. In another story, he might have delivered his judgment, as he had so many times before. He might have been set up as the old white man, the symbol of patriarchy, in opposition to the disruptive — or, at another time, wise — old hag who emerges to challenge him. But that's not Hornosty's style. In this story, the judge too signals his readiness to change. He opens the conversation to the room at large. He invites the coming of a sort of wisdom older than his own.

The old woman's storytelling is a strategy of healing. She brings a new style of proceeding to the proceedings. Her storytelling represents a therapeutic form of bearing witness, an alternative to the adversarial court mode. Her story resonates in the hearts of her listeners; it recovers deep cultural resources. Long ago, she was given a choice: "Do you want to be born?" It is a choice given, and made, many times in history, and the time seems ripe again. Hornosty structures the story-within-a-story to suggest ongoing natural cycles of complacency and renewal.

In the older woman's particular version of the story, as a young girl, she had to decide between the way of her decent grandmother and the way of her magical grandmother. In theory, Hornosty's "Disturbing the Peace" avoids any overt judgments. It seems to say to readers: "Make of this what you will." Yet, the deck of symbols is stacked. The magic realism of the polite Sunday dinner scene unmistakably reveals that the world of the decent Anglican grandmother is deadly. There is little doubt as to which choice the granddaughter should make — given the horrific fates of father — "stewed, hapless genitals" — and of mother — "whizzing around the ceiling fan in a flatulent race from her dangerous, thwarted ambition."

In contrast, the magical grandmother is surrounded by powerful, life-giving symbols — herbs, cats, colourful scarves and a loving man. During the frenzied ritual of the moonlight circle, the breach between oppositions — pumpkin and crucifix, ferocity and gentleness, pagan and Christian — is healed in a symbiotic dance. At the heart of the old woman's story is the celebration of the "healthy violence" that gives birth to new life. That's what her grandmother before her and Janina Hornosty after her celebrate too.

The opening of "Disturbing the Peace" leads the reader to expect a realistic courtroom drama. Yet, as it proceeds, the scene could be choreographed, with the witnesses, in key moments, unable to prevent their slippage from realism into ritual, their slippage from a world under rational control into a creative world of pleasure and play. Speech directs itself into chant, feet want to shed slippers. The forces of good and evil, which the court had always structured as enemies to each other, become blurred into one another. The witnesses no longer know how to speak their old lines. Instead they seem caught up in the compulsory forces of inner nature. The court room is transformed from a process of accusation and prosecution to one of cultural recovery and reinvention. The moment of transformation seems imminent. The old woman comes almost in answer to their waiting, their willing. By indirection, she invites the community — the spectators, the judge, the men in black, the young man, the young woman and the reader — to surrender to the dance, to create a new script. Is the moment right? The story ends in stillness, in a tableau. The next move is yours.

Commentator: Sylvia Bowerbank

"The Stations of the Cross"

The narrator, a woman named Grossmutti, homosexuality, the problem of death, a few other family members, and the young girl Olive — mix these ingredients and add Ingrid MacDonald. Enter the Church, and — oh, yes — cows, birds, and violence toward children! Beginning with visionary one, the work unfolds in a "dream-logic" fashion. Interwoven is the search for and expression of an inclusive form of spirituality. The result is an issue-laden, thought-provoking piece of prose/poetry, for around these characters and themes MacDonald builds a story.

When Ralph Waldo Emerson proclaimed nature as the symbol of spirit, he laid the foundation for finding religious conviction neither in scripture nor in church attendance, but in nature's depths and in diverse modes of human experience. Likewise, MacDonald's work highlights the value of everyday human events, accounts of people's lives and the process of finding God in all things. The narrator perceives "All things" — a piece of purple silk, sweetgrass, a shell — "to be sacred if we choose sacredness for them, and give them a place to be."

For the narrator, the challenge of death is both personal and religious. In her construction of an inclusive spirituality, the narrator illustrates how nature, the great spirit, the Lapps, the Haida tradition, Buddhism, a Tibetan prayer wheel, the lives of the saints, the story of Rosa de Bonheur have much to offer humankind's efforts to address such matters as death and the purpose or spiritual meaning of our lives.

The narrator describes her experience of attending the gay community church although she is uncertain that she wants to go, "sceptical of what organized religion can do" for her. In the female minister she finds a heart that is open to her, that says to her: "My sister ... remember your gifts, fill yourself with blessings here and take them with you, into the world." Suddenly, wonderfully, the narrator is moved to tears. This experience during communion reminds us that spirituality is how we stand before God in the context of our day-to-day lives. The form of spirituality advocated by MacDonald can guide us in our attempt to understand sexual diversity and the giftedness that lies herein. Her encounter with a female minister epitomizes how many women in the Church, through the way in which God has been represented by a male hierarchy, have felt deprived of access to the meaning of life, to God.

The story also raises a number of questions: are spiritual resources the same for everyone? Is holiness quantifiable or observable in terms of attitudes or actions? An overly institutional model of holiness will demand obedience. But are these values which we pass on to others, especially our children, life-affirming or life-denying? Thus, the story challenges us to allow ourselves to question and to rethink central elements of the Christian life.

For those who believe in the power of titles, here is one that is strong and suggestive of struggle. The stations of the cross, feminized in MacDonald's work, remind us that just as for Jesus, our struggle to entrust our lives and our hopes to a loving God is lifelong. A forcible and honest literary work, it will open up a discussion of the role that organized religion might perform in counteracting exclusivity and in establishing a spirituality which locates individuals within the complex and larger web of life.

Commentator: Marguerite Evans

"This Is History"

Beth Brant's story may sound to those born into patriarchy as a reversal of certain elements in more familiar creation myths. Clearly, "This Is History" is really herstory; the world was created by a woman and the first human being was a woman. Just as babies here are trained to sleep alone, to hold their cups and their food in their own fingers much younger than was the case in my village, human beings have become more and more detached from their mother earth, from the feminine elemental forces, from the cycles of life and death increasingly under human control.

To my people, it is this detachment, rather than Brant's story, that would sound strange. But, according to our beliefs, everything moves in circles and this journey will inevitably return to the Mother.

Brant's story is not what it appears to be on the surface, a story about Sky Woman, but rather a wonderful collection of stories about the Sky People, Sky Woman, First Woman, the Turtle which becomes recognizable as Turtle Island and Mother Earth, the Eagle — who watches over everything that is to be and is the "harbinger of what is to happen," the birth of the White Pine Tree, prayer, song, the drum, dance, the bleeding-place, the Three Sisters, creation of the stars and moon and the coming of the Twin Sons.

In the few minutes it took to read this story, I was flooded by the memories of hours of storytelling as a boy on my grandmother's lap. My grandmother, keeper of the "quipu," storyteller of our village in the bush of northern Brazil, would spend evenings bewitching us children with stories about the Sky People, where we come from, about how the moon came to be in the sky, why she has a fat round face and so on. Those evenings of storytelling were invoked and came to life for me while reading Beth Brant's story. Even though our stories differ somewhat there are so many common threads that they seem to be identical.

I come from a grandmother-based society, a blending of two minute, isolated tribes in northern Brazil and Venezuela. We hid from civilization in small villages of about 75 people and moved with the seasons, never returning to exactly the same spot. We have stories about the Sky People and our origins in the stars — this is where our spirit/souls come from; we have a story about Sky Woman, but in our story she falls into a great lake and later emerges from the lake to come to land. She brings forth First Woman, the first human being of flesh and spirit who later populates the earth. Sky Woman is thus the First Grandmother, as she is in Brant's story. Later, she returns to the sky as Marchi the Moon who keeps watch over her grandchildren.

In our legends, Sky Woman who later becomes Marchi is a Sky Goddess. Grandmothers in our society have a special status akin to being goddesses.

Mothers give birth and nurture children — our people — and grandmothers provide the link with the past and sow the seeds of the values for the future.

Commentator: Ala-ahuapa

"Journey into the Vortex"

Maya's story beckons. At first, a few vaguely recognizable names and terms — Xibalba, baktun, Ix Chel — call for memory and acknowledgement. A site name, Tulum, follows, and then Chichen Itza, and the vision becomes clearer. Maya, a woman's name as well as the name of a people, might have given it away immediately. In the end, it does. We have three Mayas here: Maya, the author; Maya, the main character in the latter part of the story; and Maya, the ways of the Mayan people. In this story, Maya — the author and main character — and Maya — the tradition of the Mayan people — both speak, both at once. Her voice and their voice carry on parallel recitations, and unfold parallel visions that support and maintain each other. This theme of one life informing the other, of one time, clocked in the date of 12.16.8.7.5 of the Mayan Long Count, maintaining the other, stands central in this story.

The setting and what is known about the people who occupied, and still occupy it, provide background. Tulum, a small, walled city in the northern Mayan lowlands of the Yucatán Peninsula, was settled in the Post-classic period, perhaps one hundred years before the Spanish arrived, while Chichen Itza, well known for its enigmatic archaeological offerings, spans the Classic to Post-classic periods. There has been considerable scholarly controversy regarding the cultural identity of those who occupied Chichen Itza.[1] Recent work suggests continuous occupation by a cosmopolitan nobility that manipulated diverse ritual expressions, both Mayan and non-Mayan, to consolidate and maintain political authority, providing a historic basis for some of the tensions suggested in this story. Notwithstanding the question of the conflux of Mayan and other Mesoamerican people, both sites, and indeed the entire region, were occupied by people heir to a great civilization now celebrated for sophisticated numerical skills and an extraordinary visionary understanding of time. This understanding persists today, as recent works such as Ronald Wright's *Time Among the Maya* (1990) and Barbara Tedlock's *Time and the Highland Maya* (1982) ably document.

That time should appear in both these titles is no coincidence, nor is its place in this story. As the "Journey" begins to unfold, a birthdate is given. When written according to the Mayan Long Count as 12.16.8.7.5, it appears to be from another time, another world, a past lost or discarded long ago. But, when rendered into the Gregorian calendar more familiar to North Americans, that is, 30 May 1942,[2] the date is at first startling, then revealing. It is indeed the birthdate of the author, who first saw this world under the full moon. The time of the Lords of Xibalba and Sac

Nicte runs concurrently with Maya's present. This time and that time, they are but one.

Right at the beginning of the "Journey," Sac Nicte[3] scoffs at the promise of return on the third day after her sacrifice. The time in which she lives holds out no needless promises of messianic return. She need not wait for a rebirth, a resurrection, a promised future life; instead, that life is here, ongoing and accessible. As Dennis Tedlock, translator of the Mayan *Popol Vuh* reminds us, "it is not that the time of the Mayan civilization has passed, to be followed by the time of European civilization, but that the two have begun to run alongside one another."[4]

In the story, Sac Nicte, secreted away and nurtured by her Tata, understands the flow of time and her relation to it far better than those priests who claim authority for themselves. Their hollow power is contrasted with the defiant strength of a woman who knows her own being. The expectations and regulations that ordinarily enclose a woman's life mean little to her. Instead of being trapped within a cycle of children and pounding corn every morning of her womanly life, she comes to full bloom in the expression of her sexuality. That very vitality, seemingly the source of her destruction, is exactly what this story tells us cannot be destroyed, just as time itself cannot be extinguished.

Though holding religious authority, the priests, the mediators of the Lords of Xibalba, are portrayed as knowing little of Xibalba's true nature. Usually rendered into English as Underworld, it is, according to Schele and Freidel, "perhaps closer to the original Maya understanding to think of Xibalba as the parallel unseen Otherworld"[5] inextricably linked to this world. The "waking dream" of the Lords of the Xibalba is the world in which humans live, and vice versa. As David Stuart has convincingly argued on the basis of his study of Mayan glyphs,[6] each realm of existence is sustained through the rituals and visions undertaken by the inhabitants of the other. Yet, the priests of this story cannot see what Sac Nicte is able to sense. The priests' view resembles the way Xibalba was transformed by seventeenth- century Spanish friars who worked through the Popol Vuh into a source of oppression.[7]

Like the priests, Can Ek participates in Sac Nicte's destiny. Here our author reminds us that men and women need not always struggle, but can fulfil each others' lives. At least three Can Eks figure in early colonial Mayan history. One greeted Cortez in 1525, one spurned Spanish fathers' attempts at conversion in 1618 with the words that the time had not yet come to relinquish the Mayan gods, and the third met the Spanish in 1695 and again in 1697 and recognized that it was the end of an era. It was, for a cycle within the Mayan Long Count had come to an end. That particular Can Ek, the last Mayan king to reign independently, was taken in chains to Guatemala City. In the story, however, Can Ek is transformed, maybe to an eagle, maybe a jaguar.[8]

Echoing Can Ek, the Kanuk of Maya's — the character's — life lets us not forget that the lives of women and men in this world, in Canada, as well as Mexico, also participate in the events of other worlds and other times. The vortex of time serves up the past along with the present, even those pasts we sometimes try to leave unacknowledged. The final message of the author, residing in Canada for the past fourteen years, but born in Mexico of ancestry from two other great continents, is one of worlds intertwined, and of relationships that outlive any individual's life.

Notes

1. See Linda Schele and David Freidel, *A Forest of Kings: The Untold Story of the Ancient Maya* (New York: William Morrow and Co., 1990), 352-57, for further discussion.
2. The Mayan Long Count is based on the actual counting of days from a fixed starting day. The days are then organized into a calendar of increasingly larger cycles. A *tun* is the equivalent of a 360-day year; it is made up of eighteen months of twenty days. A *katun* is twenty *tuns*, a *baktun* is twenty *katuns*, or four hundred *tuns*. The date provided in the story reads day 5 (*kin*) of the seventh month (uinal) of the eighth year (*tun*) of the 16th katun of the 12th *baktun*. Though there is disagreement as to the beginning of the present cycle, 11 August 3114 BCE is a generally accepted date. 12.16.8.7.5 is thus 1,846,225 days since that starting date. I used two dates, one, 12.18.12.8.0 (for 24 October 1985, provided by Ronald Wright, p.34) and 12.19.6.15.0 (1 January 2000, provided by Schele and Freidel, p.83) as anchoring points and calculated backwards to read the date given in the story. I then verified the date with the author. There is apparently an easier way to make the calculation, namely with the help of a computer on site at Chichen Itza.
3. A body of folktale exists about Sac Nicte. Some of this material has been reworked by Antonio Mediz Bolio, *La Tierra del Faisán y del Venado* (Mérida, Yucatán: Ediciones Dante, 1983). The work was originally published in the 1920s and is considered a fine example of Yucatec writing.
4. Introduction, *Popul Vuh* (New York: Simon and Schuster, 1895), 13, cited in Ronald Wright, *Time Among the Maya* (Penguin Books, 1990), 205.
5. Schele and Freidel, 66.
6. David Stuart, "Blood and Symbolism in Mayan Iconography," in *Maya Iconography*, ed. Elizabeth Benson and Gillett Griffin (Princeton: Princeton University Press, 1988), 175-221. Cf. Schele and Freidel, 66-67 and 424-26.
7. See Delia Goetz and Sylvanus G. Morley, *Popol Vuh: The Sacred Book of the Ancient Quiché Maya* (Norman: Oklahoma Press, 1972, 1950), n109. The Spanish translators saw Xibalba as an inferno, a place of the "enemy of man."
8. The reference to either an eagle or jaguar is significant, as the eagle is more closely associated with non-Mayan Mexican cultures, whereas the jaguar finds

a place among Mayan motifs. To live on either as eagle or jaguar suggests continuity, either Mayan or Mesoamerican.

Commentator: Kay Koppedrayer

"Between Ebony and Ivory"

I encountered Martine Jacquot's short story "Ebony and Ivory" when rereading Margaret Laurence's *The Diviners*. Despite differences of length and language (Jacquot's story was written in French), notes of resonance between the texts immediately sounded from their shared interest in the themes which are the subject of this volume. *The Diviners'* protagonist, novelist Morag Gunn, discovers that, the limits of language notwithstanding, writing is possible and necessary. Confronted with life's contradictions and the challenge of love, writing is for Morag a form of faith — not the divine sort but that of the diviner, an act that defies logic. This insight about life applies to love as well. "You have to take it on faith," Morag observes of her relationship with Metis Jules Tonnerre. "They smile, then, at each other. Like strangers who have now met."

The narrator of Martine Jacquot's "Ebony and Ivory" also perceives writing as a necessary recourse for a story of love between two other strangers who meet at a party winding down at dawn "on a 27th. No matter which one." Details of time and place seem superfluous to the telling, for as Jacquot's narrator reveals, this love is doomed. The unnamed couple does not yet know this as they stroll through a park toward dawn in "the uncertain moment," "that fine border between ebony and ivory." But they have decided that their "fiction would become real."

There is little logic to this love or its narration, Jacquot's narrator insists. Unfolding amidst uncertainty, doubt, and hesitation, but with amazement and passion, this love/story is "[b]eyond all reason." It is not, however, beyond language, and "[o]rdinary words, usually meaningless, but suddenly so laden with meaning they're almost unbearable."

Thus the narrator writes the couple's story, "so that we may believe it really took place. So that these lovers who never made love together and probably never will ... won't be forgotten." Writing re/members and re/stores the lost, and the loved — the lovers of Ebony and Ivory, whose story speaks "for all the impossible loves that have existed if only in a passing glance, because of the others, of a world that is too large." The story of love and its writing are intimately and lyrically linked by Jacquot:

Write this story because it had become so important that no other could compare.... Write their story as an excuse for a love which does not have any right to live, but never wants to die.... Write how impossible it is to explain anything when the characters themselves do not understand.... Write their unintelligible, incoherent story, to mask the incomprehensible, uncontrollable truth.... Write it to make it immortal.

Writing transforms "what could have been into what is, since what has been written is the only proof that [the couple] ever met"; "[o]nly the written words will bear witness." Moreover, in making "this love come alive in a story," Jacquot's characters transcend "everyday life, ... the washed-out faces of faded, paltry relationships legitimized by society ... turn[ing] it into a true story."

Even if their love is doomed, Jacquot's lovers succeed inasmuch as the fiction of their love becomes a reality of language. Since the 27th, since their inevitable separation, they write in their notebooks. In Jacquot's words, "[t]hey write about the abundance of love with meagre words." They write with love and faith, in the divine-r spirit of Laurence's novel, and Jacquot's short story.

Commentator: Christl Verduyn

"Second Solitude"

When we look at people who have reached what we, perhaps disingenuously, call their golden years, we may think of them as having come to the end of a journey or as having fulfilled their mission on earth. There is nothing left for them to do; they are simply waiting for the end.

To all appearances, Lucinda, the principal character of Lorraine Coyle's "Second Solitude," is one of these people. Seventy-five years old, widowed for three years almost to the day, she is left to her memories and her faded dreams. Life seems to be reduced to such rituals as immaculate housekeeping and monthly visits from children and grandchildren. It seems that all that remains is to hear someone say to her, "Well done, good and faithful servant."

Yet Lucinda's journey is, in fact, far from over, and her mission is not yet complete. We meet Lucinda in her kitchen, waiting for a visit from her daughter and family. Just before they arrive, however, she has a stroke, and Coyle uses this event to initiate two narratives: one, focused on Lucinda in the world — as her family worries over her, in hospital; the other, centred on the recollections and experiences of her spirit or true self, now "out of time."

It is the latter narrative that dominates "Second Solitude," alternating between an account of Lucinda's simple out-of-body experiences and the reliving of fragments of her life. We learn that, despite what she sees as the confines of a male-dominated material and spiritual order, throughout all of her life Lucinda has been on a search for purpose and meaning — for what she calls "the divine or infinite love." While outwardly acknowledging traditional religion, first implicitly, then explicitly, she abandons religion and finds in solitude and in meditation an access to a more personal, more profound spirituality.

The spiritual principles that Lucinda has come to recognize are not entirely opposed to the essence of the Christianity of her youth, but they are certainly more than those reflected in traditional religious practice. Lucinda shuns Christianity's — specifically, Catholicism's — apparent aloofness and dogmatic, didactic and patriarchal character. Like many, what she finds to be particularly restrictive in organized religion is its maleness. Under the guise of religion, men have challenged and hindered her search for the infinite. Men have insisted on the necessity of a mediation, by men, of the absolute. Coyle suggests that this is nothing less than another way of controlling women's lives. And so we see why Lucinda has turned to a more person-centred spirituality — one that emphasizes the insights of women and is independent of all particular religious traditions. It is a spirituality shared with, and inherited from, her mother, but it is also one that comes, ultimately, from all women.

In the narrative describing Lucinda's out-of-body experience, we find a reaffirmation of the legitimacy of her search for the infinite and the divine. But both Lucinda and the reader also encounter certain truths — principles half remembered or, perhaps, never fully grasped. Coyle presents them to us by drawing our attention to three basic contrasts: between body and soul, spirituality and religion, and self and other.

Yet these contrasts are not opposites. For example, Lucinda notes that her body is not her "self," and it is by leaving the body that she not only better understands, but has access to, the transcendent. Still, the physical dimension cannot and must not be ignored. Her encounter with the transcendent is compared to a number of sensuous experiences — eating, intimacy with her husband, feeling the texture of her clothing and of her body. (Here, one cannot help but see in Coyle's erotic imagery a parallel to the great thirteenth-century English nun and mystic, Julian of Norwich.) And to be human is, of course, to have both a body and a spirit. Not surprisingly, then, Lucinda's first reaction after her stroke is to resist separation from the body.

Or again, consider the contrast Coyle draws between spirituality and religion. Catholicism — a faith that continues "the oppression of women by fathers" — is nevertheless one that Lucinda recognizes as giving a key role to the mother — Mary, the mother of Jesus. Lucinda may not take seriously Christianity's claim to being the unique truth, but she does not claim that it is entirely false. In fact, Lucinda's spiritual journey reflects many principles found in traditional Christianity — the distinction of soul and body, the description of soul or spirit as the "real" self, and the recognition of the value of personal mystical experience.

Or, yet again, consider Coyle's contrast between "self" and "other." Lucinda yearns to be free of the demands and the expectations of others, and she understands the need for solitude in her spiritual development. Still, her own spirituality is one that is rooted in the experience of other women, it is enriched as she comes to know women who are marginalized — particularly the senile and the mentally handicapped — and she is eventually drawn back into the world by the claims of others on her. In fact, it is the recognition of negligence in her service to others that leads to her return to the physical world.

Coyle's story is particularly instructive, reminding us that the search for the infinite and the divine is not just an individualistic and ego-centred enterprise.

When we begin this journey, we are indebted to others — though not as mediators, but as trail-blazers — and although we travel alone, we are supported both by those close to us and by chance encounters. Coyle reminds us, as well, of the importance of recognizing that even the most disadvantaged and the most humble may know the truths we seek more clearly than we ever can.

"Second Solitude" also insists that the search for the infinite can be achieved only by working in the finite world; the search for infinite love can only be realized, for example, through a sacrificial love for others. We must die to ourselves in the here and now, in order that we may be what we have it in ourselves to become. And finally, but perhaps most importantly, Coyle's story reminds us of the need for each of us to set aside time for our own search for the transcendent.

Commentator: William Sweet

"Beginning in Summer"

The summer, season for bringing all to fruition, is also a time of rebirth for the narrator of "Beginning in Summer." She enters into a new job as a student minister somewhere on the prairies. In her new setting she is able to begin to pick up the pieces of her shattered former self and mend them to heal them into a more unified whole.

The narrator's past has been one of disruption and fragmentation. Brought up in a family of alcoholic men she chooses a husband who is also an alcoholic, but one who brings her wealth in comparison to her poor farming family. We hear hints of the pain of her past, of being treated as stupid, of abuse, of rape. When she begins to develop a feminist consciousness and finally is able to extricate herself from her marriage, she is left on her own with nothing but the recognition that her survival depends on making the difficult choices of leaving both relative affluence and her children.

Maude and Belle, in their attitudes toward the narrator in many ways portray her own past and future, as well as pointing to two different attitudes to church and clergy. Maude is what the narrator is leaving. "Charles ... will want his morning coffee." Maude also points to the fear of the body and of sexuality that is symptomatic of the fragmentation both of the narrator and of the church. Maude demonstrates concern for how things will look. She is more watchdog than friend. "The board prefers it if you have no overnight company, men or women."

Belle, on the other hand, cares little about appearances and seeks to lead an integrated life. She offers unconditional friendship. She is a teacher and a thinker. The life of the mind/spirit and the life of the body is one and the same.

The narrator is initially wary of Peter, wary of being alone with a strange man. Part of her own fragmentation and her very real fear arises from the fact that as a high school student she was raped by someone she knew, and she experienced the conspiracy of a society that punishes its victims. "I would drop these charges, no one will believe you, and there are people saying you were with someone earlier."

But Peter is not a threat. Like Belle, his mother, he understands the interconnectedness of life and thought. He understands how political and personal intertwine. He too offers friendship. In the end, the narrator learns with him to reclaim the goodness of embodied existence.

Curiously, in a story where institutionalized religion provides the central setting, God, formally named, only appears at the very end. The narrator's salvation from fragmentation, fear and self-blame is not effected, directly by "God." What happens to her happens through the agency of others, of Belle and Peter, and through her own recognition of who she is and what she lacks. Wholeness happens in relatedness. As the summer begins she does not understand confession, because life has always been something that has happened to her rather than being something over which she has had control. We can only wonder if that changes when she begins to take responsibility for herself.

The patterns of pain in the life of the narrator show signs of becoming patterns of grace. She learns to take responsibility for her own thoughts and feelings. She learns to reclaim her body as her own. She learns to sing. As the summer ends she has a sense of new beginnings, of new ways of seeing, of new hope.

Commentator: Pamela Dickey Young

"Blood and Chestnuts"

Reading this piece brought back some very strong memories centred on that time in my own life. The author brings home vividly the mine field of ambivalent emotion that a young woman confronts, as she comes to a profound physical and emotional landmark in her life. A monumental change, which in the best of all possible worlds would be marked with celebration/ritual, welcoming her into an authentic community of women. The message conveyed is that her menses is something shameful from which she must separate. She must use her mind to split from her body.

The heroine's attempts in her daydream, and in the actual world, to invest bleeding with vital pride, to talk about what it feels, looks like, are rejected or ridiculed. Periods are a nuisance. The only bond that the young woman finds with other women (her peers, aunt, and mother) is in silence. For example, her friend's mother's attempt to make something of worth out of the event, for herself and her daughter, is dismissed as childish. Her mother deals with the mechanics of what to use, "the stuff." No sharing of what this means emotionally, spiritually, or culturally. Her friends do not encourage her curiosity in wanting to see a used "sanitary napkin," the very description of which implies the sterility of the process.

Ultimately Ms. O'Grady decides " ... my head moves on to more important matters."

For this reader, "Blood and Chestnuts" is a story which brought home my own sense of alienation from my body, and from other girls and women at menses. Menstruation was shameful and marked us as Other, in a totally negative sense. It was to be kept hidden at all costs. Any show of blood through an "accident" was mortifying. The process leading up to "the curse" was vaguely described in pamphlets or books, read secretly. Menses was related to procreation, but also to craziness. It meant women were (at least once a month) nuts, that we could not be trusted to work in the real world (of men). My mother, sister, peers and I accepted this as a given. The primary source of this design was Catholicism. The Virgin Mother Mary was our model, to compensate for Eve. Sterility as opposed to sensuality. Eve wanted knowledge, Mary wanted to be an instrument. You couldn't be both. The post-war period in which I grew up reinforced these models in every aspect of society. The context for myself, my mother, peers, was uniform in that respect.

I am perplexed that Ms. O'Grady doesn't address the issue of her mother's, her peers', and her own silencing in a more complex way. For example, to suggest that her mother, whom she herself stated was always there for her, was silent around this issue, because she was just old, is far too simplistic, as well as offensive. I wondered why the only male who she remembered (in a negative way), specific to menses and religion, was a Native. How did she know that what he said devalued menstruation? Why was her own (white) religion not able to sustain her power? Also, I feel it is skating on thin ice to equate girls and women with the nether world rather than with the world at large. We are relegating ourselves to an old stereotype in which we are once again defined only by our biology, rather than by a unity of mind and body, at each other's service. Where there is such integration, we are not then at the mercy of technology or the moon. The silence is broken, and we become visible and connected in our unique worldview.

Writing this response was, I felt, part of that sharing of the authentic woman's voice by Ms. O'Grady. I was right there with those daydreams, the anticipation, the curiosity, the desire to be heard. The falling into the disappointment and pain at the lack of power, and separateness from Self, peers, and saddest of all, mother. It is so palpable here. I am now living with menopause, and it was enriching to know that a younger woman could make me think so intensely about menses.

Commentator: Patricia Campbell

"Gifts"

What is "pure lust?" I found myself pondering this question as I read for the fifth, the sixth time this magical short story. Magical because of its craftiness, its deceptive intimacy, its tenderness and humour. Magical, too, in that the diaphragm-in-the-drawer works like a charm to prevent the birth of the third child until the right time, the third-time-lucky-time.

What does pure lust mean for a woman? Jouissance — unalloyed pleasure? Not in the 1950s in Tunisia when she worries about unwanted pregnancies. Come to think of it, not in Canada in the 1950s: no "magic" pill as yet, only leaky condoms, and the "rhythm method," which was more a matter of faith than method. Of course, there was always the cap or the diaphragm — clumsy, often uncomfort-able, not sexy. Who can blame the narrator for leaving hers in the drawer?

She has her children in another country, another language. A deliberate lack of context here raising more questions — how did the narrator and her family survive in Germany during the Second World War? What is she doing in Tunisia? How did she come to Canada?

Also absences in the text — her male partners are not present or only present in a fragment of dialogue, a phrase. This allusive/elusive style gives us glimpses, hints of darker currents running underneath. Fear, anger, the loneliness of exile, the writer creating texts in one, two, three languages.

Continuity comes through the mother's gift, a shifty signifier displaced, in the end, by the magic mother of memory and longing as the daughter becomes the mother of a daughter.

Pure lust? No. But much pleasure for the reader.

Commentator: Donna E. Smyth

"The Birth Circle"

The experience of pregnancy and giving birth, seldom described in fiction, is paradoxically intensely personal and universal. It provides a powerful sense of "knowing" identification with all women, everywhere, past and present who have gone through the same ordinary, but always extraordinary, biological experience. I have found women (myself included) eagerly sharing details of their birth experiences, the most intimate and often public of acts, even with strangers, at the slightest provocation. Thus, I was immediately drawn into Louise Holland's story, "The Birth Circle," ready to recall my own experiences as I read about Elizabeth's.

I, too, was unexpectedly pregnant six months after marriage and initially filled with ambivalence — but not about my mother's reaction.

The story, told in the third person but focusing on Elizabeth's point of view, centres on Elizabeth's estrangement from her mother, Margaret.

This estrangement is a source of anguish to Elizabeth. The means to its resolution are unclear to, and feared by, her. "Nothing I do makes her happy," Elizabeth says resignedly, and, later, "I'm tired of trying." Pinned to Elizabeth are all the thwarted plans, hopes and desires of her embittered, divorced mother. In turn, Elizabeth is starving for her mother's love and approval. Mother and daughter are locked in a pattern of mutually unhappy disconnectedness. When Elizabeth finally announces her pregnancy to Margaret, the only potential grandparent, the mother is predictably reproachful.

Towards the end of the pregnancy, at the point when a new life (new possibilities) is about to demand its emergence, the connection between mother and daughter-about-to-be-mother suddenly begins to be restored. Mother has brought Elizabeth a christening gown made by Margaret's mother for Elizabeth, but never worn. The gown intended for Elizabeth has been quietly kept all these years and Elizabeth, in a moment of epiphany, realizes that her mother's love was also "intended" for her, if not quite delivered. By moving back into ancestral memory and forward into regenerative hope threaded by shared experience (the primal experience of birth and physical nurturing), the fissures in the mother/daughter relationship can be healed. Grandma Emily "stopped their arguing"; daughter/granddaughter Emily has unwittingly done the same.

The role of the midwife as mediator, while not developed in the story, is also suggestive of recovery. Emotionally absent at her own daughter's birth (probably anesthetized too), Margaret is inadvertently present at her granddaughter's. Thus she can reclaim the whole experience in a positive way. For Elizabeth, the birthing and nursing of her first child has become a source of empowerment and mystery, enhanced by the fact that she "took charge" of the birth, engaging a midwife at home rather than submitting to the indifferent authority of hospital space and personnel.

The circle is the recurring motif made explicit at the opening. The reader is told that, "The darkness encircled and cloaked them, this circle of nurturing and birth, a link in the eternal chain of life that imprisons and gives freedom to us all." The circle is an old and still potent symbol of wholeness and completion; of unity or a return to unity from multiplicity; of cycle, repetition and continuity.

This symbol is effectively used by Holland in various ways. First, the narrative structure of the story itself is circular, beginning and ending with a description of the new mother suckling her newborn, in awe and amazement. Second, images of roundness abound: the pregnant belly, the birth passage, the globular breasts, the fragile sphere of the baby's head. Holland also conveys the interchangeableness of images and roles in such lines as, "Feeling smothered, Elizabeth sucked at the air heavily, gasping for approval," as a nursing baby can feel smothered by a bursting breast. And, as she labours, mother becomes baby: "Immersed in the wave of birth-force, surroundings become blurred by the emerging and receding roar. Swallowed in a corridor of blackness ... " In name, baby becomes great-grandmother; naming the possibility of rapprochement.

Finally, Holland employs the motif of the circle as she sets up the protagonist's experience of self-transcendence. She and her mother come to recognize the larger chain of which they are links — each of which, while unique, is the same shape as the ones before and after, and which, like every other link, is necessary for the integrity of the whole.

Birth "is the rhythmic participation in an order that transcends and embraces the human. It is the common denominator of being human. It reaches behind meaning into unspeaking sensuous life. It overcomes the false dichotomy between the physical and the spiritual" [1] and allows no place for alienation.

Note

1. Inglis, Laura L. and Peter K. Steinfeld, "Birth Space: Feminist Pedagogy and Maiieutics, " unpublished paper, 1986, p.11.

Commentator: Anne M. Pearson

"The Spirit of a World without Spirit"

I am simultaneously attracted to and frightened by the aloneness of this woman. Late at night, without anyone to help, death is with her three times over. There is her own death, heralded by signs of cancer in inconclusive hospital tests. There is this month the anniversary of her mother's death, still recent enough to deny. And there is this day her daughter's death, a stillbirth unmourned. Her husband is in some far-off land; her young son is asleep. Unable to sleep herself, she undertakes a vigil. On account of her vigil the spirits come to her. Her vigil is the writing of the story we are reading.

In my first reading of "The Spirit of a World without Spirit," I was struck less by the things that are spiritual resources for the narrator and more by the things that are not. Her husband is too far away, his voice too distant to comfort her. Her son is asleep and when he is awake, he clings to her, her impatience reminding her that she is not a Good Mother. The Roman Catholic Church, which she forswore when sixteen, provides some uncomfortable yet nourishing memories (first communion, first confession, "holy cards instead of gold stars"), but little by way of "spirit" that she can pass on to her son. Her memories of Ave Maria cannot speak to his singing of "the national anthem with new words." God remains "unapproachable," the driver of a commuter train on a narrow track with only scheduled stops, "enclosed in glass and steel."

It should be, she knows, her ancestors who come to offer support — the spirit-memories of her father's French mother and Iroquois father. "Their selves are surfacing and they identify themselves in my speech, mannerisms, instinctual memories." But there is something wrong. The words do not "flow and flow" from her as usual. Her expectations are blocked by her inability to connect with her

French and Iroquois roots — a legacy of her father's decision to assimilate the family coupled with the racism of the hegemonic society. Thus while the "golden age of childhood" is supposed to ground and energize the odyssey for the ethnic writer, this writer's childhood is so painful she seldom talks of it. Despite this, the memories begin to come, and thus it is we learn that some of the spirits who come to her bring distress rather than aid.

It is her male ancestors who are useless ... or worse. Her memories of her father are mixed. The most vivid father-memory that she shares with us, however, is one of violence. Nearly at the top of the CN Tower, axis mundi of anglophone Canada, her father — laughing, nasty — shoves her against the green plexiglas window. Knowing that he was sexually abused by priests at residential school does little to heal the wounds caused by this violence, and it suggests more secret abuse. The effects of this violent encounter remain with the narrator.

Her father's father is more difficult to understand. I expected him to be the wise Indian elder, dispensing pithy sayings to his granddaughter at his knee. He is not. She remembers him as unable or unwilling to help her grandmother, either with running the small store that was their livelihood or with child care. When he appears in her memories in his armchair telling stories, he seems improbable: arrayed in full headdress, an inauthentic (Plains) get-up for an Iroquois, telling an Inuit story. The story — the one in which Sedna becomes the guardian of the undersea animals — turns on a father's violence towards his daughter. He pushed her out of the boat, and, as "[s]he clung desperately to the side of the boat, ... her father hacked off her fingers." This "secret" story implicates the grandfather in the pattern of violence against women that his granddaughter experiences in the CN Tower. It is not to her male ancestors that she can turn as she faces death on her lonely vigil.

How does she make it through the night? How was the spirit passed on to the narrator? It was passed. By the end of her first night (and her story) she says that the words flow from her like blood. Something has changed; something is different. For one thing she has confronted some of the violence of her past. But she has not done this alone. Her memories of her father's mother — who gave herself to family as she never can, who had a depth of faith she cannot know, who died courageously, barricaded away from the life-prolonging techniques of modern medicine of uterine cancer in a way she never will — these memories somehow sustain her. Against cool logic, these memories are the passing of spirit she wants so much. She mourns her grandmother and through her is able to see the budding male dominance of her son and is able to grieve the death of her daughter. The healing is small, but the vigil is not over; this is only night number one.

Commentator: Thom Parkhill

"What She Remembered and What She Forgot"

I found this an incredibly powerful story. A woman writing in the present (and the present tense) is recreating in her journal the abuse she suffered as a child. Her writing is prescribed by primal therapy, "the therapy of last resort because it is so painful." Reclaiming these memories gives the writer the tools for the reclamation of her lost self.

But to state baldly the "facts" of this story, its process and purpose, is to recess the impact. First, there are the three voices: a third-person narrator whose comments provide setting and voice-over for the work as a whole; Joanna the journal-writer, whose memories these are; and a third voice, which becomes increasingly confident as the narration continues. This is the lost voice of the child who was there, the abused one erased from the story by the grown Joanna.

Joanna's memories set up the dichotomies of abuse, rather the way the happy family paradigm works to eclipse its darker side. There are two parallel worlds inhabited by the young Joanna. One is the world of normality, structured around the day church with Reverend Tanner and Sunday School, angels and nice ladies. Then there is night church with the crooked cross and the pentangle, people with hidden faces, darkness and dead animals. This scene is dominated by Hern the Hunter, the terrible father who creates and kills, and whose power is terrifying. There is no life beyond this father. In the adult Joanna's memories, the child she was becomes The Spook banished from the memories of the adult and daylight world. It is this spook who haunts the text, from whose dark and recessed place Joanna's memories eventually emerge. This return of the repressed child brings with it recollections of the forgotten mother, long dead of cruelty and cancer, who was powerless to protect her children, though she tried. When Joanna's memory resurfaces as the mother-light and energy behind a painted false God, it is a testament to the efficacy of the healing process.

What makes this text so relevant is its concept of the way in which patriarchy works to reinforce only the safe childhood memories. The abused child Joanna is also daddy's priestess, his good little girl. That the priestess participates in Satanic rituals only alluded to makes its attraction all the more horrifying. The banished child, The Spook, labours for years to break through the priestess/princess paradigm, so powerful in our culture is this stereotype of the good daughter whose worth is measured by her loyalty to the father. Joanna's childhood is informed by fairy tales; her life structured within a Walt Disney world of good fairies and good children, like the child Shirley Temple, whom she resembles.

When the banished spook self breaks through, she represents not only triumph for the journal-writer, who is healing, but also victory over the false representations of childhood in which our culture encourages us to believe. Joanna's personal triumph is a triumph of the female spirit over false images. Her story represents a willingness to engage in re/writing the myths of patriarchal culture for the sake of our children and our selves. The voices of these newly formed and darker selves are thus given a place in language, our most powerful signifying system. This story, then, represents another way of assessing the mother/Goddess, through returning the voice of one of her lost children.

Commentator: Lorna Drew

"Black Moon"

"Black Moon," by Hélène Turcotte, deals with the relationship between a desire for death and the unhappy childhood of the narrator, on one hand, and, on the other, with the narrator's mother, who oppresses her out of a need to rid herself of her feelings of guilt in any way possible. The author introduces the image of the Goddess as a reference point in the journey towards female self-actualization and an affirmation of life. The story is well paced and well structured in its progression and in its selection of images.

From the beginning, we are struck by the way the idea of death has taken hold of the narrator: "Death, becoming obsessive, continues to follow me, crossing the street, lurking in the shower ... I have wanted to die for a long time." But we do not understand the source of death's power over her until later in the story. Later, we learn that the narrator has bitter memories of her childhood, and that her self-actualization was incomplete in childhood. Finally, we discover that her desire to die originates in the stifling influence of her mother who, wanting to be forgiven for the fact that she did not want a child when conception took place, ends up asphyxiating her daughter's personality and life. This might be called a "psychological infanticide." But who is ultimately the guilty party in this situation? We cannot point our fingers at the mother as being solely responsible. The intense feelings of guilt did not arise from nowhere, but rather from a patriarchal society which cannot accept that a woman might wish to contravene the "maternal instinct" which supposedly characterizes all women and which cannot, by any sort of analogy, be transposed to a man. It is in patriarchy, functioning as a system of psychological, social and cultural oppression of women, that the fundamental explanation of psychological infanticide lies. The way to be, to think and to act are defined by and for men in patriarchal society: it is the Man-ner of being that is condoned. Social models and roles, imposed by the patriarchy, are responsible not only for psychological infanticide, but also for gynocide or the genocide of women and for female antifeminism; cf. Mary Daly, *Gyn/Ecology: The Metaethics of Radical Feminism*, Boston: Beacon Press, 1978.

The narrator sees Claude as a model of masculinity better suited to her needs. He possessed both feminine gentleness and masculine aggression. But the aggressivity dominates over the gentleness in case of doubt. This is an *androgynous* model. The narrator does not develop a feminine model of this "hybrid culture" (gentleness-aggressiveness), which would be *gynandry*, in which gentleness would take precedence over aggressiveness. Furthermore, the narrator insists on the existence of a Goddess situated inside her feminine self, figuring in women's collective unconscious, as an archetype. The Goddess is the "Great ... of life and death." The narrator attributes a sacred power or "mana" to human existence. In this sense, the Goddess is the source of all spirituality. She is the neglected origin of all religions. So, could we not say that all patriarchal religions (Christianity, Judaism, Islam, etc.) have often been afflicted with this patriarchal tendency when they refuse to acknowledge the sacred powers of women and of the Goddess, because such acknowledgement would be unacceptable historically, culturally and socially? Monotheistic religions are not the only patriarchal religions. Polytheistic religions, while allowing for the existence of goddesses, are often equally patriarchal in their contents and practices. Allowing a goddess into the procession of gods who decide human destiny is an effort to suppress systematically the feminist revolution by granting some heavenly seats to women, and by allocating to them a token place in a religion dominated by men. This is a means of appropriating liberation movements which address the needs not only of women but also of other socially and culturally oppressed groups. However, what distinguishes sexism (like racism, for that matter) is the way that oppression attacks that person in that her or his sex or race makes that person interchangeable with any other member of the group. Sexism and racism are also based on an intentional and systematic misunderstanding of an individual's alienation: "Woman," in the singular and with a capital W, does not exist. Women exist, but without any model or social role that can be imposed on all women any more than it could be on all men; no such model is part of women's nature. Men's and women's roles are cultural and social constructions rather than "esoteric" projections of the fundamental nature of the sexes. There is only a single human being, with physical and psychological differences whose cultural origins we have yet to uncover. A dualist anthropology (which foregrounds distinct masculine and feminine natures), supporting the idea of gender-specific tasks, is not scientifically defensible. The narrator understands anthropology in a more appropriate manner, for she chooses a universal conception of human beings, where each man and woman can develop his or her own resources to be, to think, and to act.

Commentator: Michel Dion

"A Day in the Life of a Warrior, or Safe in the Body of Goddess"

The title of this powerful and disturbing story tells its theme: a woman's fight against the forces of division and ambivalence and her realization that she can be safe in the body of "Goddess."

Adult Laura, who has, through pain and trial, made herself into a warrior-hero, descends into the depths of her own fearsome past to rescue, give birth to, "little ell," her "childbody." As a result of incest and sexual abuse, little ell may be dead, disintegrated. In response to what her father was doing to her, the being that became Laura split from little ell's battered body and damaged spirit and subsequently "hovered over reality, separate, safe." Actually, however, Laura, holding herself "untouched, untouching, untouch-able," has been living a life haunted by unexplained horrors. Laura is aware that within herself she has beings whom she calls Savage, Retard, and Dead; eventually, the agony of this "fractured self" forces her to remember and rebirth little ell. In the process Laura rediscovers yet another part of her self, Goddess, whom little ell had known and loved "when she herself was pure goddess." From then on, Goddess serves as her ally, and to realize herself as goddess becomes Laura's goal, though she is acutely aware that it is impossible for "a divided woman" to "become goddess."

An inner monologue of self-analysis, Laura's account of her descent/ascent uses recurring metaphors, through which Laura begins to reconcile the divisions and ambivalences that have plagued her since little ell's "murder." Night and blackness are both safe and dangerous, as are the caverns of sea and earth she has to plumb. Birds also indicate Laura's progress as they change from protective predators to gentler flyers. Above all, the sea surrounds and transforms the psychological action. Laura's pilgrimages to the ocean after her visits to the sacred and wretched pool of her psyche cleanse and bless her for further forays. The way in which the writer has used the sea in this story is reminiscent of Kate Chopin's use of the sea in "The Awakening," but here the sea is Goddess, giver of safety that is necessary to life.

Through her expert handling of metaphor, the author signals that the story means more even than the heroine-quest, the harrowing and inspiring rescue/rebirth of little ell from disintegration as a result of male violence and abuse. She clearly demonstrates that the real enemy, the Original Sin, is the force that divides and disintegrates: "division itself is the only evil." The binary thinking of our patriarchal world with its oppositions and dichotomies has successfully divided women from each other and, above all, from ourselves. In her remembering, Laura draws spiritual strength from other women's stories, her woman friend Andrea, and, after she rediscovers her, Goddess. Thus, this story is a powerful, feminist testimony to a valiant and winning battle against these forces that divide in order to rule. It is not all surprising, then, that Laura's primary support should prove to be Goddess, she who first manifests herself to Laura as Mary, "the ocean that embraces all the continents." By the end Goddess is not only all of nature, but wholeness and unity, "that which is greater even than disintegration."

Commentator: Johanna H. Stuckey

The Poems

Di Brandt, Elizabeth Brewster, Lorna Crozier, Travis Lane, Carol Rose, Gail Taylor. These poets were obviously not chosen to illustrate a particular tendency.

But if anthologists believe they have the power and the knowledge to select representative works, to design a pseudoscientific sample of "Canadian women's poetry" or "contemporary writing," they are, of course, working under misguided notions. On the other hand, Colin and I went to the poets more often than the poets came to us; more than half of the poems were previously published elsewhere. So they are hardly a random sample, either. It would be more accurate to say that many of the poems here are works that we had the happy fortune of happening across, and all are texts that I have somehow carried with me since my first reading.

Being a comparatist, however, my *déformation professionnelle* is such that I like to find patterns, and there are, indeed, commonalities among these poems. All revolve around the task of situating women in the world. While this is far from being an unusual theme in literature, these poems suggest that there is a distinctive common ground for women artists.

We all know what patriarchy looks like; often it seems that that is all there is, as far as the eye can see. But, of course, it is simply a question of perspective. When "you stand alone / at the world's edge," as Di Brandt writes, "the air is full of messages," in the plural, to be made sense of. Although Brandt may be addressing "you," the (woman) reader, here, it seems more likely that there is a distancing taking place, as though an outsider is introduced into the landscape to observe the observer.

However, the frequent use of "I" or "we" in other poems is both interesting and significant, and reinforces the importance of the subject's voice and point of view. Far from standing outside a ritual borrowed from another culture, Travis Lane finds that "the fire smudge centers us." The "I" or "we" is whole: "It was as if one spirit leaped." In contrast, the outside world is divided or divisive, full of walls and barriers: the "cloud / that lion-tawny crept toward us, / ... divided us ... / as absolute as that clear wall." This is not to say, though, that disparate objects cannot be brought together by the subject. Elizabeth Brewster introduces herself immediately into the poem: "I find consolation in both" the bible and the Tarot pack, merging Judeo-Christian images with those of another belief system to which many New Age feminists have recently turned. In Carol Rose's "hallel," the poet, unlike, some of the women wailing at the wall, is not tongue-tied; her right hand is not withered. She can speak and write. But even the wailing has double meaning; wailing is the opposite of silence, the female noise of labour and birthing, lamentation and praise.

In Gail Taylor's poems, art is clearly an act of faith and complaint against harsh world, the bees and mosquitoes, or frostbite, the "two pests / [that] Come never together" but alternate to make both young Eric and Ivaluartjuk, an Arctic singer/storyteller, miserable much of the year. Writers and artists deliver a message of unity here: "It is I." In "Thee," the forest similarly speaks for itself:

This is a forest: this
is not arable   land that
you may use,

    once razed,   to support
    your elaborate
    domestic arrangements.

The loggers are like the builders of "the father's house," laying foundations upon dead women's bodies, raped land, epitomizing male destruction. The men dismember trees, but the forest remembers. The spirit of the goddess flees to take refuge in their trunks as the patriarchal god is establishing his dominion, "sacrificing mercy in return for power / to raven   after   her." Women's spirits grounded in earth, rooted, aware "that bounty   comes / from underground." Women are still there, "unsettling the land": a beautifully evocative description of women's place in the patriarchal landscape.

     Images of shifting soil, of flowing water, of movement and flight, are found in several poems. Carol Rose speaks of a different conception of power, like that of grandmother-based cultures or the talking cure, with stories providing individual guidance as well as a basis for community. This is a world ruled by "lore / instead of / law." Rules sprout "butterfly / wings / moist / and full / of light"; nothing is fixed or solid. Lorna Crozier, trying to situate her self in the creation story, is attracted by the "wet, salty body" plucked up by the swan or on a dolphin's back; not the "thin, dry rib / white and bare as if chewed and sucked / by a small dog." The story of the prototypical couple of Adam and Eve, the basis for the gender polarization underlying patriarchy, is rewritten. Erotic love is once more associated with creation, rather than destruction: "We dreamed each other / at the same time and we dreamed a garden." The artist is creating a new creation story: "This is a story I could believe."

     Elizabeth Brewster's weaned child parallels women in patriarchal society, out of place, her undernourished soul taking "whatever food it finds / or bitter brew," but still remembering, dreaming always of a "land overflowing / with [the] milk and honey" of the mother's breast. The old women suggest using wormwood to make the fussing, sobbing child "turn away, / drink water, eat bread / as he was supposed to." Once again speaking from and for her self, however, the poet introduces her own mother, who "never did that. / Her breasts were never bitter."

     Like Lorna Crozier, Elizabeth Brewster has revised the story of women, of mothers, in patriarchy, returning them to that land of milk and honey we once knew, and carry in our bodies, always. It is impossible not to be struck by the affirmative language of so many of these works: "This is a forest"; we / stand, well planted"; "I am alive, Ai! / It is / I"; "This Is History"; "This is a story I could believe." A new tale is, indeed, being written; the self is strong and whole.

                                                           Commentary: Jo-Anne Elder

List of Contributors

Marguerite Andersen is a francophone writer, translator, university teacher of French and Women's Studies and Gestalt therapist. In 1971 she edited the Canadian bestseller, *Mother was not a person*. In 1996, her novel, *La Soupe*, obtained the Grand Prix du Salon du livre de Toronto. The same year, her critically acclaimed play, *Christiane: Stations in a Painter's Life*, based on the painter Christiane Pflug, was produced by Factory Theatre Café.

Gisele Marie Baxter is a writer and academic who is currently living in Halifax and teaching in the Department of English at Dalhousie University.

Sylvia Bowerbank teaches in the Arts and Science Programme at McMaster University and has published widely on British literature. Her interests include many areas of women's studies, including women's writing and gender issues.

Di Brandt is a Winnipeg poet who grew up in a Mennonite village in Manitoba. She has received wide recognition for *questions I asked my mother* (1987) and *Agnes in the sky*, published by Turnstone Press in 1990, from which this poem is taken.

Beth Brant is a Bay of Quinte Mohawk from Tyendinaga Mohawk Territory in Ontario. She is the editor of *A Gathering of Spirit*, a collection of writings and artwork by Native women (Firebrand Books and Women's Press, 1988), the author of *Mohawk Trail, Food and Spirits*, short fiction, *Writing as Witness*, essays, *I'll Sing Til the Day I Die: Conversations with Tyendinaga Elders* and more than 70 publications. She is a mother and grandmother and lives with her partner of twenty years, Denise Dorsz.

Alan D. Bulley is a PhD candidate in Theology at Saint Paul University, Ottawa. His research interests include Greco-Roman rhetoric, early Christianity, and Second Temple Judaism.

Elizabeth Brewster was born in New Brunswick and now lives in Saskatchewan, where she taught English at the University of Saskatchewan for many years. Since her *East Coast*, in 1951, she has published more than a dozen collections of poetry, as well as some novels and short story collections. The poems reprinted here appeared in *Spring Again*, her thirteenth book of poetry (Oberon, 1990).

Anne Ricard Burke is the literary editor of *The Prairie Journal of Canadian Literature* and has contributed poetry, drama, stories, essays and reviews to such venues as *Poetry Canada, Cross-Canada Writers' Quarterly* (now *paragraph*), the Calgary Women's Writing Project, *Speaking in the Enemy's Language* (Joy Harjo, ed.) and *Places of the Heart* (Don Bailey and Daile Ulruh, ed.), *Prairie Fire, Prism International, The Annotated Bibliography of Canada's Major Authors* (ECW Press), *Canadian Poetry* and the womanstrength Alberta festival.

Patricia Campbell lives in Fredericton, NB, where she is a much-appreciated member of a vibrant community of artistic women. She is a photographer, and her recent work has focused on women throughout the life-cycle.

Donna Caruso is a 47-year-old single parent from Saskatchewan, the mother of Jason and Elliot Hicks. She has worked in the arts since 1980, performing as a singer and comedian and writing for radio, stage and television. Her work has been broadcast on the CBC, national and provincial, including *Morningside, Gabereaux* and *Between the Covers*, performed at the Saskatoon Fringe Festival, and published in *Prairie Fire, NeWest Review*, and the anthologies *Out of Place* and *Studio One*. And yes, Enrico is her uncle.

Ann Copeland has recently published her sixth collection of fiction, *A Season of Apples* (Goose Lane, 1996) and a book on the art of writing, *ABCs of Fiction Writing* (McGraw-Hill Ryerson, 1996). She is currently living in Salem, Oregon, where she is writer-in-residence at Willamette University and also the first holder of the Hallie Brown Ford Chair in English. Her life in a convent and afterwards formed the basis of such works as *At Peace, The Golden Thread* and *Strange Bodies on a Stranger Shore*.

Lorraine Coyle is a New Brunswick writer, who has, for the past 35 years, lived closer to the Irish culture than the Acadian from which she is descended, but always with a yearning for a more open and universal society. She has published articles as well as a short story in *Shout and Speak Out Loud* (J. Blades and M. McLeod, eds., Wild East) and is working on a novel.

Lorna Crozier was born in 1948 in Swift Current, SK. Her books include *No Longer Two People*, with Patrick Lane (1981), *Humans and Other Beasts* (1980), *The Weather* (1984) and *The Garden Going On Without Us* (McClelland and Stewart, 1985), from which this selection is reprinted.

Pamela Dickey Young teaches at Queen's Theological College in Kingston, ON. She is a scholar in the field of women and religion and editor of the journal *Studies in Religion*.

Michel Dion is associate professor in the Faculty of Theology, Ethics and Philosophy at the Université de Sherbrooke in Sherbrooke, QC. His research interests include business ethics, government ethics, peace studies, feminist studies and cultural theology. In 1995, he published a book on Mary Daly and Paul Tillich (*Libération féministe et salut chrétien*, Montreal: Bellarmin, 1995).

Lorna Drew lives in Fredericton, NB. She is a poet, a feminist community worker, cultural animator and a member of the Department of English of the University of New Brunswick, where she completed her PhD.

Jo-Anne Elder is a writer and literary translator whose research focuses on Canadian women writers and the reception of translated texts. Her translations include *Unfinished Dreams: Contemporary Poetry of Acadie* (Goose Lane, 1990), books on Acadian art and history, and poetry in *ellipse*. She writes postcard stories while travelling with Carlos Gomes and their eight children in a custom camper.

Marguerite Evans, RN, PhD, is a clinical ethicist at Sisters of Charity of Ottawa Health Service, a theologian and registered nurse. She has taught bioethics at Saint Paul University, Ottawa, and has worked extensively in psychiatry and chronic care.

Sharon Ferguson-Hood completed her master's degree in Divinity at St. Andrew's College in Saskatoon, was ordained in 1995, and is now doing pastoral ministry with the United Church of Canada. She lives in Kelvington, SK, with her son. Her publications include a poem, "Woman Weaving," a short story, "From Silence to Freedom," and two stories "Until Death Us Do Part" and "The Last Dance" in Carol Morrell and Hilary Clark's forthcoming anthology.

Deborah Fleming is a stained-glass artist, art educator and community organizer. Aside from a brief stay in the West, her home has been in Hubbards, in rural Nova Scotia. *The Illuminated Series*, of which the cover illustration is part, has shown in group and one-person shows in several towns and cities, at informal gatherings, and in postcards available from the artist.

Claudia Gahlinger is a writer and environmental activist living in northside Victoria County, Cape Breton. She has published short stories in *Fireweed, Room of One's Own, Pottersfield Portfolio* and other publications. This story has also been published as a chapbook and in the anthology *Shout and Speak Out Loud* (both by Wild East Publications, 1992) and in *Woman in the Rock*, a collection of short stories (gynergy books, 1993). Claudia is working on her first novel, *The House of Junk*.

Carlos Gomes (Ala-ahuapa) has Aboriginal roots in northern Brazil and Venezuela. He is the father of eight children and grandfather of two. Destined to be a healer and a counsellor, he is a human rights activist, community worker, and a practitioner of holistic therapies, tai chi, yoga, dance, music, drumming, and the visual arts. He has spent most of his life near the Atlantic Ocean.

Melissa Hardy, daughter of activist and novelist William Hardy, has spent many summers on the Qualla Boundary reservation, where her second novel, *Constant*

Fire (Oberon, 1995) is set. In the twenty years after the publication of *A Cry of Bees* (Viking Press, 1970), she completed graduate studies in post-classical history, recovered from Guillian Barré Syndrome, raised three children, won the Journey Prize for "Longman the River" and worked as a business communicator in London, ON. Forthcoming are two novels, *Demon Barrow* (Quarry Press) and *Broken Road and The Drifts*, a story cycle.

Louise Holland is a mother of three, a social worker, and a writer who resides in Northern BC. The publication of "The Birth Circle" will coincide with the unforeseen birth of her fourth child.

Janina Hornosty lives with her husband and son in Nanaimo, BC. She teaches in the Liberal Studies and English Departments at Malaspina University College. She has published short stories in *Event, Prism International, Canadian Fiction Magazine*, and *Best Canadian Stories* ('89 and '94). A collection of her short stories, *Snackers*, will be published soon by Oolichan.

Joyce Howe has taught English since 1958 while mothering a family and learning to write. She is currently editing her journals and beginning a book about her life in a cult family.

Martine Jacquot is a writer based in the Annapolis Valley, NS. She writes poetry, short stories, novels, and essays, and has published nine books so far. Her poetry collection, *Cet autre espace,* as well as her book, *Duras ou le regard absolu,* are scheduled for publication in 1997. She gives writing workshops and lectures on literature on a regular basis.

William Closson James, a professor of Religious Studies at Queen's University, Kingston, ON, earned his doctorate in Religion and Literature (Chicago, 1974). He has written on religious aspects of Canadian literature, native peoples, and the academic study of religion. His forthcoming book, *Locations of the Sacred*, will be published by Wilfrid Laurier University Press.

Morny Joy is associate professor in Religious Studies at the University of Calgary. Her recent publications include "Feminism and the Self," (Psychology and Theory 3/3 [1993]) and "God and Gender: Some Reflections on Women's Explorations of the Divine," in *Religion and Gender* (Blackwells, 1994). Morny has also co-edited (with Eva Dargyay) *Gender, Genre and Religion* (Wilfrid Laurier University Press, 1995). She is past president of the Canadian Society for the Study of Religion.

Susan Kerslake is a Halifax writer who has published two novels, *Middlewatch* (Oberon, 1976) and *Penumbra* (Aya Press, 1984) and two collections of short stories, *Blind Date* (Pottersfield Press, 1989) and *Book of Fears* (Ragweed Press,

1984) which was nominated for a Governor General's Award. Her fiction and poetry have appeared in many magazines and anthologies.

Maya Khankhoje was born in Mexico to an Indian father and a Belgian mother, and has travelled extensively. Her published material includes fiction, poetry, articles and reviews in *Montreal Serai, Shakti, inter alia, vice versa, New Canadian Review, Harper's* and *diva*, and in such anthologies as *Aurat Durbar: The Court of Women and Frictions*. She has won the Quetzalcóatl Prize as well as prizes in other international contests.

Kay Koppedrayer has been teaching in the Department of Religion and Culture at Wilfrid Laurier University since 1987. Her publications include work on medieval South Indian religious institutions, studies of women's biographical and autobiographical material, ritual aspects of traditional archery, and Gandhian studies. Recently her research interests have turned to Native/non-Native relations in North America, and she is working on a volume that explores the participation of non-Native Vietnam veterans in the Lakota sundance.

Travis Lane lives in Fredericton, NB, where she is an honorary research associate with the Department of English at the University of New Brunswick. Her most recent books are *Temporary Shelter* (Goose Lane) and *Night Physics* (Brick). *Divinations*, from which this poem is taken, won the Pat Lowther prize in 1980.

Ingrid MacDonald is the author of *Catherine, Catherine* (Women's Press, 1991), several short stories variously published, and a play, *The Catherine Wheel*, which has been produced in Toronto and Chicago. Ingrid lives in Toronto where she works as a writer and illustrator.

Margaret McLeod is a writer and editor from Fredericton, NB, where she belongs to a number of boards, committees, and cultural and community organizations. She has been editor of *Pottersfield Portfolio* and co-editor of *Shout and Speak Out Loud* (Wild East Publishing Co-Op). Her poetry and fiction have been published in literary magazines across Canada.

Colin O'Connell is a former professor of religious studies and has published widely in western religious thought. He has also served as a commentator with the Canadian and Australian Broadcasting Corporations. He recently co-authored *Liberal Education and Value Relativism*. Currently, he serves in Ottawa as associate editor of *The Focus Report*.

Kathleen O'Grady is a doctoral student at Cambridge University in the UK, where she is completing a dissertation on the linguistic philosophy of Julia Kristeva. She has published articles on Kristeva, Cixous, Irigaray and others, and is co-editing *A Sweet Secret: Telling the Story of Menstruation* (forthcoming from Second Story Press).

Thom Parkhill, trained in Hindu religious history, now researches the study of Native American religions and teaches in the Department of Religious Studies at St. Thomas University in Fredericton, NB. His latest publication is *Weaving Ourselves into the Land: Charles Leland, the "Indian" and the Study of Native American Religions* (SUNY, 1997).

Anne M. Pearson has a PhD in Religious Studies from McMaster University. She has recently published *Because it Gives Me Peace of Mind* (New York: SUNY Press, 1996). She is the mother of three daughters and lives in Dundas, ON.

Liza Potvin speaks four languages and reads ten. Her PhD thesis (from McMaster) was on "Women's Spirituality and English Canadian Poetry," and she now teaches at Malaspina University College in Nanaimo. Her publications include scholarly articles, reviews, short stories in *The Malahat Review* and poetry in *Contemporary Verse II* and *A Room of One's Own* and *White Lies (for my mother)* (NeWest Press, 1992), for which she was awarded three prizes.

Carol Rose has published widely, including articles in *Healing Voices: Feminist Approaches to Therapy with Women* and *Living the Changes* (Joan Turner, ed., Turnstone Press with whom she is co-editor of *Spider Women,* an anthology); poetry in *Vintage '96* (as a finalist in the League of Canadian Poets competition), *Prairie Fire, Celebrating the New Moon: a Rosh Chodesh Anthology, Quarry Magazine, Parchment Magazine,* etc. Her poetry manuscript, *Behind the Blue Gate,* is forthcoming from Beach Holme Publishers, Vancouver.

Gloria Sawai lives in Edmonton, AB, and is a writer of short stories and plays. Her stories have been published in numerous anthologies. "The Day I Sat With Jesus..." has been recently translated into Japanese and published in Tokyo, and has also been published in Denmark, the US, and England.

Jamie S. Scott received his PhD in Religion and Literature from the Divinity School of the University of Chicago. He is the editor of, and a contributor to, *And the Birds Began to Sing: Religion and Literature in Post Colonial Cultures* (Rodopi, 1996) and author of *Christians and Tyrants: The Prison Testimonies of Boethius, Thomas Moore and Dietrich Bonhoeffer* (Peter Lang, 1995). He has also published essays on various topics in religion and literature and geography and religion in scholarly journals and periodicals. He teaches English and Geography in the Division of Humanities at York University.

Donna E. Smyth lives on an old farm in Hants County, NS. Her other writings include: *Subversive Elements* (a novel) and numerous short stories and poems as well as *Giant Anna* (a puppet play for children) and *Loyalist Runaway* (a young adult novel). She is the co-author of *No Place Like Home* (a collection of diaries and letters of Nova Scotia women). She teaches English and Creative Writing at Acadia University, Wolfville.

Johanna Stuckey, PhD Yale, University Professor Emerita in Women's Studies and Religious Studies at York University in Toronto, still teaches courses in her field of specialization, Goddess worship and female spirituality, at York and at the School of Continuing Studies, University of Toronto. She was a member of the Guest Editorial Board of *Canadian Woman Studies / les cahiers de la femme* for their recent issue on "Female Spirituality," and is working on a book tentatively entitled *Goddesses and Dying Gods in the Ancient Eastern Mediterranean.*

William Sweet is associate professor of Philosophy at St. Francis Xavier University in Antigonish, NS. He is the author of *Idealism and Rights* (1996) and of some 50 articles, principally in the philosophy of religion and in British idealism. He is editor of the journal *Maritain Studies / Etudes maritainiennes* and of several collections: *The Bases of Ethics* (1997), *Religion, Modernity and Post Modernity* (1997), and *La philosophie de la religion à la fin du vingtième siècle* (1993).

Gail Taylor is a professional writer, editor, curriculum designer, and adult educator specializing in English language studies in Fredericton. She has contributed to *1993: A Woman's Almanac: Voices from Atlantic Canada, Human Studies, The Atlantic Anthology* (Ragweed Press, 1985), *The New Brunswick Reader, Contemporary Verse 2,* and the film *Fred Cogswell* (TVO/Access Alberta, 1984).

Hélène Turcotte has written a collection of short stories, *Les Passantes*, for her master's degree in creative writing from Laval. Her PhD thesis is a study of women journalists and writers in Québec from 1885-1925. She has published stories and articles in *la Parole Métèque and L'écrit Primal.*

Christl Verduyn holds a PhD in French Studies from the University of Ottawa and teaches Women's Studies and Canadian Studies at Trent University in Peterborough, ON. She has published extensively on anglophone and francophone women writers in Canada, including Margaret Laurence, Marian Engel, and Québec immigrant writers.

Source Notes

The following poems and stories have appeared in other collections and magazines:

Di Brandt
> "already there is no going back," copyright Di Brandt, reprinted, by permission, from *Agnes in the Sky* (Winnipeg: Turnstone Press, 1990).

Beth Brant
> "This Is History" has been published in several anthologies and magazines, including her own collection *Food and Spirits* (Firebrand Books and Press Gang), *Akwesasne Notes, River Styx, Woman of Power* and *Clockwatch Review*, and is reprinted here with the permission of the author.

Elizabeth Brewster
> Elizabeth Brewster's "The Weaned Child" and "Parallel Images," in *Spring Again: Poems*. Reprinted with permission by Oberon Press, 499-350 Sparks Street, Ottawa K1R 7S8.

Anne Ricard Burke
> Some of this work appeared in another form in *Prism International* and *Eating Apples*, published by NeWest Press. An excerpt of it was accepted by *Anna's House*. Reprinted with the permission of the author.

Anne Copeland
> Parts of "Through a Glass Darkly" appeared as "My Vision" in *Compass*, July/August 1995 and were broadcast as "Visions" on the CBC National Radio Program *Writers and Company* on March 31, 1991.

Lorna Crozier
> "Mother is Sewing" and "Myths" are reprinted from *The Garden Going On Without Us* (1985, reprinted 1987). Reprinted with the permission of McClelland and Stewart.

Claudia Gahlinger
> Claudia Gahlinger, from *Women in the Rock*. Reprinted with the kind permission of the publisher, gynergy books, P.O. Box 2023, Charlottetown, PEI, C1A 7N7. Also published in the Salamanca Series and in the anthology *Shout and Speak Out Loud* by Wild East Publishing Cooperative.

Melissa Hardy
> "Discriminatio Spirituum," by Melissa Hardy, published in *Quarry* vol. 40 no. 3 (Summer 91). Reprinted with the permission of the author and Acacia House Publishing Services.

Martine Jacquot
> The French version of "Ebène et ivoire" was published in Martine Jacquot's collection *Sables mouvants* (Grand-Pré, NS: Editions du Grand-Pré, 1994). The translation is by Jacquot and her students.

Susan Kerslake
> "Margaret's Dreams," in *Blind Date* (Porters Lake, NS: Pottersfield Press, 1989). Reprinted with the permission of the author.

Travis Lane
> Travis Lane's "Last Picnic," in *Divinations and Shorter Poems* 1973-1978, published by Fiddlehead Poetry Books and available through Goose Lane Editions. Reprinted with the permission of the author.

Carol Rose
> "hallel" was published in *The Jewish Women's Literary Annual*, 1995, and in *Celebrating the Moon: A Rosh Chodesh Anthology*, Susan Barrin, ed. (New York: Josh Aronson Publishers, 1996). All poems are forthcoming in *Jerusalem: Another Version of the Story* (Victoria, BC: Beach Holme Publishers Ltd., 1997).

Gloria Sawai
> Reprinted with the permission of the author.

Hélène Turcotte
> The translation is by Uta Doerr.

Selected Bibliography

Women — Christianity and Judaism

Alfaro, Juan. "The Mariology of the Fourth Gospel and the Struggles for Liberation." *Biblical Theology Bulletin* (1980).

Bertell, Rosalie. "Humanity at Risk." *Canadian Catholic Review* (1984).

Carmody, Denise Lardner. *Feminism and Christianity: A Two-Way Reflection.* Nashville: Abingdon, 1982.

Daly, Mary. *The Church and the Second Sex.* New York and Evanston: Harper & Row, 1968.

Doely, Sarah Bentley, ed. *Women's Liberation and the Church.* New York: Association Press, 1970.

Declaration on the Question of the Admission of Women to the Ministerial Priesthood. Vatican City, 1976.

Fischer, James A. *God Said: Let There Be Woman.* New York: Alba House, 1979.

Gilman, Charlotte Perkins. *His Religion and Hers: A Study of the Faith of Our Fathers and the Work of Our Mothers.* Westport: Hyperion Press, 1976 (reprint of 1923 edition).

Heschel, Susannah. *On Being a Jewish Feminist.* New York: Schocken Books, 1983.

Jacobs, Malina. *Beyond Patriarchy: The Images of Family in Jesus.* New York: Paulist Press, 1993.

Maguire, Daniel. "The Feminization of God and Ethics." *Christianity and Crisis,* 42 (1982).

Moltmann-Wendel, Elisabeth. *The Women Around Jesus.* Trans. John Bowden. New York: Crossroad Publishing Co., 1980.

Neu, Diann L., and Mary E. Hunt, eds. *Women-Church Sourcebook.* Silver Spring, MD: WATERworks Press, 1993.

Phillips, John A. *Eve: The History of an Idea.* San Francisco: Harper & Row, 1984.

Ruether, Rosemary Radford. *Contemporary Roman Catholicism: Crises and Challenges.* Kansas City: Sheed and Ward, 1987.

_____. *Mary: The Feminine Face of the Church.* Philadelphia: Westminster Press, 1977.

_____. *New Woman, New Earth: Sexist Ideologies and Human Liberation.* New York: Seabury, 1975.

_____. *Religion and Sexism: Images of Woman in the Jewish and Christian Traditions.* New York: Simon and Schuster, 1974.

Schneider, Susan Weidman. *Jewish and Female: Choices and Changes in Our Lives Today.* New York: Simon and Schuster, 1984.

Schüssler Fiorenza, Elisabeth. *In Memory of Her: A Feminist Theological Reconstruction of Christian Origins.* New York: Crossroad Publishing Co., 1986.

Stanton, Elizabeth Cady. *The Woman's Bible.* New York: Arno Press, 1974 (reprint of 1895 edition).
Wahlherg, R. *Jesus According to a Woman.* New York: Paulist Press, 1975.
Warner, Marina. *Alone of All Her Sex: The Myth and the Cult of the Virgin Mary.* New York: Pocket Books, 1976.

Women — Other Religions

Carmody, Denise Lardner. *Women and World Religions.* Nashville: Abingdon, 1979.
Chen, Ellen M. "Tao as the Great Mother and the Influence of Motherly Love in the Shaping of Chinese Philosophy." *History of Religions,* 14 (1974): 51-64.
Emerson, Ellen R. *Indian Myths: Or, Legends, Traditions, and Symbols of the Aborigines of America Compared with Those of Other Countries including Hindostan, Egypt, Persia, Assyria, and China.* Minneapolis: Ross and Haines, 1965.
Gill, Sam D. *Mother Earth: An American Story.* Chicago: University of Chicago Press, 1987.
Hardesty, Nancy A. *Great Women of Faith.* Nashville: Abingdon, 1980.
Kinsley, David. *Hindu Goddesses: Visions of the Divine Feminine in the Hindu Religious Tradition.* Berkeley: University of California Press, 1986.
_____. *The Goddesses' Mirror: Visions of the Divine from East and West.* Albany: State University of New York Press, 1989.
Sharma, Arvind, ed. *Women in World Religions.* Albany: State University of New York Press, 1987.
Srivastava, M.C.P. *Mother Goddess in Indian Art, Archaeology and Literature.* Delhi: Agam Kala Prakashan, 1979.
Steltenkamp, Michael F. *The Sacred Vision: Native American Religion and Its Practice Today.* New York: Paulist Press, 1982.
Vecsey, Christopher, ed. *Religion in Native North America.* Moscow, ID: University of Idaho Press, 1990.
Ywahoo, Dhyani. *Voices of Our Ancestors.* Boston: Shambhala, 1987.

Goddess Worship, New Age and Neopaganism

Adler, Margot. *Drawing Down the Moon: Witches, Druids, Goddess-Worshippers and Other Pagans in America Today.* New York: Viking, 1979.
Berger, Pamela. *The Goddess Obscured: Transformation of the Grain Protectress from Goddess to Saint.* Boston: Beacon Press, 1985.
Bolen, Jean Shinoda. *Goddesses in Everywoman: A New Psychology of Women.* San Francisco: Harper & Row, 1984.
_____. *Websters' First New Intergalactic Weckedary of the English Language.* Boston: Beacon Press, 1987.

Christ, Carol P. *Laughter of Aphrodite: Reflections on a Journey to the Goddess.* San Francisco: Harper & Row, 1987.

Ehrenreich, Barbara, and Deirdre English. *Witches, Midwives and Nurses.* Old Westbury, New York: The Feminist Press, 1973.

Farber, Thomas. *The Midwife and the Witch.* New Haven: Yale University Press, 1966.

Gimbutas, Marija. *The Language of the Goddess.* San Francisco: Harper & Row, 1989.

Noble, Vicki. *Motherpeace: A Way to the Goddess through Myth, Art and Tarot.* Harper & Row, 1983.

_____. *Shakti Woman: Feeling Our Fire, Healing Our World: The New Female Shamanism.* Harper Collins, 1991.

Perera, Sylvia Brinton. *Descent to the Goddess: A Way of Initiation for Women.* Toronto: Inner City Books, 1981.

Read, Donna, producer. *Goddess Remembered.* Studio D, National Film Board of Canada, 1989.

Starhawk. *The Spiral Dance: A Rebirth of the Ancient Religion of the Great Goddess.* San Francisco: Harper & Row, 1979.

_____. *Truth or Dare.* New York: Harper & Row, 1987.

Stein, Diane. *The Women's Spirituality Book.* St. Paul, MN: Llewellyn Publications, 1995.

Swidler, Arlene, ed. *Sistercelebrations: Nine Worship Experiences.* Philadelphia: Fortress Press, 1974.

Walker, Barbara G. *The Woman's Encyclopedia of Myths and Secrets.* San Francisco: Harper & Row, 1983.

Whitmont, Edward C. *Return of the Goddess.* New York: Crossroad Publishing Co., 1982.

Feminist Spirituality

Alder, Margot. *Drawing Down the Moon: Witches, Druids, Goddess-Worshippers and Other Pagans in America Today.* New York: Viking, 1979.

Anderson, Sherry Ruth, and Patricia Hopkins. *The Feminine Face of God: The Unfolding of the Sacred in Women.* New York: Bantam Books, 1992.

Atkinson, C.W., C.H. Buchanan, and M.R. Miles, eds. *Immaculate and Powerful: The Female in Sacred Image and Social Reality.* Boston: Beacon Press, 1987.

Bolen, Jean Shinoda. *Websters' First New Intergalactic Weckedary of the English Language.* Boston: Beacon Press, 1987.

Carson, Anne, ed. *Feminist Spirituality and the Feminine Divine: An Annotated Bibliography.* Freedom, CA: The Crossing Press, 1985.

_____. *Goddesses & Wise Women. The Literature of Feminist Spirituality 1980 - 1992: An Annotated Bibliography.* Freedom, CA: The Crossing Press, 1992.

Christ, Carol P. *Diving Deep and Surfacing: Women Writers in Spiritual Quest.* Boston: Beacon Press, 1980.

_____, and Judith Plaskow, eds. *Womanspirit Rising: A Feminist Reader in Religion.* San Francisco: Harper & Row, 1979.

Daly, Mary. *Gyn/ecology: Towards a Metaethics of Feminism.* Boston: Beacon Press, 1978.

_____. *Beyond God the Father: Toward a Philosophy of Women's Liberation.* Boston: Beacon Press, 1973.

_____. *The Church and the Second Sex.* New York and Evanston: Harper & Row, 1968.

Daly, Lois K., ed., *Feminist Theological Ethics: A Reader.* Louisville, KY: Westminster John Knox Press, 1994.

Doely, Sarah Bentley, ed. *Women's Liberation and the Church.* New York: Association Press, 1970.

Goldenberg, Naomi R. *Changing of the Gods: Feminism and the End of Traditional Religions.* Boston: Beacon Press, 1979.

Joy, Morny, and Eva K. Neumaier-Dargyay, eds. *Gender, Genre and Religion: Feminist Reflections.* Waterloo, ON: Wilfrid Laurier University Press, 1995.

Hoch-Smith, Judith, and Anita Spring, eds. *Women in Ritual and Symbolic Roles.* New York: Plenum Press, 1978.

Ochs, Carol. *Behind the Sex of God: Toward a New Consciousness Transcending Matriarchy and Patriarchy.* Boston: Beacon Press, 1977.

Ochshorn, Judith. *The Female Experience and the Nature of the Divine.* Bloomington: Indiana University Press, 1981.

Plaskow, Judith, and Carol P. Christ, eds. *Weaving the Visions: New Patterns in Feminist Spirituality.* San Francisco: Harper & Row, 1989.

Porterfield, Amanda. *Feminine Spirituality in America from Sarah Edwards to Martha Graham.* Philadelphia: Temple University Press, 1980.

Rabuzzi, Kathryn Allen. *The Sacred and the Feminine.* New York: Seabury, 1982.

Rosoff, Ilene, ed. *The WomanSource Catalog & Review.* Berkeley, CA: Celestial Arts, 1995.

Snow, Kimberley. *Keys to the Open Gate: A Woman's Spirtuality Sourcebook.* Berkeley, CA: Conari Press, 1994.

Spacks, Patricia Meyer. *The Female Imagination.* New York: Avon, 1976.

Walker, Alice. "In Search of Our Mother's Gardens." *In Working It Out.* Sara Ruddick and Pamela Daniels, eds. New York: Pantheon, 1977.

Feminist Literary Criticism and Women's Writing

Auerbach, Nina. *Communities of Women: An Idea in Fiction.* Cambridge: Harvard University Press, 1978.

Byrne, Lavinia, ed. *The Hidden Tradition: Women's Spiritual Writings Rediscovered.* New York: Crossroad Publishing Co., 1991.

Christ, Carol P. *Diving Deep and Surfacing: Women Writers in Spiritual Quest.* Boston: Beacon Press, 1980.

Davidson, Cathy N., and E. M. Broner, eds. *The Lost Tradition: Mothers and Daughters in Literature.* New York: Ungar, 1980.

Flack, Audrey. *Art and Soul: Notes on Creating.* New York: E.P. Dutton, 1986.

Fryer, Judith. *The Faces of Eve: Woman in the Nineteenth-Century American Novel.* New York: Oxford University Press, 1976.

Gilbert, Sandra, and Susan Gubar. *The Madwoman in the Attic: The Woman Writer and the Nineteenth-Century Imagination.* New Haven: Yale University Press, 1979.

Godard Barbara, ed. *Gynocritics / La Gynocritique: Feminist Approaches to Writing by Canadian and Québécoise Women.* Toronto: ECW Press, 1985.

Olsen, Tillie. *Silences.* New York: Dell Publishing Co., 1989.

Pratt, Annis. *Archetypal Patterns in Women's Fiction.* Bloomington: Indiana University Press, 1981.

Rigney, Barbara Hill. *Madness and Sexual Politics in the Feminist Novel: Studies in Bronte, Woolf, Lessing, and Atwood.* Madison: University of Wisconsin Press, 1978.

Smart, Patricia. *Écrire dans la maison du père: l'émergeance du féminin dans la tradition littéraire au Québec.* Montreal: Québec/Amérique, 1988.

Snow, Kimberley. *Writing Yourself Home: A Woman's Guided Journey of Self-Discovery.* Berkeley, CA: Conari Press, 1992.

Turner, Joan, ed. *Living the Changes.* Winnipeg: University of Manitoba Press, 1990.

Matriarchy and Ancient Goddess Religions

Bachofen, J. *Myth, Religion, and Mother Right.* Trans. Ralph Manheim. Princeton: Princeton University Press, 1954.

Barstow, Anne L. "The Prehistoric Goddess." In Carl Olson, ed., *The Book of the Goddess Past and Present: An Introduction to Her Religion.* New York: Crossroad Publishing Co., 1983.

Berger, Pamela. *The Goddess Obscured: Transformation of the Grain Protectress from Goddess to Saint.* Boston: Beacon Press, 1985.

Bukert, Walter. *Ancient Mystery Cults.* Cambridge: Harvard University Press, 1987.

Campbell, Joseph. *The Masks of God: Primitive Mythology.* New York: Viking Press, 1959.

Fluehr-Lobban, Carolyn. "A Marxist Reappraisal of the Matriarchate." *Current Anthropology* 20 (June 1979): 341-60.

Gimbutas, Marija. *The Language of the Goddess.* San Francisco: Harper & Row, 1989.

_____. *The Goddesses and Gods of Old Europe: Myths and Cult Images.* Berkeley: University of California Press, 1982.

Graves, Robert. *The White Goddess: A Historical Grammar of Poetic Myth*. New York: Farrar, Straus & Giroux, 1966.

Harding, Esther. *Woman's Mysteries, Ancient and Modern*. New York: Bantam, 1973.

Jayne, Walter. *The Healing Gods of Ancient Civilization*. New Haven, CT: Yale University Press, 1925.

Neumann, Erich. *The Great Mother: An Analysis of the Archetype*. Trans. Ralph Manheim. Princeton: Princeton University Press, 1955.

Pearson, Carol. *The Hero Within: Six Archetypes We Live By*. San Francisco: Harper & Row, 1986.

Stone, Merlin, *When God Was a Woman*. New York: Dial Press, 1976.

_____. *The Paradise Papers: The Suppression of Women's Rites*. London: Virago, 1976.

Women and Culture: Women and Religion

Bainton, R.H. *Women of the Reformation from Spain to Scandinavia*. Minneapolis: Augsburg Publishing House, 1977.

_____. *Women of the Reformation in Germany and Italy*. Minneapolis: Augsburg Publishing House, 1971.

Beer, Frances. *Women and Mystical Experience in the Middle Ages*. Woodbridge, Suffolk, UK: Boydell Press, 1992.

Bernard, Jessie. *The Female World*. New York: Free Press, 1981.

Bolen, Jean Shinoda. *Goddesses in Everywoman: A New Psychology of Women*. San Francisco: Harper & Row, 1984.

Brownmiller, Susan. *Against Our Will: Men, Women and Rape*. New York: Simon and Schuster, 1975.

Chesler, Phyllis. *Women and Madness*. New York: Avon, 1972.

_____. "Nothingness and the Mother Principle in Early Chinese Taoism." *International Philosophical Quarterly* 9 (1969): 391-405.

Chicago, Judy. *The Dinner Party: A Symbol of Our Heritage*. New York: Doubleday Anchor Books, 1979.

Davis, Elizabeth Gould. *The First Sex*. New York: Putnam, 1971.

de Beauvoir, Simone. *The Second Sex*. Trans. H. M. Parshley. New York: Bantam, 1961.

Diner, Helen. *Mothers and Amazons: The First Feminine History of Culture*. New York: Anchor/Doubleday, 1973.

Dinnerstein, Dorothy. *The Mermaid and the Minotaur: Sexual Arrangements and Human Malaise*. New York: Harper, 1976.

Ehrenreich, Barbara and Deirdre English. *Witches, Midwives and Nurses*. Old Westbury, NY: The Feminist Press, 1973.

Falk, Nancy Auer, and Rita M. Gross. *Unspoken Worlds: Women's Lives in Non-Western Cultures*. New York: Harper & Row, 1980.

Firestone, Shulamith. *The Dialectic of Sex: The Case for a Feminist Revolution.* New York: Bantam, 1971.

Friedan, Betty. *The Feminine Mystique.* New York: Norton, 1970.

Fuller, Margaret. *Woman in the Nineteenth Century.* New York: Norton, 1971.

Gray, Elizabeth Dodson. *Patriarchy as a Conceptual Trap.* Wellesley, MA: Roundtable Press, 1982.

Kolbenschlag, Madonna. *Kiss Sleeping Beauty Good-Bye: Breaking the Spell of Feminine Myths and Models.* New York: Doubleday, 1979.

Laidlaw, Toni and Cheryl Malmo, eds. *Healing Voices: Feminist Approaches to Therapy with Women.* San Francisco: Jossey-Bass, 1990.

Lauter, Estelle. *Women as Myth Makers.* Bloomington: Indiana University Press, 1984.

Lerner, Gerda. *The Creation of Patriarchy.* New York: Oxford University Press, 1986.

Merchant, Carolyn. *The Death of Nature: Women, Ecology, and the Scientific Revolution.* San Francisco: Harper & Row, 1979.

Nunnally-Cox, Janice. *Foremothers.* New York: Seabury, 1981.

O'Faolain, Julia and Lauro Martines, eds. *Not in God's Image: Women in History from Greeks to Victorians.* New York, Evanston, London: Harper & Row, 1973.

Pellauer, Mary. "Violence Against Women: The Theological Dimension." *Christianity and Crisis* (1983).

Porterfield, Amanda. *Feminine Spirituality in America from Sarah Edwards to Martha Graham.* Philadelphia: Temple University Press, 1980.

Redekop, Gloria Neufeld. *The Work of Their Hands: Mennonite Women's Societies in Canada.* Waterloo, ON: Wilfrid Laurier University Press, 1995.

Reik, Illeodor. *The Creation of Woman: A Psychoanalytic Inquiry into the Myth of Eve.* New York: McGraw-Hill, 1973.

_____. "Feminism and Peace." *The Christian Century* (1983).

Russell, Letty M. *Human Liberation in a Feminist Perspective.* Philadelphia: Westminster Press, 1974.

Schneir, M., ed. *Feminism, the Essential Historical Writings.* New York: Vintage, 1972.

Stuard, Susan Mosher, ed. *Women in Medieval Society.* Philadelphia: University of Pennsylvania Press, 1976.

Turner, Joan, ed. *Living the Changes.* Winnipeg: University of Manitoba Press, 1990.

Woodman, Marion. *The Pregnant Virgin: A Process of Psychological Transformation.* Toronto: Inner City Books, 1985.

Gender and Sexuality: Women's Body

Barnhouse, R. Tiffany and U.T. Holmes, eds. *Male and Female: Christian Approaches to Sexuality.* New York: Seabury, 1976.

Bird, Phyllis. "Male and Female, He Created Them: Gen. I :27b in the Context of the Priestly Account of Creation." Harvard *Theological Review* 74 (1981).

Bruce, Michael and G.E. Duffield. *Why Not? Priesthood and the Ministry of Women.* Abingdon, England: Marcham Manor Press, 1972.

Bruns, J. Edgar. *God as Woman, Woman as God.* New York: Paulist Press, 1973.

Declaration on the Question of the Admission of Women to the Ministerial Priesthood. Vatican City, 1976.

Farber, Thomas. *The Midwife and the Witch.* New Haven: Yale University Press, 1966.

Gaskin, Ina May. *Spiritual Midwifery.* Summertown, TN: Book Publishing Company, 1980.

Gilman, Charlotte Perkins. *His Religion and Hers: A Study of the Faith of Our Fathers and the Work of Our Mothers.* Westport: Hyperion Press, 1976 (reprint of 1923 edition).

Grahn, Judy. *Blood, Bread and Roses: How Menstruation Created the World.* Boston: Beacon Press, 1993.

Griffin, Susan. *Woman and Nature: The Roaring Inside Her.* New York: Harper & Row, 1978.

Harding, Esther. *Woman's Mysteries, Ancient and Modern.* New York: Bantam, 1973.

Jewett, Paul K. *Man as Male and Female.* Grand Rapids, Michigan: Eerdmans, 1975.

Maguire, Daniel. "The Feminization of God and Ethics." *Christianity and Crisis* 42 (1982).

McFague, Sallie. *Metaphorical Theology: Models of God in Religious Language.* Philadelphia: Fortress Press, 1982.

Ochs, Carol. *Behind the Sex of God: Toward a New Consciousness Transcending Matriarchy and Patriarchy.* Boston: Beacon Press, 1977.

Rich, Adrienne. *Of Woman Born: Motherhood as Experience and Institution.* New York: Bantam, 1977.

Rowan, John. *The Horned God: Feminism and Men as Wounding and Healing.* New York: Routledge and Kegan Paul, 1987.

Tomm, Winnie. *Bodied Mindfulness: Women's Spirits, Bodies and Places.* Waterloo, ON: Wilfrid Laurier University Press, 1995

Trible, P. *God and the Rhetoric of Sexuality.* Philadelphia: Fortress Press, 1978.

Language and Liturgy: Rhetoric, Feminization and Sexism

Bolen, Jean Shinoda. *Websters' First New Intergalactic Weckedary of the English Language*. Boston: Beacon Press, 1987.

Daly, Mary. "After the Demise of God the Father: A Call for the Castration of Sexist Religion." *Women and Religion* 1972. Missoula, MT: American Academy of Religion, 1973.

Miller, Casey and Kate Swift. *Words and Women: New Language in New Times*. New York: Anchor Books, 1977.

Ruether, Rosemary Radford. *Sexism and God-Talk: Toward a Feminist Theology*. Boston: Beacon Press, 1983.

_____, ed. *The Liberating Word: A Guide to Nonsexist Interpretations of the Bible*. Philadelphia: Westminster Press, 1976.

_____. *New Woman, New Earth: Sexist Ideologies and Human Liberation*. New York: Seabury, 1975.

Vetterling-Braggin, M., ed. *Sexist Language: A Modern Philosophical Analysis*. Littlefield: Adams & Co., 1981.

Series Published by Wilfrid Laurier University Press for the Canadian Corporation for Studies in Religion / Corporation Canadienne des Sciences Religieuses

Editions SR

1. *La langue de Ya'udi: description et classement de l'ancien parler de Zencircli dans le cadre des langues sémitiques du nord-ouest*
   Paul-Eugène Dion, O.P.
   1974 / viii + 511 p. / OUT OF PRINT
2. *The Conception of Punishment in Early Indian Literature*
   Terence P. Day
   1982 / iv + 328 pp. / OUT OF PRINT
3. *Traditions in Contact and Change: Selected Proceedings of the XIVth Congress of the International Association for the History of Religions*
   Edited by Peter Slater and Donald Wiebe with Maurice Boutin and Harold Coward
   1983 / x + 758 pp. / OUT OF PRINT
4. *Le messianisme de Louis Riel*
   Gilles Martel
   1984 / xviii + 483 p. / OUT OF PRINT
5. *Mythologies and Philosophies of Salvation in the Theistic Traditions of India*
   Klaus K. Klostermaier
   1984 / xvi + 549 pp. / OUT OF PRINT
6. *Averroes' Doctrine of Immortality: A Matter of Controversy*
   Ovey N. Mohammed
   1984 / vi + 202 pp. / OUT OF PRINT
7. *L'étude des religions dans les écoles : l'expérience américaine, anglaise et canadienne*
   Fernand Ouellet
   1985 / xvi + 666 p. / OUT OF PRINT
8. *Of God and Maxim Guns: Presbyterianism in Nigeria, 1846-1966*
   Geoffrey Johnston
   1988 / iv + 322 pp. / OUT OF PRINT
9. *A Victorian Missionary and Canadian Indian Policy: Cultural Synthesis vs Cultural Replacement*
   David A. Nock
   1988 / x + 194 pp. / OUT OF PRINT
10. *Prometheus Rebound: The Irony of Atheism*
    Joseph C. McLelland
    1988 / xvi + 366 pp. / OUT OF PRINT
11. *Competition in Religious Life*
    Jay Newman
    1989 / viii + 237 pp.
12. *The Huguenots and French Opinion, 1685-1787: The Enlightenment Debate on Toleration*
    Geoffrey Adams
    1991 / xiv + 335 pp.
13. *Religion in History: The Word, the Idea, the Reality / La religion dans l'histoire : le mot, l'idée, la réalité*
    Edited by/Sous la direction de Michel Despland and/et Gérard Vallée
    1992 / x + 252 pp.
14. *Sharing Without Reckoning: Imperfect Right and the Norms of Reciprocity*
    Millard Schumaker
    1992 / xiv + 112 pp.

Comparative Ethics Series /
Collection d'Éthique Comparée

Dissertations SR

Studies in Christianity and Judaism /
Études sur le christianisme et le judaïsme

3. *Society, the Sacred, and Scripture in Ancient Judaism: A Sociology of Knowledge*
   Jack N. Lightstone
   1988 / xiv + 126 pp.
4. *Law in Religious Communities in the Roman Period: The Debate Over*
   Torah *and* **Nomos** *in Post-Biblical Judaism and Early Christianity*
   Peter Richardson and Stephen Westerholm with A. I. Baumgarten,
   Michael Pettem and Cecilia Wassén
   1991 / x + 164 pp.
5. *Dangerous Food: 1 Corinthians 8-10 in Its Context*
   Peter D. Gooch
   1993 / xviii + 178 pp.
6. *The Rhetoric of the Babylonian Talmud, Its Social Meaning and Context*
   Jack N. Lightstone
   1994 / xiv + 317 pp.
7. *Whose Historical Jesus?*
   Edited by William E. Arnal and Michel Desjardins
   1997 / vi + 337 pp.

The Study of Religion in Canada /
Sciences Religieuses au Canada

1. *Religious Studies in Alberta: A State-of-the-Art Review*
   Ronald W. Neufeldt
   1983 / xiv + 145 pp.
2. *Les sciences religieuses au Québec depuis 1972*
   Louis Rousseau et Michel Despland
   1988 / 158 p. / OUT OF PRINT
3. *Religious Studies in Ontario: A State-of-the-Art Review*
   Harold Remus, William Closson James and Daniel Fraikin
   1992 / xviii + 422 pp.
4. *Religious Studies in Manitoba and Saskatchewan: A State-of-the-Art Review*
   John M. Badertscher, Gordon Harland and Roland E. Miller
   1993 / vi + 166 pp.
5. *The Study of Religion in British Columbia: A State-of-the-Art Review*
   Brian J. Fraser
   1995 / x + 127 pp.

Studies in Women and Religion /
Études sur les femmes et la religion

1. *Femmes et religions**
   Sous la direction de Denise Veillette
   1995 / xviii + 466 p.
   * Only available from Les Presses de l'Université Laval
2. *The Work of Their Hands: Mennonite Women's Societies in Canada*
   Gloria Neufeld Redekop
   1996 / xvi + 172 pp.
3. *Profiles of Anabaptist Women: Sixteenth-Century Reforming Pioneers*
   Edited by C. Arnold Snyder and Linda A. Huebert Hecht
   1996 / xxii + 438 pp.
4. *Voices and Echoes: Canadian Women's Spirituality*
   Edited by Jo-Anne Elder and Colin O'Connell
   1997 / xxviii + 237 pp.

SR Supplements

1. *Footnotes to a Theology: The Karl Barth Colloquium of 1972*
   Edited and Introduced by Martin Rumscheidt
   1974 / viii + 151 pp. / OUT OF PRINT
2. *Martin Heidegger's Philosophy of Religion*
   John R. Williams
   1977 / x + 190 pp. / OUT OF PRINT

3. *Mystics and Scholars: The Calgary Conference on Mysticism 1976*
   Edited by Harold Coward and Terence Penelhum
   1977 / viii + 121 pp. / OUT OF PRINT
4. *God's Intention for Man: Essays in Christian Anthropology*
   William O. Fennell
   1977 / xii + 56 pp. / OUT OF PRINT
5. *"Language" in Indian Philosophy and Religion*
   Edited and Introduced by Harold G. Coward
   1978 / x + 98 pp. / OUT OF PRINT
6. *Beyond Mysticism*
   James R. Horne
   1978 / vi + 158 pp. / OUT OF PRINT
7. *The Religious Dimension of Socrates' Thought*
   James Beckman
   1979 / xii + 276 pp. / OUT OF PRINT
8. *Native Religious Traditions*
   Edited by Earle H. Waugh and K. Dad Prithipaul
   1979 / xii + 244 pp. / OUT OF PRINT
9. *Developments in Buddhist Thought: Canadian Contributions to Buddhist Studies*
   Edited by Roy C. Amore
   1979 / iv + 196 pp. / OUT OF PRINT
10. *The Bodhisattva Doctrine in Buddhism*
    Edited and Introduced by Leslie S. Kawamura
    1981 / xxii + 274 pp. / OUT OF PRINT
11. *Political Theology in the Canadian Context*
    Edited by Benjamin G. Smillie
    1982 / xii + 260 pp. / OUT OF PRINT
12. *Truth and Compassion: Essays on Judaism and Religion
    in Memory of Rabbi Dr. Solomon Frank*
    Edited by Howard Joseph, Jack N. Lightstone and Michael D. Oppenheim
    1983 / vi + 217 pp. / OUT OF PRINT
13. *Craving and Salvation: A Study in Buddhist Soteriology*
    Bruce Matthews
    1983 / xiv + 138 pp. / OUT OF PRINT
14. *The Moral Mystic*
    James R. Horne
    1983 / x + 134 pp.
15. *Ignatian Spirituality in a Secular Age*
    Edited by George P. Schner
    1984 / viii + 128 pp. / OUT OF PRINT
16. *Studies in the Book of Job*
    Edited by Walter E. Aufrecht
    1985 / xii + 76 pp. / OUT OF PRINT
17. *Christ and Modernity: Christian Self-Understanding in a Technological Age*
    David J. Hawkin
    1985 / x + 181 pp. / OUT OF PRINT
18. *Young Man Shinran: A Reappraisal of Shinran's Life*
    Takamichi Takahatake
    1987 / xvi + 228 pp. / OUT OF PRINT
19. *Modernity and Religion*
    Edited by William Nicholls
    1987 / vi + 191 pp. / OUT OF PRINT
20. *The Social Uplifters: Presbyterian Progressives and the
    Social Gospel in Canada, 1875-1915*
    Brian J. Fraser
    1988 / xvi + 212 pp. / OUT OF PRINT

Available from:

WILFRID LAURIER UNIVERSITY PRESS

Waterloo, Ontario, Canada   N2L 3C5